Our Vampires, Ourselves

Our Vampires, Ourselves

NINA AUERBACH

The
University
of
Chicago
Press

*Chicago and
London*

Nina Auerbach, the John Welsh Centennial Professor of English at the University of Pennsylvania, is the author of *Communities of Women; Woman and the Demon; Ellen Terry, Player in Her Time;* and *Private Theatricals: The Lives of the Victorians.* She has coedited, with U. C. Knoepflmacher, *Forbidden Journeys: Fairy Tales and Fantasies by Victorian Woman Writers* (also published by the University of Chicago Press), and has written many articles about nineteenth-century literature, theater, and culture.

The University of Chicago Press, Chicago 60637
The University of Chicago Press, Ltd., London
© 1995 by The University of Chicago
All rights reserved. Published 1995
Printed in the United States of America
04 03 02 01 00 99 98 97 96 95   1 2 3 4 5
ISBN 0-226-03201-9 (cloth)

Library of Congress Cataloging-in-Publication Data

Auerbach, Nina, 1943–
    Our vampires, ourselves / Nina Auerbach.
        p.   cm.
    Includes index.
    1. Vampires—History.   2. Vampires—Psychological aspects.   3. Gays in popular culture.   I. Title.
    GR830.V3A92   1995
    820.9'375—dc20   95-1044
                                                                         CIP

♾ The paper used in this publication meets the minimum requirements of the American National Standard for Information Sciences—Permanence of Paper for Printed Library Materials, ANSI Z39.48-1984.

Contents

Acknowledgments

For me, the best vampires are companions—perhaps because, long before my guilty obsession with them took scholarly shape, they cemented so many of my friendships. I would especially like to thank Elaine Bernstein, Sue-Ellen Case, Virginia Crane, Betsy Feist, Beth Kalikoff, Peter Ross, Lee Sterrenburg, and Judith Wilt for the horror we have shared.

The University of Pennsylvania is, in its staid way, rich in vampires. My students there taught me that every generation creates and embraces its own. In a course that led me to this book, I learned with the help of my shrewd teaching assistants Deborah Schizer and Bronwyn Beistel to appreciate fiends I at first found suspiciously strange. I could not have imagined this book without the vampires I met through my students John Bartland, Elizabeth Broadwell, Dorothy Burns, Jill Cunningham, and Amy Robinson. My friends and colleagues Susan Foster, Jennifer Brody, Joan Gordon, Jonathan Grossman, Victoria Kirkham, Robert Lucid, Cary Mazer, Thaïs Morgan, Talia Schaffer, Carroll Smith-Rosenberg, Rebecca West, and Georgianna Ziegler provided invaluable food for this book, though some of them look down on vampires—or claim to.

I am especially grateful to Carroll Smith-Rosenberg and Elaine Terranova, who read drafts of the manuscript with an empathy and wisdom that transcended their initial distaste for its subject. Along with two anonymous monster-loving readers for the University of Chicago Press, my editor, Alan Thomas, provided inspiring encouragement and assistance.

So many friends, students, and associates have given so much to this book that whether they like vampires or not, they bring to life my central idea: that vampirism springs not only from paranoia, xenophobia, or immortal longings, but from generosity and shared enthusiasm. This strange taste cannot be separated from the expansive impulses that make us human.

Introduction: Living with the Undead

WE ALL KNOW DRACULA, or think we do, but as this book will show, there are many Draculas—and still more vampires who refuse to be Dracula or to play him. An alien nocturnal species, sleeping in coffins, living in shadows, drinking our lives in secrecy, vampires are easy to stereotype, but it is their variety that makes them survivors. They may look marginal, feeding on human history from some limbo of their own, but for me, they have always been central: what vampires are in any given generation is a part of what I am and what my times have become. This book is a history of Anglo-American culture through its mutating vampires.

From the beginning of nineteenth-century England through the close of twentieth-century America, vampires have been popular confederates of mortals. As parasites, they stretch back through folklore to the beginnings of recorded history, but they began their significant literary life in 1816, with the self-creations of Byron. The Byronic Lord Ruthven has something in common with his American cousin today, Anne Rice's Lestat, who preys on 1980s and '90s America. Both are enchanting companions; both are media stars; but each feeds on his age distinctively because he embodies that age. Why, for instance, does Ruthven attach himself to mortals, while Lestat is enthralled only by his fellow vampires? The differences that keep vampires alive are my subject.

THIS BOOK TOOK SHAPE between 1989 and 1992—the span of George Bush's presidency—when impalpable fears afflicted America. Nationally, we were assaulted by plenty of devils we knew, but the most potent may have been the devils we had lost: a designated enemy in the seemingly almighty Soviet Union, and a designated patriarch

1

in Ronald Reagan, who during the eight years of his presidency consummately played America's father. Suddenly stripped of its heroes and villains, shorn of a script for its national morality play, America (as the press orchestrated it at least) turned its fears on itself. Among the most popular targets of a mounting backlash against the social gains of the 1970s were women, especially feminists, and university professors, especially feminists. As all of the above, I found myself living in a climate of intensifying hostile mutterings. In that ugly time, I began to imagine a book about fear.

Initially I was going to call it *Fear Itself* in tribute to the lost patriarch who had cast a beloved aura over my childhood, President Franklin D. Roosevelt. The fact that FDR was already dead when I was born made him, for me, incorruptible. In the spirit of his wonderful exhortation, "The only thing we have to fear is fear itself," I began thinking about fear as a phenomenon that could be contained and understood from without. Encompassing and unwritable, *Fear Itself* was not yet focused on vampires, but on all terror, which I thought I could explain.

But as fear took on a local habitation, especially in Republican rhetoric, my book narrowed itself down as well. In his 1968 presidential campaign, Richard Nixon had already enlisted FDR's embracing counsel in the service of a less expansive America: "Freedom from fear is a basic right of every American. We must restore it."[1] This campaign promise pits "every American," or "us," against darkly unspecified but presumably non-native agents of terror, embodied in any "them" the quaking voter imagines. Nixon didn't free Americans from fear; he taught his political heirs to relish it. The late 1980s and early '90s was an era of manipulated hate that came to define our national life: to name was to demonize. By the 1992 presidential campaign, a political cartoonist mordantly imagined George Bush inverting FDR's stirring words: sitting in front of a placard reading "BASH CONGRESS, BASH LAWYERS, BASH HILLARY, BASH CULTURAL ELITE, BASH SINGLE MOTHERS, BASH GAYS, BASH LESBIANS, BASH FEMINISTS," and so on, Bush growls: "We have nothing to fear— but fear it sells."[2] The president has gone from exorcist of fear to its agent.

Vampires and American presidents began to converge in my imagination, not because I think all presidents are equally vampiric (though all do absorb power from the electorate), but because both are personifications of their age. In the spirit of a changing America, I became increasingly implicated in this book as I wrote it: in the American half especially, I saw myself not so much explaining as expressing. My final title, *Our Vampires, Ourselves,* makes fear an ongoing cultural and personal presence, one no rational, Rooseveltian goodwill can dispel. I am not saying that vampires can be reduced to their political component; they are too mutable to be allegories. But the nervous national climate in which I imagined this book taught me that no fear is *only* personal: it must steep itself in its political and ideological ambience, without which our solitary terrors have no contagious resonance.

Since I loved vampires before I hated Republicans, this book also reflects my idiosyncrasies, not only as a citizen, but as a woman. As a teenager chafing against the 1950s, an elated student in the 1960s, an academic in the '70s and '80s, I thought of vampires as my confederates, but most women I know are less accepting: I was received with polite revulsion at a Women's Studies symposium when I gave a paper on undeath. The leaders of the group, stalwart fighters all, claimed they never read horror—because they found it either too frightening or, in comparison to "real" fears like abuse, not frightening enough. Jane Austen's *Northanger Abbey* reminds us that in the eighteenth century, horror was by definition a woman's genre, but today, many women disclaim it (or try to), finding its alternative world alien, almost insulting. Here as so often, though, women's supposed resistance may unwittingly obey a taboo that originates in male exclusivity.

The most sophisticated and best-known experts on American popular horror insist that it is and always has been a boy's game.[3] Twitchell, Skal, and Kendrick construct a compelling paradigm of adolescent boys chafing against the smug domestication of the 1950s, but this paradigm assumes by definition that girls were contented domesticators. What about those of us who weren't? When I was twelve or thirteen, some enterprising ghoul began to televise 1930s horror movies on Saturday nights. These shadowy monsters were a revelation to my best friend and me. Trying to make us popular, our worried parents forced us away from Transylvania to dances and parties, where we spent most of the evening making vampire faces at each other with horrible contortions. We weren't popular (that beatifying condition of the mid-1950s); the monster-loving boys now supposed to have been prevalent in those years never showed up at our parties; but we did feel we had found a secret talisman against a nice girl's life. Vampires were supposed to menace women, but to me at least, they promised protection against a destiny of girdles, spike heels, and approval. I am writing in part to reclaim them for a female tradition, one that has not always known its allies.

When I subverted those parties, or thought I did, it had not yet occurred to me that vampires also personified the fears within the supposed national bliss of those years—fears of communism, of McCarthyism, of nuclear war, of not being certified sexually normal by paternalistic Freudian authorities—fears that fueled the ghastly compulsion to be liked. When I made vampire faces in wholesome settings, I thought I was rebelling against my milieu. I know now that I expressed it—a knowledge that inspired this book.

Vampires changed with my life and times. In the 1960s, like so much else that had been denied in the '50s, they burst out of the underground crypts that had confined Bela Lugosi into the light of brightly colored Hammer films. In the 1970s, like American women, they broke out of their preordained plot to create self-generated new stories. If we each have a halcyon decade, the 1970s was mine; it saw the burgeoning of the women's movement; the beginning of my career (and of the frightening, exhilarating moves around America this career made possible); the end of the war in Vietnam; the end (we thought) of corrupt old ways in the fall of Nixon's presidency. It also saw the assimilation of horror into mainstream culture.[4] My exhilarating memories of the '70s are entwined with its innovative and self-defining vampires; my depression, in the '80s, about Ronald Reagan's grinning descent over the American imagination colors my memory of vampires newly subdued. The alacrity with which vampires shape themselves to personal and national moods is an adaptive trait their apparent uniformity masks.

There is no such creature as "The Vampire"; there are only vampires. Walter Kendrick emphasizes the formulaic stasis of a horror genre that responds monotonously to a universal fear of death, a genre reducible to an "apparently endless recycling of a few scant materials, all assembled two hundred years ago" (p. 255). But since vampires are immortal, they are free to change incessantly. Eternally alive, they embody not fear of death, but fear of life: their power and their curse is their undying vitality. From Varney to Dracula (particularly as Bela Lugosi intones him), from Chelsea Quinn Yarbro's disenchanted idealist, Count Saint-Germain, to Lestat and his friends, vampires long to die, at least in certain moods, infecting readers with fears of their own interminable lives. Kendrick's formula may hold for most monsters, but vampires are wily enough to evade it.

Because they are always changing, their appeal is dramatically generational. In 1991 and 1993, I taught large classes at the University of Pennsylvania on the evolution of vampires. In none of my other courses have age differences been so central. Aficionados all, the students acknowledged my favorite vampires more or less politely, but had to teach me to appreciate theirs. Moreover, the 1991 class searched with obsessive unanimity for the rules governing vampirism, rules that bored students in 1993, who were enchanted by the less governable world of Anne Rice and didn't care much for anything outside. There may have been political reasons for this shift; between 1991 and 1993, the anxieties of the Persian Gulf War gave way to the looser, more amorphous climate of the Clinton administration. Whyever it happened, the vampires covered in these courses took life from generational debates: along with the differences between two groups of students, between myself and both groups, there were the distinctive perspectives of my teaching assistants, women in their twenties who were devoted to the vampires of the 1980s.

To the jaded eye, all vampires seem alike, but they are wonderful in their versatility. Some come to life in moonlight, others are killed by the sun; some pierce with their eyes, others with fangs; some are reactionary, others are rebels; but all are disturbingly close to the mortals they prey on. I can think of no other monsters who are so receptive. Vampires are neither inhuman nor nonhuman nor all-too-human; they are simply more alive than they should be.

Ghosts, werewolves, and manufactured monsters are relatively changeless, more aligned with eternity than with time; vampires blend into the changing cultures they inhabit. They inhere in our most intimate relationships; they are also hideous invaders of the normal. I am writing about vampires because they can be everything we are, while at the same time, they are fearful reminders of the infinite things we are not.

VAMPIRES GO where power is: when, in the nineteenth century, England dominated the West, British vampires ruled the popular imagination, but with the birth of film, they migrated to America in time for the American century. My book follows them, concentrating on nineteenth-century England in the first half and resettling in twentieth-century America in the second.

England did not lose its taste for vampires in the twentieth century, but monsters, like other imports, became subject to the dominant American market. For this reason, in the second half of the book, I view through an American prism the films that swarmed out of England's Hammer Studios in the 1960s, and the mordant "alternative history" that British horror writers have been producing in the 1980s and '90s. As author I became, like many vampires, a time traveler, attempting to reconstruct a nineteenth-century perspective in the first half of this book, relying in the second half on my own experience as that was colored by my country and time.

In England (at least until the coming of Dracula), vampires offered an intimacy that threatened the sanctioned distance of class relationships and the hallowed authority of husbands and fathers. Vampires before Dracula were dangerously close friends. When they became charismatic stage performers, theatrical technology suffused them with a spectral aura, and popular mythology bestowed on them mystic lunar affinities, safely dissipating the erotic implications of their intimacy. At the end of the century, Bram Stoker's Dracula—animal rather than phantom, mesmerist rather than intimate, tyrant rather than friend—safely quarantined vampires from their human prey, foreclosing friendship and opening the door to the power-hungry predators so congenial to the twentieth century.

Vampires in the American century embody seditious urbanity rather than dangerous intimacy. Unlike their insinuating British counterparts, they gravitate to leadership, aping the tyrants they parody. In the vacuum of authority that afflicted and energized the 1970s, they devised innovative exhibitions of undeath. When Ronald Reagan's powerful persona took control of the American imagination in the 1980s, vampires began to die. Intimidated by ideological reaction and the AIDS epidemic, they mutated, as a species, into unprecedented mortality, lacking the tenacity of the Victorian theatrical phantoms they resembled. The best of them took on the holy isolation of angels, inspiring awe in a humanity they could no longer govern.

Despite these differences, their stories have much in common. In both England and America, vampires oscillate between aristocracy and democracy, at times taking command with elitist aplomb, at times embodying the predatory desires of the populace at large. In both cultures, vampires turn to women to perform the extreme implications of their monstrosity—erotic friendship in England, social rebellion in America. In general, with striking exceptions (particularly in the American 1970s), vampires are male creations; their most stellar incarnations are male; but in their well-bred inhibitions, many need women to act out their natures for them. Even solitary luminaries like Dracula turn their demonic designs into female plots.

In nineteenth-century England and twentieth-century America, vampires end their story and their century in retraction and reaction, collaborating to restore the patriarchy they had menaced. Stoker's *Dracula* is a compendium of fin-de-siècle phobias. Dracula's lonely rigidity repudiates the homoerotic intimacy with which earlier vampires had insinuated themselves into mortality. In America, Reaganesque vampires, increasingly ghettoized, wilt, dissipate, and even shed undeath when challenged by the paternal authorities they had mocked in the '60s and '70s. In fin-de-siècle conservative reversions, vampires prop up the ideologies and institutions they had undermined when they (and their centuries) were in their prime. Posing as revolutionaries, they are consummate turncoats, more formidable in their flexibility than in their love, their occult powers, or their lust for blood. It is impossible either to exorcise or to trust a species whose immortality has given them supreme adaptability.

THIS BOOK TELLS only some of the many possible vampire stories; there are so many vampires that tracking them necessitated arbitrary exclusions I regret. National boundaries forced me to ignore those of France, China, Russia, Spain, and Scandinavia. The boundaries of my subject—to trace an evolving myth through two centuries of cultural history—have forced me to ignore crucial distinctions of genre. Vampires thrive in poetry, tales, novels, songs, and movies. Obviously they adapt differently to each narrative form, but for my purposes I have collapsed these forms into episodes in a single story, leaving others to explore the borders between genres and to explain vampires' special affinity for long novels and films.

"The Vampire" is a popular if nonexistent abstraction, but many particular vampires are frustratingly difficult to find. While *Dracula* has never been out of print, some of his most interesting progeny exist only in specialized science fiction/horror publications, ephemeral paperback originals, and rarely seen films. Along with loftier ambitions, I hope my book will revive interest in works I particularly like, such as Dan Simmons's *Carrion Comfort;* Chelsea Quinn Yarbro's historical horror series featuring Count Saint-Germain; Gabrielle Beaumont's 1989 television adaptation of Sheridan Le Fanu's *Carmilla; Blood Is Not Enough* and *A Whisper of Blood,* stunning collections of psychic vampire stories edited by Ellen Datlow; and Kathryn Bigelow's vampire western, *Near Dark.* Two recent anthologies by Alan Ryan and Christopher Frayling[5] have made some marvelous tales easily available, but many wonderful novels and films are in limbo. Popular though vampires are in general, commercial perishability has defeated some of the most vivid.

Individual vampires may die; after almost a century, even Dracula may be feeling his mortality; but as a species vampires have been our companions for so long that it is hard to imagine living without them. They promise escape from our dull lives and the pressure of our times, but they matter because when properly understood, they make us see that our lives are implicated in theirs and our times are inescapable.

Giving Up the Ghost: Nineteenth-Century Vampires

"Ha! what a delightful thing is friendship!"

Varney the Vampire

Byron's Ghost

VAMPIRES WERE NOT DEMON LOVERS or snarling aliens in the early nineteenth century, but singular friends. In those days it was a privilege to walk with a vampire. They were not yet the specialized creatures we know today, recognizable by distinguishing characteristics—fangs, fruity accents, eccentric clothes—and killable by experts on their many limitations. In those early days, few vampires were defined enough to die; not all of them sucked blood to stay alive. They were indeterminate creatures who flourished, not in their difference from their human prey, but through their intimate intercourse with mortals, to whom they were dangerously close.

Byron in his most congenial mood modeled for the first literary vampire to captivate the popular imagination: he depicted himself as a lordly comrade entitled to supplant such drearily sanctioned forms of love as family and marriage. His traveling companion, the enthralled narrator of the fragmentary tale, endows Augustus Darvell with a glamour at once familiar and unattainable: "We had been educated at the same schools and university; but his progress through these had preceded mine, and he had been deeply initiated into what was called the world. . . . He was a being of no common order, and one who, whatever pains he might take to avoid remark, would still be remarkable."[1]

The charmed narrator is not repelled by this remarkable being: he hopes implicitly to become equally uncommon. Darvell is a compelling contemporary and glamorous traveling companion, not—as Count Dracula will be to Jonathan Harker—a repulsive old man who terminates a lonely journey. Like Dickens's Steerforth traveling to Yarmouth with the adoring David Copperfield, Darvell is his friend's sinister, superior sharer.

13

His compelling closeness has something in common with the contemporaneous genre Eve Sedgwick wittily calls "paranoid Gothic," in which male homosexual anxiety infuses fears of power: "Each [instance of paranoid Gothic fiction] is about one or more males who not only is persecuted by, but considers himself transparent to and often under the compulsion of, another male."[2] But Darvell is too liberal to persecute a man he likes. So are the vampires he spawned; their main characteristic is congeniality. Presumably Darvell does feed on people, but Byron never shows him doing so; Byron's short fragment stops before Darvell's presumptive rebirth as a vampire. Darvell's menace lies not in sadistic persecution, but in his offer of "intimacy, or friendship, according to the ideas of him who uses those words to express them" (p. 3).

Intimacy and friendship are the lures of Romantic vampirism. In Polidori's amplification of Byron's fragment, the vampire, now more euphoniously named Lord Ruthven, seals his bond with his traveling companion by his repeated admonition, "Remember your oath." In the first half of the nineteenth century, these words were as inevitable a vampire refrain as Dracula's "the children of the night. What music they make!" became in the twentieth. Dracula, however, proclaims his vampirism by pledging allegiance to wolves, while Ruthven's is his human bond.

This oath—to preserve Ruthven's honor by concealing his predatory life and apparent death—has absolute binding power in Polidori's *The Vampyre* and its many offshoots. The oath is frightening because it involves not raw power, but honor and reciprocity. It avoids the compulsion inherent in Sedgwick's "paranoid Gothic"; the oath signifies instead a bond between companions that is shared and chosen, one far from the Dracula-like mesmeric coercion we associate with vampires today.[3] Byronic vampires are only incidentally interested in blood, or for that matter in life. Their egalitarian promise is intensified by their relative indifference to animals and their persistent flirtation with ghosts. The origin of their intensity was a friendship that never occurred.

The Byronic vampire who was to proliferate through the nineteenth century was shaped less by folklore or Romantic intimations of immortality than by irritation: Byron's journey through Brussels to Geneva in 1816 was punctuated by squabbles with his physician and traveling companion, Dr. John Polidori. Their dislike was formed and fueled by class antagonism: the letters of both insist on their identities as master and servant, lord and vassal, bard and poetaster. In the end, they played out the hierarchical roles that galled them both. Byron released his many tensions by making Polidori's poetic, athletic, and medical ineptitude the butt of his lordly jokes with the Shelleys; after Polidori was dismissed from Byron's retinue, he wrote with a pretense of dignity, "There was no immediate cause, but a continued series of slight quarrels. I believe the fault, if any, has been on my part, I am not accustomed to have a master, & there fore my conduct was not free & easy."[4] When Byron heard two years later that Polidori had had a serious accident, he wrote to his publisher with conspicuous scorn: "I am as sorry to hear of Dr. Polidori's accident as one can be for a person for whom one has a dislike—and—something of contempt" (quoted in Macdonald, p. 153).

But the vampires that rose out of their tense journey transcended class contempt. When Byron and Polidori wrote fantasies about each other, they wrote not about masters and servants, but about friends. In 1819, Polidori defended his *Vampyre* from groundless attributions to Byron, elevating himself from servant to gentleman: "Lord Byron is *not* the author—I . . . am that author I was the '*Gentleman*' who travelled with his Lordship and who wrote the whole of that trifle" (quoted in Macdonald, p. 180; Polidori's italics). The vampire is an equalizer, turning vassals into peers. His monster raises the mocked servant to collaborative dignity.

The vampire fragment Byron began at Villa Diodati in 1816 and Polidori's 1819 tale, *The Vampyre,* are symbiotic. Polidori pervades Byron's fragment. In his poetry, Byron generally displays himself in all the flair of the first person, but his Darvell has no existence independent of his traveling companion's awe. The real Polidori watched his master's histrionics with diagnostic resentment; the companion Byron creates brims with a tenderness that consecrates the apparent death in Turkey of his brilliant, strangely debilitated friend. The fragment is less a tale of terror than an account of a romantic friendship only a vampire could inspire.

Polidori's *The Vampyre,* which was instantly attributed to Byron, is a sardonic development of Byron's material. The tale is Polidori's own, but it is steeped in Byron and Byronism. Aubrey, through whom the tale is told, is a bookish naïf like Jane Austen's Catherine Morland; like her, Aubrey lives in a heightened world of books, making Ruthven into "the hero of a romance, [determining] to observe the offspring of his fancy, rather than the person before him" (p. 8). Soon, Aubrey tries to extricate himself from his perverse hero, but separation is impossible. Ruthven, who unlike the sketchy Darvell is a full-fledged vampire, binds the reluctant young man with his oath, kills the woman he loves, and marries his sister in order to glut his thirst with her on their wedding night. Unlike the vampires he spawned, Ruthven not only survives the end of his story: he is so irresistible and elusive that Aubrey, who alone knows what he is, never dreams of killing him. Ruthven's dreadful power springs from his oath of friendship.

Byron and Polidori suffused each other's vampire tales as indelibly as they had each other's identities on their unhappy journey. Polidori's *Vampyre* not only elaborates on Byron's sketch: the name "Ruthven" alludes to the Byron character in Lady Caroline Lamb's satiric roman à clef, *Glenarvon.* A strained journey generated a mutual obsession that created a monster, in a collaboration as authentic, if disaffected, as the one that produced Wordsworth and Coleridge's *Lyrical Ballads.* Out of a hating, needing companionship between men came not only Romantic poetry, but the Romantic vampire. Later vampires are more indiscriminately evil and disgusting than the ones Byron inspired, but licentious as they are, few have been allowed to embark on a journey with another male.

This journey had no precedent. In Slavic folklore, the main repository of vampires before the Romantics began to write about them, vampires never ventured beyond their birthplace.[5] Byron used their clannishness to ghoulish effect in another fragment, his Turkish tale *The Giaour* (1813). The "false Infidel" of *The Giaour* is blasted by the curse of returning to family life as a vampire:

> But first, on earth as Vampire sent,
> Thy corse shall from its tomb be rent;
> Then ghastly haunt thy native place,
> And suck the blood of all thy race;
> There from thy daughter, sister, wife,
> At midnight drain the stream of life. . . .[6]

In a lurid climax, the vampire devours his favorite daughter, who nevertheless blesses the name "father" as she dies. The vampire in *The Giaour* is a patriarchal, incestuous spirit who eats his dependent women. The vampire's restriction to his family plot anticipates the sentimental folklore of the twentieth century: in Thornton Wilder's beloved family play *Our Town* (1938) and the beloved movie *Ghost* (1990), undead protagonists return like folklore vampires, to embrace the confined spaces they had lived in.[7] The hell Byron's *Giaour* envisions is the traditional folkloric hell—and American heaven—of domestic confinement, which is never free from revenants.

The prose tales of Byron and Polidori discard this stationary familial hell.[8] Darvell is by nature and definition itinerant, springing to life "on a journey through countries not hitherto much frequented by travellers" (Byron, in *Penguin*, p. 2). Ruthven is equally vagrant but more social, thriving on "the dissipations attendant upon a London winter," where his sepulchral gloom ensures popularity: "His peculiarities caused him to be invited to every house; all wished to see him, and those who had been accustomed to violent excitement, and now felt the weight of *ennui*, were pleased at having something in their presence capable of engaging their attention" (Polidori, in *Penguin*, p. 7). Ruthven haunts everyone's home, but unlike folkloric vampires, he has none of his own to prey on.

Since these vampires go everywhere *but* home, they are indifferent to incest. Their hunger, like their itinerant lives, explores realms beyond family definition.[9] Darvell, who devours no one and so withers mysteriously, finds death and presumptive renewal in a mysterious Turkish cemetery far from England; Ruthven drinks Aubrey vicariously through his women, but he makes no move toward a sister, mother, or daughter of his own. Romantic fiction licenses folkloric family devourers to reach into uncharted spaces. The friendship itself is "a journey through countries not hitherto much frequented by travellers," removing vampirism from licensed homes and categorizable intimacies. They slide so deftly beyond classification that their stories are unanchored by that later obligatory antagonist, the vampire expert who knows how to kill them.

Vampires make draining friends in the nineteenth century, but as we shall see, only when vampires are women do their friends become literal prey: Coleridge's Geraldine and her prose descendant, Sheridan Le Fanu's Carmilla, leap from homoerotic friendship to homosexual love, but male vampires refuse to love their food. For most of them, the need to feed on women is an annoying distraction from their political or metaphysical concerns. Vampiric hunger is incidental to men who have their most complex identities as friends.

Vampire friendship as Byron and Polidori imagined it was so single-minded that popular adaptation had to force their rapacity into conventional channels. The theater subdued its intensities by shifting the emphasis to marriage. J. R. Planché's melodrama, *The Vampire; or, The Bride of the Isles* (1820), a loose adaptation from Polidori, invented the rule that the vampire must marry his maiden before fortifying himself with her. Accordingly Planché's Ruthven is as indiscriminately thirsty for a wedding as Jane Austen's proper clergyman Mr. Collins; his need for bridal blood leaves him little energy for friendship. Offstage, however, Romantic vampires saw marriage only as a conduit to human men. In their allegiance to an unattainable male friend, these yearning vampires were truer than melodrama's predators to the obsessions of canonical Romantic poetry.

Romantic heroes as well as vampires often yearn less for marriage than for impossible friendships. Wordsworth and Coleridge's collaboration on the *Lyrical Ballads* seems to have been as symbiotic, as tormented by fearful identification and repudiation, as was Byron and Polidori's chafing journey to Geneva. Wordsworth never wrote a vampire story about Coleridge, but his most sustained poetic self-definition, *The Prelude*, abounds in plangent addresses to "Friend!"; the poem continued to spin itself out long after the souring of the friendship and the death of Coleridge. The absent friend who understands is a more vivid and moving presence in Wordsworth's *Prelude,* and throughout his work, than are the rocklike mentors, the flowing sisters or spouses, in whom he tries to find sustenance.

Sanctioned marriage is as emotionally vacant in much canonical Romanticism as it is in vampire stories.[10] Haunted by thirst and by vampire-like variations on living death, Coleridge's *Rime of the Ancient Mariner* nullifies the ceremony toward which the Wedding Guest dutifully trudges, exploring instead a darker, stronger bond, one of repelled identification with a terrible friend who, like Wordsworth perhaps, forces him to hear the story of his life—or life in death.[11] In the same spirit, Victor Frankenstein's wedding is annulled by his most intimate friend, his creature, whose tale Victor cannot choose but hear; the creature's oath, like Ruthven's, vitiates the wedding by killing the bride. Even the canon of that slyly self-effacing Romantic Jane Austen rings constant changes on her early thematic play between "Love" and "Freindship" [*sic*]: her obligatory weddings are sickeningly hollow, if not inhuman, without the assurance the story gives that their essence is complex friendship. Weddings may be narrative necessities, but only a friend can show you, if horribly, who or what you are.

In societies where families are inescapable and marriage is enforced, friendship may be a more indelible taboo than incest. In a dreadful way, the Byronic vampire/friend fulfills the promise of Romanticism, offering a mutuality between subject and object so intense that it overwhelms conventional hierarchies and bonds. The interfusion, as Wordsworth might have called it, between vampire and mortal makes familiar boundaries fluid, offering a wider world than home and a larger self than one sustained by sanctioned relationships.

The association of Darvell and Ruthven with a free-floating Orientalism that had not quite become a rationale for imperialism dissolves constraints of place:[12] Darvell finds his spiritual home in Turkey, Ruthven his in Greece, making them in a psychic sense amalgams of West and East. Drawing their identities from England and the East but belonging to neither, Darvell and Ruthven dissolve, at climactic moments, into phantoms, discarding altogether their transgressing bodies.

As revenants, the once-living returned, vampires and ghosts

were originally scarcely distinguishable. The first use of *vampire* the *Oxford English Dictionary* records, in 1734, defines them as "evil Spirits" who animate the "Bodies of deceased persons." Folklorists use *vampire* interchangeably with *revenant* or *ghost*.[13] Only gradually did vampires lose their identification with the human world to acquire the menace of a separate species.

"'We will each write a ghost story,' said Lord Byron; and his proposition was acceded to. There were four of us."[14] So, according to Mary Shelley, began the famous competition in 1816 that produced Frankenstein and Dracula, our two great modern monsters, neither of whom looks like a ghost today.[15] The ghosts born at the Villa Diodati are not mere shadows of the formerly living. They have bodies of their own and independent identities. Nevertheless, they appropriate the majesty of phantoms, borrowing spiritual authority from England's most imposing ghost, King Hamlet.

Darvell and Ruthven whisper "swear" as persistently as the ghost of Hamlet's father, who brooded over the Villa Diodati. Mary Shelley remembers the house party reading a French translation of a German tale about "the sinful founder of his race, whose miserable doom it was to bestow the kiss of death on all the younger sons of his fated house, just when they reached the age of promise. His gigantic, shadowy form, clothed like the ghost in Hamlet, in complete armour, but with the beaver up, was seen at midnight, by the moon's fitful beams, to advance slowly along the gloomy avenue" (Shelley, intro. to *Frankenstein*, 3d ed., p. 224). Byron and his friends evoked the ghostly power of patriarchs, but they never embodied it. Like Frankenstein's hulking adolescent creation, Byronic vampires are quintessential sons, aging schoolboys wandering beyond patriarchal regulation, who nevertheless borrow the dignity of a famous ghostly father.

King Hamlet's "gigantic, shadowy form" permeates and dignifies nineteenth-century vampires. The motto on the title page of the mid-Victorian thriller *Varney the Vampire; or, The Feast of Blood* (1847) invokes the ghost of Hamlet's father before Varney's bloody escapades begin, turning Hamlet's vow, "Be thou a spirit of health or goblin damned, . . . I will speak to thee" (I, iv, ll. 40–44), into a nagging ontological question: "Art thou

a spirit of health or goblin damned?" Varney is haunting because no one quite knows what he is: a vampire at midcentury
can be many things at once. Similarly, in 1856, with no apparent inconsistency, Dion Boucicault changed the name of his
popular 1852 melodrama *The Vampire* to *The Phantom.* When
they abandoned homoerotic journeys at the end of the nineteenth century, vampires sank into matter (Dracula is notable
for hairiness, foul breath, affinity with animals and corpses),
but in their Byronic beginnings, they flirted with mortal men
and with disembodiment. As semi-phantoms, vampires traveled
easily with the living. Immaterial seducers made acceptable
friends.

Byron's Turkey reinforced his ghostliness: a delicious, if dangerous, reservoir of homoerotic, even transvestite, possibility,[16]
his Orient offers release not merely from gender restrictions, but
from the body's boundaries. Unlike Frankenstein's lumbering
creature, who is inseparable from his overdeveloped anatomy,
Darvell and Ruthven are only half-encumbered by bodies; thus
they are relatively immune to the rules of physical existence
that will shackle later vampires.[17] Since they are scarcely physical, the friendship they offer need never commit itself to bodily
incarnation. The "oath" they impose is associated with travel,
with liminality, with evasion. Darvell and Ruthven are only
half-hungry because they are by implication half-ghosts. Since
they are only half-alive, they do not have to resolve their stories
by dying. But in the public arena of the theater, "intimacy, or
friendship" metamorphosed into heterosexual marriage and the
vampire's dissolution into ghostliness.

Polidori and the Phantoms

J. R. Planché's gorgeous theatrical adaptation relegated homoerotic journeys to the half-light of the Byronic imagination.
Planché cast a respectable veneer over Polidori and his more
faithful French adapter by making Lord Ruthven marriageable.[18]
Planché's Ruthven, like Boucicault's later on, is less a glamorous
companion than a would-be bridegroom. Aubrey, along with his
undefined yearning for the vampire, dwindles safely to an offstage corpse: Polidori's susceptible young man becomes the pa-

triarch Lord Ronald, Baron of the Isles, the *father* of Ruthven's dead friend and of his intended bride Lady Margaret. Lord Ronald loves Ruthven only for his solicitude toward his dying son. Planché's French source does retain Aubrey in his original role, but in the English melodrama, the male bond and the indelible oath become safely filial and hierarchical. A responsive friend turns into a caretaking father; an uncharted allegiance acquires safely familial contours.

Planché transplants Polidori's action from Turkey to Scotland, in part because Scottish costumes were available to his company, but also, perhaps, in search of chillier, rockier coasts that would be bracingly free of Byronic perversities. The now-kilted Ruthven pursues the servant Effie as well as Margaret in order to get the blood he needs before the moon sets. Whatever emotional complexity Planché's melodrama contains lies in Margaret's mixed fear of and devotion to Ruthven; translated to the stage, the yearning revulsion of Polidori's Aubrey becomes heterosexual and safely titillating.[19]

Plot and characters, however, have little to do with Planché's *Vampire*, which relies on song and spectacle. The story begins with the sleeping Margaret's "Introductory Vision" in "the Interior of the Basaltic Caverns of Staffa," where exotic spirits sing warnings about the spectral man she may love. The singing spirits make clear that Planché's Ruthven scarcely exists as a body: he is a spirit like those of the dream-vision, a product of reincarnation, not resurrection. Moreover, he is our first vampire exotic enough to require expert explanation. Spectacle can't stand still for the painstaking exposition of a Van Helsing, so the poster advertising the melodrama at the Theatre Royal clarifies his legend:

> THIS PIECE IS FOUNDED ON the various traditions concerning THE VAMPIRES, which assert that they are *Spirits*, deprived of all *Hope of Futurity*, by the Crimes committed in their Mortal State—but, that they are permitted to roam the Earth, in whatever Forms they please, with *Supernatural Powers of Fascination*—and, that they cannot be destroyed, so long as they sustain their dreadful Existence, by imbibing the BLOOD of FEMALE VICTIMS, whom they are first compelled to marry.[20]

This insistence that vampires are spirits answerable to esoteric laws removes Ruthven from his Byronic context of gentlemen's schools and comradely journeys: this vampire is an alien invader from occult orders of being. Unda, Spirit of the Flood, makes clear at the outset that Ruthven is really the spirit of "Cromal, called the Bloody," reincarnated as a vampire "in the form / Of Marsden's Earl" (pp. 15–16). Ruthven is only a shell; the essence of the vampire is his cursed spirit, transforming him, onstage, from friend to ghost. His incorporeality is reflected in the technological innovation for which *The Vampire* has entered theater history: the invention of the Vampire (or Vamp) Trap.

Depending on its placement, the vampire trap made the actor alternately body and spirit. The trap propelled the vampire either up and down through the stage floor (allowing Ruthven to rise from the tomb of Cromal, to sink back tombward in the dream vision, and to fall raging into the abyss at the end) or through invisible doors in the flats, allowing him to make imperceptible, phantomlike intrusions into or out of domestic space. The ghost was more theatrically viable than the descending crypt-bound or soaring batlike creatures of our own popular mythology. The trap was most frequently used, not in the floor, but as an instrument of domestic disembodiment, "a pair of spring-controlled doors cut into the scenery, which allowed the fiendish Ruthven to disappear through apparently solid walls."[21]

In their nineteenth-century incarnations, vampires were theatrically identifiable as spirits. While Victorian scripts emphasize rises and falls, Victorian stagecraft preferred a vampire who scarcely had a body at all, infiltrating alien matter. Nineteenth-century Gothic stage machinery favored ghostly defiance of physical laws. In 1852, the theater acquired a still more celestial ghost trap: the Corsican Trap, designed to allow the spectral brother in Dion Boucicault's *Corsican Brothers* to glide across the stage while gradually ascending to ghost music.[22] The elaborate technology of nineteenth-century theatrical horror aimed at a highly sophisticated disembodiment of the actor, making the stage vampire a particularly versatile ghost.

The recurrent rising and sinking of the moon in Planché's *Vampire* and its mid-Victorian progeny enhances the vampire's ritual disembodiment. The vampire may need marriage and blood, but the governing body of his life is lunar: not only must he find a bride or die before the full moon sets, but the climax of the play, the oath he imposes on Lord Ronald before his apparent death at the end of Act I, involves his exposure to the moon's restorative magic. For Polidori, the oath itself was magically binding. Planché transfers its power to the moon that gains precedence over male bonds: "Remember your oath. The lamp of night is descending the blue heavens; when I am dead, let its sweet light shine on me. Farewell! Remember—remember your oath" (I, iii, p. 32). Ronald obediently *lays the body of Ruthven on a bank in the garden, R. U. E., and kneels mournfully beside it— the moon continues descending, till the light falls upon the corpse* (p. 33). By the beginning of Act II, Ruthven is alive again, gliding through the vampire trap into Lord Ronald's apartment. Not blood but the moon has restored him.

The presiding moon is Planché's most important addition to the vampire legend. Byron and Polidori were too absorbed in themselves to notice skies. Darvell does make his acolyte swear to perform an elaborate ritual with his dead body, but Byron's magic involves time and numbers, not astronomy, and it flowers in daylight, not night: "On the ninth day of the month, at noon precisely (what month you please, but this must be the day), you must fling this ring into the salt springs which run into the Bay of Eleusis; the day after, at the same hour, you must repair to the ruins of the temple of Ceres, and wait one hour" (Byron, in *Penguin*, p. 9). Travel and friendship, developing through time and place, are Byron's primary sources of power. The realm of heavenly bodies is too inhuman to matter.

Polidori does align the vampire's life with the moon, but only incidentally. After Aubrey swears to conceal the activities of the apparently dying Ruthven, the corpse mysteriously disappears. A fortuitously encountered robber (not a strikingly reliable informant) explains that Ruthven's body has been "conveyed by himself and comrades, upon his retiring, to the pinnacle of a neighbouring mount, according to a promise they had given his lordship, that it should be exposed to the first cold ray of the moon that rose after his death" (Polidori, in *Penguin*, p. 18). Polidori's moon never reappears, but his descendants played on vaster fears: the forgettable moon of Polidori's robber became central to imaginations of the vampire for decades, as two mutually attracted young men were erased from the foreground of a tale that evolved into a legend.

The moon plays no role in Planché's French source (White, "Two Vampires of 1828," p. 25), but it dominates his English melodrama, heightening Ruthven's immateriality. For at least fifty years after Planché's *Vampire,* the moon was the central ingredient of vampire iconography; vampires' solitary and repetitive lives consisted of incessant deaths and—when the moon shone down on them—quivering rebirths. Planché's Ruthven, Rymer's Varney, and Boucicault's Alan Raby need marriage and blood to replenish their vitality, but they turn for renewed life to the moon. Like the moon, they live cyclically, dying and renewing themselves with ritual, predictable regularity. A corpse quivering to life under the moon's rays is the central image of midcentury vampire literature; fangs, penetration, sucking, and staking are peripheral to its lunar obsession.

Boucicault's vampire Alan Raby is still more moonstruck than Planché's Ruthven; in the sensational first-act climax of *The Phantom,* Alan Raby, apparently shot, is carried up Mount Snowdon, where his ceremony of lunar resurrection ends the act:

> *The Peaks of Snowdon. —No vegetation whatever is visible, but a sinister, tender, bluish light gives a desolate character to the scene. . . . The moonlight is seen to tip the highest peaks and creeps down the mountain side; it arrives at the ledge, and bathes the body of* ALAN RABY *in a bright white light. —After a moment his chest begins to heave and his limbs to quiver, he raises his arm to his heart, and then, revived completely, rises to his full height.*
>
> *Alan. (Addressing the Moon.)* Fountain of my life! once more thy rays restore me. Death!—I defy thee![23]

The moon in nineteenth-century literature typically takes its nature from Shakespeare, particularly *A Midsummer Night's Dream:* it licenses an enchanted eroticism, an extension of human power into a nonhuman realm, a lowering of the boundaries between fairies and mortals. The vampire comes to life under the same moon that gives Bottom an animal's head so that he can have intercourse with a fairy: it unites disparate orders of being. Coleridge's gloss to that subtly vampiric epic of thirst, *The Rime of the Ancient Mariner*, allows "the moving Moon" to preside over a healing, if fleeting, vision of harmony unavailable in the poem itself, hallowing an impossible union of motion and rest, home and journeying: "In his loneliness and fixedness [the Mariner] yearneth towards the journeying Moon, and the stars that still sojourn, yet still move onward; and everywhere the blue sky belongs to them, and is their appointed rest, and their native country and their own natural homes, which they enter unannounced, as lords that are certainly expected and yet there is a silent joy at their arrival." "By the light of the Moon he beholdeth God's creatures of the great calm."[24] But this lunar calm is an illusory hope. Like the vampires who come after him, Coleridge's Mariner turns to the moon for renewed life, but it denies him—perhaps because though the Mariner may no longer be entirely human, he has not quite managed to attain the blessed status of "creature" by turning into a vampire. Fearful, mindless, and predatory, Coleridge's men aspire to the charmed status of a creatureliness beyond the human, but as *Christabel* reveals, only his women live in that enchantment.

The mid-Victorian moon is the magic fusion among species, the balm that joins human to preterhuman, death to life. In the last year of *Varney the Vampire*'s serial publication, Jane Eyre expanded under the moon into a fairy, witch, or otherwise magically empowered creature. Like Polidori's Aubrey and the other obsessed innocents of vampire fiction, Jane finds her lunar friend, one distant and repellent, but beloved: her doomed foreign agent Bertha Mason Rochester, who tames for Jane the marrying predator Rochester, and whom Jane likens to another foreigner, "the foul German spectre—the Vampire."[25] The moon that energizes vampires bestows on Jane Eyre all the blended powers inaccessible in ordinary English life.

This moon aspires to make vampires safely eternal, but its primacy was brief in vampire iconography. Alan Raby's aspirations have little in common with those of the biologically sophisticated vampires who displaced him. In 1897, *Dracula* would bequeath bloody sexy animals to twentieth-century vampire mythology; in a new climax, the vampire loomed, baring his fangs, over the bed of a ripe woman, rather than raising himself to drink life from moonbeams. Twentieth-century vampires lose their affinity for the moon and for unearthliness in general. Though they become creatures of the night, the sun, an enemy that scorches them, is the only heavenly body they notice. From 1820 to 1870, however, vampires' affinity is not with life and its liquids, but with the bloodless, the inorganic, the ghostly, and the lunar.

When Hollywood appropriated literary mythology, it disposed of the moon's aggrandizing powers, taking the moon away from the vampire and assigning it to the werewolf, a less versatile hybrid in whose story the moon is a simple, mechanical index of transformation, no different from a magic wand. Larry Talbot in *The Wolf Man* (1941) finds no glory in being a werewolf. His new identity springs not from his mobile soul; it is dictated by a lunar jingle.

> Even a man who's pure in heart
> And says his prayers by night
> May become a wolf when the wolfbane blooms
> And the autumn moon is bright.[26]

By 1941, the moon in American popular mythology is no longer an agent of release, but an instrument of mechanistic coercion. In mid-nineteenth-century England, however, it spiritualizes the vampires who respond to it, aligning them with fairies or phantoms rather than animals. Like the vampire trap, it turns body into spirit, devourer into ghost. This potent agent of non-humanity preserves the mystery of the first vampire with a common touch, James Malcolm Rymer's snarling, suffering Varney.

Varney's Moon

The theater detached vampires from the aristocratic solipsism of Byronism, exposing them to the general gaze; *Varney the Vampire*, a wildly popular serial that ran for two years, made them mass-market commodities for an England turning self-consciously and ambivalently toward capitalism and democracy. James Malcolm Rymer, *Varney's* author, tried vainly to dissociate himself from his mass audience, the new vehicle of literary fear: "It is the privilege of the ignorant and weak to love superstition. The only strong mental sensation they are capable of is *fear*. . . . There are millions of minds that have no resource between vapid sentimentality, and the ridiculous spectra of the nursery."[27] Though Lord Ruthven would never court "millions of minds," Rymer's sprawling, structurally incoherent, but extraordinary novel is faithful to the key attribute of Polidori's vampire: the lure of his friendship, which Planché, and later Boucicault, refused to dramatize. But Varney's friendship, like his audience, is broader than Byronic intimacy; it embraces not a sole chosen spirit, but an entire society.

Friendship with vampires is permissible to readers of novels and tales, but it is taboo to theater or film audiences: from Polidori's to Anne Rice's, vampires on the page seduce the reader into sharing their condition, while stage (and later movie) vampires embody the alienation of theatricality itself, stunning us with the things our own bodies will not do. Only the moon, in *Varney the Vampire*, reminds us of the vampire's status as a creature closer to enchantment than to us. In the three volumes of his long story, Varney does his best to look preternatural, but he continually, helplessly, reverts to the more unsettling human condition of friendship.

The Varney we meet in the first scene is the corpse-like, fanged, long-nailed creature who will become decades of movie monsters, beginning with Max Schreck in *Nosferatu*. This horrible figure crawls into the bedroom of lush, sleeping Flora Bannerworth, desecrating her neck and bosom with his glittering eye before sinking his fangs into her neck. But the motto on the book's title page—"Art thou a spirit of health or goblin damned?"—has already problematized that monster, giving him the ambiguous authority of King Hamlet's ghost, hinting at an identity beyond the repulsive face we watch watching Flora.

Varney's status as indeterminate spirit tempers the repellent neck-biter, as does the quite different appearance of Sir Francis Varney, the urbane gentleman we, and the Bannerworths, meet shortly thereafter: "There was the lofty stature, the long, sallow face, the slightly projecting teeth, the dark, lustrous, although somewhat sombre eyes."[28] Gentleman and vampire scarcely share a body. The lividity, the long nails and fangs, remain only as shadows in his suggestive eyes: "The only thing positively bad about his countenance, was to be found in his eyes. There was a most ungracious and sinister expression, a kind of lurking and suspicious look, as if he were always resolving in his mind some deep laid scheme, which might be sufficient to circumvent the whole of mankind" (p. 148).

Varney's eyes may be suspicious, but they don't give his character away; in fact, they are astonishingly mobile. Even the mercurial Ruthven declared his nature by dead eyes that were the same in deserts and drawing rooms; Varney's glittering eyes are as mutable as Varney is himself. Varney's physical changes may result in part from the exigencies of rapid serialization— even the gentleman Sir Francis becomes more repulsively corpse-like as the story proceeds, suggesting either that vampires deteriorate if they are sufficiently guilt-stricken, or that the author was getting too tired to maintain fine physical distinctions—but they enhance the vampire's perplexing amorphousness. Is he spirit or goblin, gentleman or fiend, human or creature, predator or friend? The mutations of his relations with Flora Bannerworth reflect his own tantalizing mobility. Though Varney seemed to have disposed of Flora in the first scene, monstrosity gives way to complex affinity.

Flora turns out to be alive but, since Varney is the first vampire who can transform his victims into his kind,[29] she is potentially infected. The good men who love her are terrified at the thought of a transformed Flora preying on her own children, but this anti-Flora never emerges. Stoker will build his *Dracula* around this fear of a condition utterly alien to domesticated identity (especially female identity), exposing bourgeois virtue as sufficiently frail to turn into its own destroyer, but *Varney* refrains from violent contrasts: instead, the vampire and the socialized characters become increasingly difficult to distinguish. Varney's power to transform his victims, which he scarcely exercises, mimics Rymer's own transformation of apparent humanity. The central, sophisticated fear of *Varney the Vampire* is not aberration, but kinship. Varney can turn good citizens into vampires, not because civilization is fragile, but because it has always licensed vampirism. Whether he is gentleman or fiend, Varney becomes an increasingly representative interloper in a predatory society.

As Varney comes to trust the Bannerworth family, he admits that his interest is not in Flora's blood or her soul, but in the fortune her father has concealed in Bannerworth Hall. The power he seeks is neither sexual nor theological; unlike Frankenstein's creature or Dracula, he has no Darwinian ambitions for the triumph of his species over humans; like most middle-class mid-Victorian males, he wants only money, "that greatness which I have ever panted for, that magician-like power over my kind, which the possession of ample means alone can give" (p. 151). What blood will be to Dracula, money is to Varney; his acquisitiveness makes him, as Tennyson might put it, one with his kind. His hunger for money—he eventually acquires the lost fortune by a quite unsupernatural trick—softens his bond with the Bannerworths from infection to friendship. He revokes his monstrous entrance into the novel, assuring Flora that he hasn't attacked her enough to transform her into a vampire; eventually he claims not to have taken any blood from her at all. Instead of turning the Bannerworths into monsters, he melds his identity with theirs: "I am a desperate man, and what there is at all human in me, strange to say, all of you whom I sought to injure, have awakened" (p. 391).

The climax of the first volume is incongruent with the Grand Guignol opening, for it is an act of human fellowship rather than a monstrous invasion: Varney releases Flora's fiancé, Charles Holland, from the dungeon to which he had lured him. The volume ends with the narrator's praise of vampire domestication: "We are pleased to find that Sir Francis Varney, despite his singular, and apparently preternatural capabilities, has something sufficiently human about his mind and feelings, to induce him to do as little injury as possible to others in the pursuit of his own objects" (p. 277). But this "something sufficiently human" makes Varney the gentleman more frightening than the fanged monster who crawled through Flora's window.

For Varney is scarcely alone in a vampiric society. Like *Vanity Fair,* which was serialized at the same time, *Varney the Vampire* plays on the typicality of its supposedly monstrous parasite. A violent mob tramps through the first volume and a half, pursuing Varney, burning both his house and Bannerworth Hall, and, for diversion, killing suspicious strangers on the theory that "who knows, if he ain't a vampyre, how soon he may become one?" (p. 339). In their frenzy of superstition they desecrate a corpse with relish. Vampirism is, for the first time, a communal activity, not an esoteric rite. Thus, unlike theatrical melodramas, *Varney* needs no vampire specialist like Planché's Unda or Boucicault's Dr. Rees to mediate between humanity and the occult: like American teenagers today, the mob are thorough initiates in a condition no longer foreign. Rymer's narrator explains that "the dim and uncertain condition concerning vampyres, originating probably as it had done in Germany,[30] had spread itself slowly, but insidiously, throughout the whole of the civilized world" (p. 188). Realizing that Varney is the lesser predator, the Bannerworths shelter him from socialized murder.

After the mob plays itself out and Varney acquires the Bannerworth fortune, paying his friends back by finding lost property deeds that ensure the family's "comfort and independence," he sets out to buy a bride who will supply him with virgin blood. His misadventures in the marriage market associate him with parents (and some daughters) who are subtler, more skilled predators than the vampire-hunting mob. Next to the sophisticated bartering of polite women—and a Count Polidori who tries to force his daughter into marriage with Varney—his demonism seems innocent. By the time he is cast out of the marriage market, Varney has been thoroughly entangled in mercenary games. The sardonically named Count Polidori enmeshes the vampire further in commercialism; by the last volume the demon has become the commodity we know today. In Rymer's witty metafiction, Polidori, the first storyteller to inject his vampire into popular culture, becomes a possessive father aspiring to feed his daughter to the friend he adores.

From mob to middle class to monarchy, Varney is only one increasingly weary member of a predatory society, the paradigmatic citizen of a decade that named itself the "Hungry '40s." During *Varney*'s serialization, Karl Marx was in London preparing his *Communist Manifesto* (1848). His *Capital* (1867) sealed the vampire's class descent from mobile aristocrat to exploitative employer: "Capital is dead labour which, vampire-like, lives only by sucking living labour, and lives the more, the more labour it sucks."[31] Like Varney, the capitalist vampire is no outsider, but the epitome of licensed unnatural acquisitiveness.

Varney's killer contemporary Sweeney Todd shares the vampire's capitalist avarice. In the 1979 American musical, Stephen Sondheim and Hugh Wheeler romanticized Sweeney into a symbol of crushed love and social despair, but in George Dibdin Pitt's *The String of Pearls; or, The Fiend of Fleet Street,* which opened at the Britannia Theatre in 1847, the demon barber is no rebel; feeding the hunger of unsuspecting Londoners with meat pies composed of his victims, he justifies these ghoulish meals with his own hunger for money: "When a boy, the thirst of avarice was first awakened by the fair gift of a farthing: that farthing soon became a pound; the pound a hundred—so to a thousand, till I said to myself, I will possess a hundred thousand. This string of pearls will complete the sum."[32] Sweeney's greed unites him with the good citizens he feeds.

By the end of Varney's long story, this creation of capitalist democracy is understandably tired of life. Despairing and on the verge of suicide, he tells a friendly clergyman his story: as Mortimer, he was cursed into vampirism during Cromwell's reign because of his inadvertent murder of his son.[33] Restored to undead life by the moon, he wakes to the sound of bells commemorating the anniversary of the Stuart Restoration. He celebrates appropriately by making his first kill, a sixteen-year-old girl: "I sprung upon her. There was a shriek, but not before I had secured a draught of life blood from her neck. It was enough. I felt it dart through my veins like fire, and *I was restored.* . . . How wonderfully revived I felt—I was quite a new creature when the sunlight came dancing into my apartment" (p. 861; my italics). Honoring the Stuart Restoration with his own, Varney acts out the vampirism in all strata of British society, from the superstitious mob to bourgeois marriage brokers to greedy kings.

Vampirism belongs to everyone. Varney is friend, not only to the Bannerworths, but to society in general. Charles Holland's nautical uncle, the Admiral, a comic, choric stock character, sums up the friendship between humanity and vampires: "Lor bless you, he is quite an old acquaintance of ours, is old Varney;

sometimes he hunts us, sometimes we hunt him. He is rather a troublesome acquaintance, notwithstanding, and I think there are a good many people in the world, a jolly sight worse vampyres than Varney" (p. 541).

The Admiral's tolerance captures the spirit of Rymer's satire. Varney is a troublesome acquaintance rather than a dangerous friend like Ruthven because Varney need not lure his prey into "countries not hitherto much frequented by travellers"; England has always known him. The mid-Victorian three-volume novel prided itself on realism and representativeness. When it uncharacteristically features a supernatural character like Varney, it normalizes its vampire by placing him in a feasting society. Like Thackeray's Becky Sharp or Dickens's skulking lawyers, Varney is the confederate of commercial society rather than its monstrous rival. Hungrier for money than for blood, Varney seems worlds away from the dead-eyed, disembodied vampires Byron spawned, but Varney too lives in intimacy with mortals, embracing not a single chosen friend of his own class, but all the greedy strata of England's hierarchy.

Varney's social flexibility brought vampires dangerously close to humanity and away from ghostliness. When, in 1852, Dion Boucicault produced *The Vampire* (retitled *The Phantom* for its 1856 revival), at least one reviewer complained of its vampire's Varney-like proximity to ordinary social life: while tolerating "an honest ghost," the reviewer balked at "an animated corpse which goes about in Christian attire, and although never known to eat, or drink, or shake hands, is allowed to sit at good men's feasts; which renews its odious life every hundred years by sucking a young lady's blood, after fascinating her by motions which resemble mesmerism burlesqued. . . . Such a ghost as this passes all bounds of toleration."[34] Ghosts are legitimate; bodies are beyond the pale. But though vampires sitting at good men's feasts repelled reviewers, these were the vampires readers responded to in the mid-nineteenth century: monsters who showed them not so much foreign lands and alien tastes as the vampirism of their own daily meals.

Boucicault's Alan Raby shares both Varney's humanity and his origin in political upheaval. Like Varney, he identifies him-

self with a particular historical period, the Cromwellian revolution, making his first entrance in stark Puritan costume. This
vampire no longer emanates from a timeless spirit world, as
Planché's Ruthven did, but from a particular historical movement associated with violated boundaries, radical bloodshed,
the division of families, violence against the monarchy. The
Puritan vampire has, for the first time, a historical reason for
being, one that entangles him in human time; in the same in-
surgent spirit, the still more solid Dracula will identify himself
with the nationalistic struggles of his country and his race.

Although *Lord* Alan Raby is even more well titled than *Sir*
Francis Varney (or *Count* Dracula later on), Puritan vampires embody not only entrenched social parasitism, but also the revolu-
tionary self-sufficiency, the integrity of will, the repudiation of
aristocratic privilege, that England's sole revolution champi-
oned. They don't plunge into British history from some other
realm: they inhabit it, simultaneously privileged and protesting.
They resurrect in the 1840s the 1640s that spawned them, re-
leasing incendiary memories in a decade whose inherited authority was undermined by expanded suffrage, a newly orga-
nized working class, the unprecedented economic and political
vulnerability of the landed aristocracy. Dion Boucicault's melodrama learns from *Varney* that history is more frightening than
the spirit world.

Stage history associates Alan Raby with Planché's Ruthven
rather than with his fictional contemporary Varney, but Boucicault's vampire is no reincarnated spirit: like Varney, he is a
walking corpse, to whom the moon gives "false life." Like Varney, Alan Raby is rooted in humanity, if dead humanity; there
is no world of spirits for him to claim as his essential home.
Since vampirism is more esoteric in the theater than in fiction,
a Dr. Rees becomes our expert informant on its peculiar life:

> It is said that if a dead person be exposed to the first rays of
> the rising moon which touch the earth, a false life is instilled
> into the corpse. . . . This creature, living against the will of
> heaven, eats not, drinks not, nor does he require the refresh-
> ment of sleep. . . . This phantom recruits its life by drawing
> the life blood from the veins of the living, but more especially

it chooses victims from amongst maidens pure and spotless.
As the body of this monster is bloodless [since his heart
does not palpitate], so his face is said to be as pale as death.
(P. 22)

This vampire's "false life" may be "bloodless"—unlike that of
Stoker's throbbing Dracula—but it is closer to Varney's reluctant
humanity than to Planché's spirit world. Ada, whose blood Alan
Raby is trying to drink, repudiates him accordingly as a body
without soul: "That breast upon which you press me, seems to
be the bosom of a corpse, and from the heart within I feel no
throb of life!" (p. 25). This vampire is, it seems, solely the body
that repelled advocates of "honest ghosts." Why, then, does Ada
turn inconsistently metaphysical, going on to denounce this
wholly material figure as "phantom! demon!"? And why did
Boucicault rename *The Vampire The Phantom?*

Just as Varney never shakes off his association with the spectral King Hamlet, Alan Raby is still in part a ghost, if not an
honest one. The fountain of his ghostly life is neither divinity
nor devil, but the ambiguous moon. The moon, not blood, is
the life of these vampires, distinguishing them from the humanity to whom they are coming too close; the "bright white light"
that causes Alan Raby's chest to heave and his limbs to quiver
at the end of the first act etherealizes his resurrection, exalting
him from corpse to phantom, raising him above history and the
human race. His position on the "Peaks of Snowdon" aligns him
with the Romantic artist: at the end of *The Prelude,* Wordsworth
stands similarly on top of Snowdon, gazing at a moon preternat-
urally large and bright, absorbing its triumphant life into his
own. But the Romantic poet turns into the Victorian vampire,
and unlike poets, stage vampires cannot remain on Snowdon;
they must finally fall to their predestined home, "the abyss."
Before they fall, however, they look upward, not outward.
Drawn to women's blood only because he must play by the arbitrary rules of the vampire game, Alan Raby finds his true affinity
with that "fountain of his life," the moon. Always uncannily
bright, it licenses vampires to cast off the body that is, in its
essence, a corpse, endowing them with the ghost's freedom from
natural laws.

Post-Stoker vampires are vulnerable to human products: rosaries and holy water, garlic, sharpened stakes. Alan Raby lifts himself beyond that manufactured world to identify with the astronomical occult. Even Varney, the most socially identified of vampires, cannot die by such human rituals as staking: only Clara, the one girl he transforms into a vampire, is sufficiently fledgling to be staked to death. When Varney is sick of life at last, he dives into Vesuvius, his own localized version of the stage abyss; he can be killed only by a fall into an energy as incessant and nonhuman as his own.

Moreover, even more frequently than Alan Raby, Varney undergoes a ritual series of lunar resurrections in the winding course of his story. The reader of *Varney* in serial form apparently expected at least one lunar resurrection per episode—if not Varney's then that of a minor character who dies only to be restored by moonlight. No matter how repetitive they became, these resurrections never seem to have bored Victorian readers. The restorative moon, which is always full, recurs, not to incite repelled hunger as *Dracula*'s fangs and blood do, but to take the reader out of the body. As the moon is about to resuscitate a vampire, the narrator soothes us into awe: "How silently and sweetly the moon's rays fall upon the water, upon the meadows, and upon the woods. The scenery appeared the work of enchantment, some fairy land, waiting the appearance of its inhabitants. No sound met the ear; the very wind was hushed; nothing was there to distract the sense of sight, save the power of reflection" (*Varney*, p. 362). The coming of the moon and the reanimation of the corpse augur purer things: "At such a time, and in such a place, the world is alive with all the finer essences of mysterious life. 'Tis at such an hour that the spirits quit their secret abodes, and visit the earth, and whirl round the enchanted trees" (p. 363).

These lunar "spirits" are not only magical, but vaguely religious. At one point, Varney and two associates ascend Hampstead Heath for a ceremony to induct a vampire fledgling. Secular spectators see three strange worshipers:

> . . . a tall, spectral-looking figure wrapped up in an immense
> cloak, but who did not seem to observe them, for his eyes

were fixed upon the moon, which at that moment again began to emerge from the clouds.

He stretched forth his arms as if he would have held the beautiful satellite to his heart.

"An odd fish," whispered the attorney.

"Very," said his companion. "I should like now to know who he is."

The attorney shrugged his shoulders, as he said, "Some harmless lunatic, most likely. They say that such often wander all night about the parks."

"That's strange; only look at him now, he seems to be worshipping the moon, and now how he strides along; and see, there is another man meets him, and they both hold up their arms in that strange way to the moon. What on earth can be the meaning of it?"

"I really don't know."

"Some religious fanatics, perhaps."

"Ah! that's as likely as not. We have all sorts of them, jumpers and screamers and tearers, and why not a few who may call themselves Lunarians. For my part I would rather worship the moon than I would, as most church and chapel going women do, worship some canting evangelical thief of a parson. . . . Of all the rogues on earth, I do detest those in surplices!" (P. 751)

As "Lunarians," no matter how rapacious or corpse-like they appear, these spectral midcentury vampires are preferable to "those in surplices," for the moon authenticates their spirituality, guaranteeing their elevation above a dreary dishonest world. The Varney who, for most of his story, embodied all levels of social rapacity becomes briefly the acolyte of an alternate religion, one that exalts its members above "the rogues on earth." As a Lunarian, Varney is no longer a creature of history, but a being as remote, pure, and alien as the sky.

Lunarians are the first of many upward-looking vampires. Their brief exaltation anticipates the angelic saviors vampires would become in the late twentieth century. In 1979, for example, two movies—*Love at First Bite* and John Badham's *Dracula* (starring Frank Langella)—featured vampire heroes who fly.

A romantic year in film, 1979 endowed grand bats with the cleansing power of Superman, sweeping the women they loved toward purer altitudes. Lunarians are more reserved. They stretch their arms upward, but they never dream of flight; they claim the moon without becoming the moon; moonlight bathes them without penetrating them. Their affinity with the sky, an affinity that never becomes identification, is equivalent to the remote energy of the friend whose intimacy dissipates in un-earthliness. Impenetrable, alluring, offering a wealth of homo-erotic promises that never quite bear fruit, vampires from Ruth-ven to Varney are as removed from the humanity they resemble as they are from the moon they aspire to. Ruthven's "Remember your oath!" is the classic tease of the male vampire, directing the obsessive energy of his victim/friend away from the present to a past bond that may or may not promise future fulfillment.

The ontological slipperiness of these vampires heightens their erotic elusiveness. Their oscillation between corpse, gentle-man, and ghost mirrors, in these works, the indeterminacy of their friendship. Neither sharer nor predator, but some compel-ling creature in between, vampires abandon their detachment only when they become women.

From Christabel to Carmilla: Friends and Lovers

Carmilla, Sheridan Le Fanu's languid and pedigreed vam-pire, sighs longingly toward Laura, her enthralled prey: "I won-der whether you feel as strangely drawn towards me as I do to you; I have never had a friend—shall I find one now?"[35] For Jane Austen, an effusive vampire might be a "freind" but never that soberer, more cherished being, a "friend." Neither Laura nor Le Fanu can afford such nice distinctions: as Laura tells her own story, she lives, motherless and exiled, with her myopic father and two silly governesses in a Styrian castle. She is cut off from England and other women. When Carmilla penetrates her household—through dreams and tricks as well as bites—she presents herself as Laura's only available source of intimacy. Everything male vampires seemed to promise, Carmilla per-forms: she arouses, she pervades, she offers a sharing self. This female vampire is licensed to realize the erotic, interpenetrative friendship male vampires aroused and denied.[36]

Ruthven, Varney, and the rest are blasphemous by definition, but their emotional life is as compartmentalized as that of any Victorian patriarch: women fill their biological needs, but men kindle emotional complexity. Women exist to be married or depleted or rescued. They are as consummately made as Frankenstein's creature, their condition a barometer of the vampire's power. When a woman becomes a vampire herself, she has no more agency than she did when she was human: Clara rises from her coffin as the pièce de résistance that finally ends *Varney the Vampire*'s feast of blood, but she has nothing to say. Her wordless appearance is testimony to Varney's evil artistry: "And now the light . . . shone on a mass of white clothing within the coffin, and in another moment that white clothing was observed to be in motion. Slowly the dead form that was there rose up, and they all saw the pale and ghastly face. A streak of blood was issuing from the mouth, and the eyes were open" (p. 837). Clara's features are no longer her own: "the" face, "the" mouth, "the" eyes are Varney's fabrications. For all the individuality it expresses, Clara's ghastly face is indistinguishable from her white clothing. Even her name is an abstraction, as is that of the snarling ingenue Clara inspired, Bram Stoker's Lucy Westenra. These girls whose names mean "light" exist only to be extinguished and relit by a vampire master.

Carmilla's is a different story. Her origins are obscure and remote; as far as Laura perceives, she sleeps, prowls, and falls in love on her own authority. If anyone directs her, it is the mother who engineers the supposed carriage accident that deposits Carmilla at the castle of Laura's father. That mother in turn may be directed by a figure only Laura's governess sees, "a hideous black woman, with a sort of coloured turban on her head, who was gazing all the time from the carriage window, nodding and grinning derisively toward the ladies, with gleaming eyes and large white eyeballs, and her teeth set as if in fury" (p. 83).

We never learn who the black woman is, where she comes from, or her degree of power over the action. Carmilla is not the product of a single maker's potency, but the spirit of an elusive female community who may be her makers or merely her confederates, and whose power only women perceive; from the beginning, Laura's father is strangely blind to the women's plot. The "hideous black woman" may be the devil herself in the form of a voodoo priestess; her exotic associations, racial and spiritual, hint at a geographic range of female magic beyond Byron's male-ruled Orient or *Varney*'s Nordic lore.[37] Remembering back through the centuries, Carmilla tells Laura of the "cruel love—strange love" that turned her into a vampire (p. 101). Though she leaves her lover's gender unspecified, the word *strange,* the Swinburnian euphemism for homosexual love, suggests that Carmilla's original maker was female.[38] But like many women—and unlike Varney and the egomaniacal Dracula—Carmilla's maker leaves no signature. As Laura tells her story, Carmilla's hunger is her own, not the projection of some megalomaniacal creator.

Carmilla has all the agency of our male vampires with none of their erotic ambivalence. Like Ruthven and the rest, she compartmentalizes her emotions, but in a subtler manner only an expert can explicate. Thus, Le Fanu brings in one Baron Vordenburg at the end to explain vampirism's "curious lore":

> The vampire is prone to be fascinated with an engrossing vehemence, resembling the passion of love, by particular persons. In pursuit of these it will exercise inexhaustible patience and stratagem, for access to a particular object may be obstructed in a hundred ways. It will never desist until it has satiated its passion, and drained the very life of its coveted victim. But it will, in these cases, husband and protract its murderous enjoyment with the refinement of an epicure, and heighten it by the gradual approaches of an artful courtship. In these cases it seems to yearn for something like sympathy and consent. In ordinary ones it goes direct to its object, overpowers with violence, and strangles and exhausts often at a single feast. (P. 136)

Leaving aside the Baron's condescending, cataloging tone, which aims, unlike Laura's narrative, to make typical Carmilla's idiosyncratic emotional ebbs and flows, the Baron locates scientifically for the first time in literature the division we have seen in male vampires between feeding and friendship. Ruthven fed on women while draining his male friend by the intangible tie of an oath. Carmilla feeds only on women with a hunger inseparable from erotic sympathy, distinguishing among her prey only on the sterling British basis of class. She preys on peasant girls but falls in love with Laura, a protected lady like herself whose relative in fact she is: Laura's dead mother was a Karnstein, part of the "bad family" that produced Carmilla. The Baron, like later Victorian sexologists, glibly turns Carmilla's passion into pathology, but he neglects to tell us that 'unlike many humans, Carmilla loves only those she understands.

Carmilla is one of the few self-accepting homosexuals in Victorian or any literature. One might assume that her vampirism immunizes her from human erotic norms, but most members of her species were more squeamish: no male vampire of her century confronts the desire within his friendship. Despite Mario Praz's portentous division between heroic male and decadent female vampires,[39] the two are interdependent: the women perform for the men. Among vampires, as in more reputable species, homosexuality itself is figured as female.[40]

In the self-conscious 1890s, females would dominate vampire iconography, but their horrible hunger is not Carmilla's: fin-de-siècle literary vampires like Dracula's three sister-brides, theatrical vampires from Mrs. Pat Campbell to Theda Bara, or pictorial vampires like Edvard Munch's *Vampire*—whose face virtually disappears as she chews on her man—are horrible because heterosexual, dreadful because they feast on men. The poem Rudyard Kipling wrote to accompany Philip Burne-Jones's powerful painting of Mrs. Pat Campbell as a vampire excoriates her sins against gender rather than God:

> The Fool was stripped to his foolish hide
> (Even as you and I!)
> Which she might have seen when she threw him aside—
> (But it isn't on record the lady tried)
> So some of him lived but the most of him died—
> (Even as you and I!)

> *And it isn't the shame and it isn't the blame*
> *That stings like a white-hot brand—*

It's coming to know that she never knew why
(Seeing, at last, she could never know why)
And never could understand![41]

To Kipling's male readers in 1897, an enraged, cohesive "us,"
female vampires are an alien gender to whom men's wrenching
adoration is incomprehensible. In 1872, Carmilla is the known.
Her story is less an account of predation than it is of the recognition that underlies all vampire literature before the close of the
nineteenth century. This erotic recognition is not a tender alternative to the coldness of male vampires, but a performance, featuring female characters, of the homoerotic identification men,
even vampires, dare not act on.

Varney plays with the affinity between vampires and humans, but an incidental aphorism denies (with characteristic
hedging) the sort of intense sharing Carmilla exemplifies: "Two
people don't dream of the same thing at the same time; I don't
of course deny the possibility of such a thing, but it is too remarkable a coincidence to believe all at once" (*Varney*, p. 796).
But Carmilla and Laura do dream the same dream at the same
time. As a child, Laura dreams of a caressing young lady entering
her bed and biting her breast. When Carmilla comes to the
castle years later, they recognize each other's faces from their
common childhood dream. Though Carmilla characterizes her
feelings by the Swinburnian code word *strange*, her enchantment is her familiarity.

Carmilla has no use for the moon that had been central to
the animation of male vampires; she drinks life only through
Laura. The moon is at its brightest just *before* Carmilla appears,
and it is analyzed to florid death by Laura's "metaphysical" governess, who declares "that when the moon shone with a light
so intense it was well known that it indicated a special spiritual
activity. The effect of the full moon in such a state of brilliancy
was manifold. It acted on dreams, it acted on lunacy, it acted on
nervous people; it had marvelous physical influences connected
with life. . . . The moon, this night . . . is full of odylic and mag-
netic influence" (pp. 78–79).

Parodying Boucicault's ornate stage effects and the pseudo-
poetry of *Varney the Vampire*, Le Fanu introduces a moon brim-

ming with signification that resuscitates no one. *Varney's* poetic commentary about the moon is an invariable prelude to a lunar resurrection, but Carmilla upstages the moon. Under her dominion, it shrinks to the decorative prop it remains in horror stories, no longer energizing Carmilla, but courteously illuminating her. "How beautiful [Carmilla] looked in the moonlight!" Laura exclaims conventionally (p. 98); at the end, vampire-killing men use moonlight to track Carmilla with no fear that the moon will resurrect her. Carmilla's hunger to absorb another life is the end of the Lunarian vampire.[42] Turning from the sky toward the living, Carmilla lets nothing distract her from the interpenetration that is the essence of the nineteenth-century vampire's hunger.

Carmilla and Laura not only share dreams or visions; they share a life even before Carmilla murmurs, "I live in your warm life and you shall die—die, sweetly die—into mine . . . you and I are one for ever" (pp. 89–90). Both have lost their mothers and their countries; each suffuses the image of the other's absent mother. In their common dream, each perceives the other as a "beautiful young lady," not another child. Like Laura's dead mother, Carmilla is a Karnstein, a vibrant remnant of an apparently extinct family. When Laura's mother breaks protectively into a vampire reverie, her message is so ambiguous that Laura misconstrues it, turning herself into Carmilla and her own mother into her friend's. Hearing a sweet and terrible warning, "Your mother warns you to beware of the assassin," seeing Carmilla bathed in blood at the foot of her bed, Laura fuses self, killer, and mother: "I wakened with a shriek, possessed with the one idea that Carmilla was being murdered" (p. 106). In the flow of female dreams, murderer and murdered, mother and lover, are one; women in *Carmilla* merge into a union the men who watch them never see.

Le Fanu's unconventional imagery brings vampirism home. There are no mediating rituals like Byron's numerology, Polidori's oath, or Varney's lunar resurrections, nor, compared to *Dracula*, does Le Fanu dwell on blood; water is the vampire's medium. "Certain vague and strange sensations visited me in my sleep. The prevailing one was of that pleasant, peculiar cold thrill which we feel in bathing, when we move against the current of a river" (p. 105). Considering the elaborate, arcane rituals in which most vampires indulge, Laura's homely sensation of swimming is neither vague nor strange. Her feelings are as familiar as Carmilla is herself, modulating into caresses and orgiastic shudders: "My heart beat faster, my breathing rose and fell rapidly and full drawn; a sobbing, that rose into a sense of strangulation, supervened, and turned into a dreadful convulsion, in which my senses left me, and I became unconscious" (p. 106).

For Le Fanu, the strangeness of vampirism is its kinship to the commonplace. Its identification with cold water rather than hot blood or spectral moonbeams releases it from both perversity and enchantment; as the lives of Carmilla and Laura flow into each other, with the voice of one spectral mother summoning both girls, so the occult flows into intimate physical sensations. Le Fanu's ghosts have been defined by their chillingly modern absurdity,[43] but his vampire invokes rather the horror inherent in the Victorian dream of domestic coziness, the restoration of lost intimacy and comfort.

In her association with bathing rather than moonbeams or blood, her play with the life of the body rather than the abstractions of magic, Carmilla is no ghost. Waking suddenly, Laura sees at her bed a collage of Carmillas, all of them solid:

> I saw something moving round the foot of the bed, which at first I could not accurately distinguish. But I soon saw that it was a sooty black animal that resembled a monstrous cat. It appeared to me about four or five feet long, for it measured fully the length of the hearth-rug as it passed over it; and it continued to-ing and fro-ing with the lithe sinister restlessness of a beast in a cage. . . . I felt it spring lightly on the bed. The two broad eyes approached my face, and suddenly I felt a stinging pain as if two large needles darted, an inch or two apart, deep into my breast. I waked with a scream . . . and I saw a female figure standing at the foot of the bed, a little at the right side. It was in a dark loose dress, and its hair was drawn and covered its shoulders. A block of stone could not have been more still. There was not the slightest stir of respiration. As I stared at it, the figure appeared to have changed its

place, and was now nearer the door; then, close to it, the door opened, and it passed out. (P. 102)

The miracle of this description, in its own time as now, is its breathtaking freedom from convention. There are no fangs, no slavering, no red eyes, no mesmerism, and no dematerialization, only a larger-than-average cat and a door that opens. The opening door is the key to this vampire: she is all body, though a mutating one, with no vampire trap to enforce transparency. Male vampires took their authority from the ghost of Hamlet's father, but Carmilla's is as cozy as a cat, though one eerily elongated.

Later on, one of the storytelling father figures who enter at the end will negate Laura's perceptions by turning Carmilla back into a phantom, equipped with the old disembodying vampire trap: "How did she pass out from her room, leaving the door locked on the inside? How did she escape from the house without unbarring door or window?" (p. 125). In her immateriality, the General's Carmilla is a monstrous mystery, while Laura's is as solid as the domestic settings. Laura's Carmilla may be strange, but her face and the sensations she arouses are indelibly familiar, and her body is as material as a door.

Laura's story is unique in its freedom from the rituals and conventions that are the usual substance of vampire tales, but its strange familiarity is an incisive comment on the vampires of its time. Carmilla differs from Ruthven, Varney, and the rest in intensity rather than kind: as a woman, the vampiric friend releases a boundless capacity for intimacy. The Byronic vampire was a traveling companion; Carmilla comes home to share not only the domestic present, but lost mothers and dreams, weaving herself so tightly into Laura's perceptions that without a cumbersome parade of male authorities to stop her narrative, her story would never end.

Carmilla initially seems devoid of authorities; Carmilla is so emotionally direct, so indifferent to occultism, that learned translators seem superfluous. Dr. Hesselius, Le Fanu's guide to the supernatural in other tales, comes on only indirectly, in a brief prologue authenticating the "conscientious particularity" of Laura's narrative; he plays no rescuing role. Like many Victorian fathers, Laura's is a venerated fool, impervious to the plot that brings a vampire to his castle, laughing ever more affably as his daughter drifts closer to death. But just as Laura's life is melting into Carmilla's, the story is forced on track by the entrance of the General, whose daughter was Carmilla's previous victim. The General is as competent a father as Laura's is idiotic. His narrative is a variant of Laura's, though its plotting mother seems to take orders, not from a voodoo priestess, but from "a gentleman, dressed in black" with a deathly pallor. The General's tale thus restores male authority on both a diabolical and a domestic plane.

More experts follow the General: a woodman expert in Karnstein revenants, a grotesque old baron who is a trove of vampire lore, a priest, and two medical men who authenticate Carmilla's decapitation, which a "report of the Imperial Commission" verifies. Laura's point of view shrivels under this invasion of experts and official language, as does the vitality of Le Fanu's story. Ruthven and Varney were credible monsters as well as seductive friends, but Carmilla has no monstrous life. Diagnosed as a horror, she dies as a presence; compared to the writhings and bloody foamings of Bram Stoker's staked Lucy, Carmilla's ritual decapitation is an abstract anticlimax to the vividness of her seduction. The Carmilla experts dispatch is as characterless as the blob the General sees attacking his daughter: "I saw a large black object, very ill-defined, crawl, as it seemed to me, over the foot of the bed, and swiftly spread itself up to the poor girl's throat, where it swelled, in a moment, into a great, palpitating mass" (p. 130).

In contrast to the General's ill-defined object, Laura's Carmilla—sharer, cat, mother, and lover—is a vividly defined subject. It is that sharing, individualized vampire—the loved and known companion, not the "great, palpitating mass"—whom nineteenth-century readers believed in and feared. In her suggestive concluding sentence, Laura restores that friend to some sort of life: "It was long before the terror of recent events subsided; and to this hour the image of Carmilla returns to memory with ambiguous alterations—sometimes the playful, languid, beautiful girl; sometimes the writhing fiend I saw in the ruined church; and often from a reverie I have started, fancying I heard the light step of Carmilla at the drawing-room door" (p. 137).

Unlike conventional vampirized ingenues—*Varney*'s Flora or *Dracula*'s Mina—Laura has no congregation of embracing men to welcome her back from the dead; she returns only to the father-ruled solitude of her pre-Carmilla existence. Her final sentence is not merely elegiac: as effectively as the moonlight under which dead male vampires quivered, Laura's memories restore Carmilla's physical life. The "light step" is as material as ever, while the final "door" reminds us that Carmilla is no phantom, but flesh, who, like us, must open doors to pass into rooms. Her oath, "I live in your warm life and you shall die— die, sweetly die—into mine . . . you and I are one for ever," is more warmly inescapable than Ruthven's was: Carmilla does live in Laura's life at the end. Her resurrection raises a lurking question about Laura's own condition: if a "strange love" transformed Carmilla into a vampire, hasn't her own love the power to transform Laura, making their lives literally one? The cryptic announcement in the Prologue that Laura "died" after writing her story (p. 72) does not preclude her being also alive—on the verge, like Carmilla, of opening the door.[44]

Ruthven's oath was formal, ritual, orchestrating his ceremonial burial; Carmilla's is a private, apparently spontaneous outburst, ensuring her continuing life. Nonetheless, in a genre that simultaneously expressed and inhibited its century's dream of homoerotic friendship, Carmilla speaks for the warier vampires who came before her. Her vampirism, like theirs, is an interchange, a sharing, an identification, that breaks down the boundaries of familial roles and the sanctioned hierarchy of marriage.

Carmilla's oath was so binding and seductive that it had no immediate progeny: for generations after Le Fanu, erotic friendship with vampires became unthinkable. Its major source, Coleridge's haunting fragment *Christabel* (1816), has a strange, scarcely cited half-life among vampire works. *Christabel* is a fantastic seduction poem whose serpent-woman Geraldine, like Carmilla, invades the castle and the identity of the motherless Christabel; like Laura's, Christabel's danger is intensified by her father's fatuous misconstructions. *Christabel,* whose main action is the interchange of identity between the two women, was one unacknowledged model for the Byronic vampire, though Byron's persona is too self-absorbed to acknowledge any play among women.

Nonetheless, *Christabel* fed Ruthven. Shortly before the famous ghost-story contest, Byron recited part of it at the Villa Diodati to terrifying effect: Geraldine's exposed bosom sent Percy Shelley shrieking out of the room, possessed by a vision of a woman "who had eyes instead of nipples." The bosoms in Coleridge's poem may or may not have eyes, but they are potent tokens of forbidden friendship. They scared a new generation of Romantics toward their own tales of terror, but no bosoms invade those manuscripts; in *Frankenstein* as well as Byron and Polidori's vampire tales, friends, villains, lovers, and sufferers all are men. Byron admitted no affinity between Coleridge's vampire and his own: his journal claims that he recited Coleridge's "verses . . . of the *witch's* breast" (Macdonald, pp. 92–93; my italics), relegating Geraldine to a different order of monstrosity than that of his own inscrutable Darvell.

Yet by her century's definition Geraldine is unquestionably a vampire: she is, like Darvell, a best friend who offers dangerous sympathy. Neither Byron nor Polidori nor their many adapters acknowledged Geraldine as a model of friendship. Until Le Fanu restored and translated into prose its erotic female plot, *Christabel* was both too strange and too disturbingly familiar to be acknowledged as the origin of the nineteenth-century vampire legend.[45]

Aside from providing the outline of a plot *Carmilla* rationalizes and develops, *Christabel,* like *Carmilla,* strips its story of occult trappings that distract from the erotic interchange of identities between vampire and prey. Intimacy arouses these vampires, not blood or the moon. Like Carmilla, Geraldine outshines the moon that rules Ruthven and Varney. As Christabel hurries to the wood at midnight, ostensibly to pray but actually to encounter Geraldine, the moon recedes: "The moon is behind, and at the full; / And yet she looks both small and dull" (*Coleridge,* I, ll. 18–19). Geraldine, on the other hand, radiates her own light. Christabel encounters a "damsel bright, / Dressed in a silken robe of white, / That shadowy in the moonlight shone" (I, ll. 58–60): the robe the moon casts into shadow nevertheless mysteriously shines. So does Geraldine's body, revealing even her veins: "Her blue-veined feet unsandaled were, / And wildly glittered here and there / The gems entangled in her hair" (I, ll. 63–65).

Geraldine eludes the decorporealizing vampire trap. Male vampires are slighter than doors, walls, and moons; female vampires are solid. The moon resurrects males, but shrinks before females. Moreover, while the power of Varney and Alan Raby takes the form of continual deaths and resurrections, Geraldine's, like Carmilla's, lies in her unquenchable life; neither woman has to die to prove she is always alive. The vitality of female vampires is an extreme embodiment of the vampire legend in the nineteenth century: these glittering companions have a corporeality men evade.

Like Carmilla, Geraldine is eerily inseparable from the spirit of her victim's mother, whom she both displaces and becomes. When she first sees Geraldine, Christabel cries, "Mary mother, save me now!"; once under Geraldine's spell, she prays ineffectually to Christ. Having brought Geraldine to her bedroom, she gives her "a wine of virtuous powers" her mother has made, adding plaintively, "O mother dear! that thou wert here!" and receiving the cryptic response, "'I would,' said Geraldine, 'she were!'" Christabel or Geraldine or the two together summon that mother's spirit, leading Geraldine to attempt an exorcism: "Off, wandering mother! Peak and pine! . . . Though thou her guardian spirit be, / Off, woman, off! 'tis given to me" (I, ll. 190–213). Having apparently expelled Christabel's mother, Geraldine exposes her own bosom, the climactic if undefined sight that transfixes Christabel and terrified Shelley. Her seduction ends in a lullaby, restoring the mother she claimed to have banished:

> And lo! the worker of these harms,
> That holds the maiden in her arms,
> Seems to slumber still and mild
> As a mother with her child.
>
> .   .   .   .

No doubt, she [Christabel] hath a vision sweet.
What if her guardian spirit 'twere,
What if she knew her mother near?
(I, ll. 296–99; 326–28)

Like Carmilla, Geraldine is simultaneously the lost mother's antagonist and her embodiment. The ambiguous exorcism in *Christabel* is the genesis of the cry in *Carmilla*—a cry that simultaneously denounces Carmilla and protects her—"Your mother warns you to beware of the assassin." These female vampires become the mothers they dispel, restoring the life they consume. In both works, moreover, when the supposedly dead mother returns, she is as subversive an outsider as the tender vampire. She does not heal the family, but dissipates its boundaries by supplanting the inept father who was its sole authority.

In *Christabel*'s cryptic second half, which takes place under the father's impercipient eye, Christabel is so imbued with Geraldine that, like Le Fanu's Laura at the end of her narrative, she can only turn into her. Laura, prosaic to the last, hears a familiar step at the door; the more baroque Christabel hisses like the serpent who is Geraldine's essence while her father caresses the lovely intruder. Vampire and victim are so entwined that, like *Carmilla*, the story has no logical end, for no character can be saved or damned. Le Fanu's experts plod in and chop Carmilla out of the narrative; Coleridge simply stops his poem. In nineteenth-century iconography, male vampires are allies of death who end their narratives by killing or dying, but females are so implicated in life's sources that their stories overwhelm closure.

Christabel and *Carmilla* isolate vampirism as an extract of alien femaleness. The itinerant Byronic vampire has the world as his stage; Geraldine and Carmilla flourish in the obscure privacy of women's bedrooms and dreams. But not all female vampires in the nineteenth century offer overpowering empathy; Keats's *Lamia* (1820) features, like *Christabel,* a vampiric serpent-woman, but the sinuously heterosexual Lamia does not mingle her identity with that of her bemused prey. She is an artist of the occult whose powers demand spectators, not sharers. Since her magic is stronger than her body, the philosopher Apollonius, Keats's male expert, easily deciphers her art and destroys her.

Christabel has no expert to decipher Geraldine, whose art is her being. Her power lies in a bosom that controls the poem, even though it may not exist at all, for its revelation enforces concealment: "Behold! her bosom and half her side— / A sight to dream of, not to tell" (I, ll. 252–53). "Behold!" is exactly what we cannot do, just as Christabel, confronted with the bosom, cannot speak: "In the touch of this bosom there worketh a spell, / Which is lord of thy utterance, Christabel!" (ll. 267–68). The bosom—or charismatic nonbosom—feeds dreams but blocks narrative. It may be large; it may drip milk; it may have shriveled into nonexistence (in part II, Christabel remembers it as "old" and "cold"); it may, like the vision that sent Shelley shrieking out of the room, be able to see you. Whatever it looks like, it is inseparable from Geraldine's body; it is neither magic to be shared nor an illusion to be dissipated, but a proclamation of femaleness.

Men acquire, through occult rigmarole, the vampirism women embody. Male vampires declare their condition by their deathly aura; Geraldine's inheres in the life of her body. Its entanglement with the source of life and with the identity of its prey may well have sent Shelley shrieking. Byron evaded Geraldine's spell by translating her bosom into the formal, purely verbal oath that binds vampire to mortal; Keats evaded it by abstracting it into a spell legible to experts. Throughout the century, male writers of vampirism followed their example: their vampires offer a friendship mystified into occult abstractions. Only among women, those specialists in romantic friendship, is vampirism embodied in a physical, psychic union the experts of the next century would label "homosexual."[46] The touch of Geraldine's bosom crystallizes the spell male vampires cast but refuse to perform.

Compared to the polished formulations and logical structure of later vampire works, Coleridge's unfinished poem is so elliptical and eccentric that its influence was easy to ignore. The ghost of Hamlet's father is a suitably stately progenitor of Darvell, Ruthven, Alan Raby, and Varney, all of whom by implication disown the touchable Geraldine. Even when Le Fanu suc-

cumbed to *Christabel* by recasting it in prose, he evaded
Geraldine's bosom. Initially, that bosom is the site not of the
vampire's power, but of the victim's wound: Laura's childhood
dream of Carmilla concludes with "a sensation as if two needles
ran into my breast very deep at the same moment" (p. 74), and
as an adult she describes "a stinging pain as if two large needles
darted, an inch or two apart, deep into my breast" (p. 102). Carmilla remembers her own transformation similarly: "'I was all
but assassinated in my bed, wounded *here*,' she touched her
breast, 'and never was the same since'" (p. 101).

But under the eyes of her father and a male doctor, Laura's
wound creeps chastely upward until it rests on the neutral neck
to which Stoker would confine vampires:

> "You mentioned a sensation, like that of two needles piercing
> the skin, somewhere about your neck, on the night when you
> experienced your first horrible dream. . . . Can you indicate
> with your finger about the point at which you think this oc-
> curred?"
>
> "Very little below my throat—*here*," I answered.
>
> I wore a morning dress, which covered the place I
> pointed to.
>
> "Now you can satisfy yourself," said the doctor. "You
> won't mind your papa's lowering your dress a very little. It is
> necessary, to detect a symptom of the complaint under which
> you have been suffering."
>
> I acquiesced. It was only an inch or two below the edge of
> my collar. (P. 111)

Considering her desperate circumstances, Laura is oddly insistent about her wound's ascent from bosom to neck. So was the
vampire literature *Christabel* inspired. A century of alluring vampire friends evade erotic sites, the shared reality of bodies, on
behalf of an abstract bond and a purely surgical violence. In
1897, *Dracula* provided a lexicon of vampirism for the twentieth
century. Predators were identifiable by their fangs, victims by
two little holes in their neck. After *Dracula*, contact between
vampire and victim is as external to the body as possible. Moving from the erotic to the clinical, from affinity to penetration,

vampire iconography abandons bosoms, fastening with scientific precision on higher, cleaner wounds.

Carmilla's Progress

Carmilla is the climax and the end of a dream of an intimacy so compelling only vampires could embody it. She survives through the twentieth century, but she shrinks to conform to our own century's embarrassed decorum. The loss of her obsessed generosity is an index of an intensifying cultural repression evident in her passage from a Victorian novel about romantic friendship through a slew of sexy twentieth-century films.

Twentieth-century adaptations abandon Geraldine's bosom. In most of these, voyeurism supplants friendship: most structure the women's story around the responses of a male watcher, explicit or implied. *Carmilla*'s men might be experts but they were incompetent watchers: Laura's father was blind to women's plots, and even the General saw the vivid Carmilla only as a blob. In twentieth-century film adaptations, by contrast, female vampires spring to life only under men's eyes. In Andrea Weiss's categorical but depressingly accurate diagnosis, "What has survived of *Carmilla* from Victorian literature and worked its way into twentieth-century cinema is its muted expression of lesbians, no longer sympathetically portrayed but now reworked into a male pornographic fantasy."[47] The physical and psychic sharing available only to women, according to nineteenth-century ideologies of gender, is scarcely possible in our own, more squeamish *Carmillas*.[48]

Carl Dreyer's stately *Vampyr* (1932) is the first canonical vampire film not based on *Dracula;* it claims to be, instead, a loose adaptation of *Carmilla*. Despite its source, *Vampyr* scrupulously avoids not only erotic intimacy, but all contact between its characters, whether they are human or preterhuman; its key images involve a solitude so solemnly intense that it is scarcely a vampire film at all. Dreyer's fastidious distance from his source guarantees his artistry for many critics: according to Pauline Kael, "most vampire movies are so silly that this film by Carl Dreyer—a great vampire film—hardly belongs to the genre."[49]

To achieve art status for his film, a director must drain away his vampires.

Dreyer's protagonist is neither Carmilla (here a blind old crone less visible than her diabolical male henchmen) nor Laura, whose character is split into two sisters: the stricken Léone, who spends most of the movie in bed, sobbing and shuddering over her own damnation, and the beleaguered Gisèle, whom the hero rescues at the end. The center of the film is the man who sees them. The opening title affirms the primacy of a male watcher: "This story is about the strange adventures of young Alan Gray. His studies of devil worship and vampire terror of earlier centuries have made him a dreamer, for whom the boundary between the real and the unreal has become dim." Like the dreamer/director Carl Dreyer, this poetic spectator retains full control over the mysterious world he observes.[50]

The story is indeed "about" Alan Gray's oblique experience of vampirism. We watch him watching the interplay between satanic shadows and human characters; intently reading experts' accounts (as have less exalted vampire-watchers from Boucicault's melodramas through Hammer films and the inhabitants of Stephen King's 'Salem's Lot); dreaming of his own burial alive, which he observes from his coffin in horror; sailing into mist with Gisèle once the crone has been staked. Vampirism here is Alan Gray's experience, his dream, or his creation. The viewer is barred from participating in it; we watch only Alan watching.

Vampirism is purged of sharing or interchange. The crone and Léone are scarcely together. When they are, the physical contrast between the massive blind woman and the frail girl is so controlling that vampirism comes to resemble self-hypnosis rather than affinity. In one dreamlike sequence, Léone wanders into the garden, where Alan and the spectators find her sprawled on a rock with the crone leaning over her. The scene freezes into a tableau that realizes Fuseli's famous painting, *The Nightmare;* its stylization deflects attention from active physical interchange toward a poetic spectator who appreciates cinematic painting.

Other scenes among women are similarly purged of affinity.

Large close-ups of Léone or Gisèle with sorrowing or stern older women—the old servant, the austere nursing nun—force the women's visual incompatibility on the viewer: old and young, imposing and frail, dark and blond, seem to inhabit different physical universes. These insistent contrasts replace the amorphous maternal spirit of *Carmilla,* who both protects against and embodies the vampire. When Léone, half-transformed, bares her teeth, Gisèle shrinks away into the nun's arms, expressing no empathy with her beloved sister. Later, we hear from behind a closed door a woman's seductive plea, "Come with me! We will be one soul, one body! Death is waiting," but we see neither speaker nor hearer. *Vampyr* is that rarity in the vampire canon, a work that forecloses intimacy.

Its two most famous sequences have little to do with vampires: in both, men experience the claustrophobic solitude of burial alive. In a vision, Alan Gray observes his own funeral, watching the grave close over him through a glass window in his coffin; at the end, the sinister doctor Marc is trapped in a flour mill, flailing helplessly as a blizzard of whiteness covers him. These splendid sequences throw the focus away from vampirism, women, or any emotional interchange; the men who helplessly, silently, watch themselves sink recapitulate the director's lonely terror at his own submergence in images. The one canonical masterpiece *Carmilla* inspired announces implicitly that female vampires are incompatible with art's mastery.

Roger Vadim's art movie *Et mourir de plaisir* (1960; released in America in 1961 under the appropriately painterly title *Blood and Roses*) is less stark than *Vampyr,* but its visual dynamic is the same: a blond and a dark woman, here more striking in their visual contrast than in their acting ability, parade erotically before the ambivalent eyes of a male watcher—Mel Ferrar, a Karnstein descendant both of them love. Carmilla, the apparent vampire, is in reality only a *reincarnation* of the eighteenth-century vampire Millarca, who in her life murdered all the mortal women male Karnsteins wanted to marry—represented here by the dark Georgia, to whom Mel Ferrar is engaged. Erotic affinity is chastely sublimated in a heterosexual romantic triangle. In the same soothing spirit, the vampire is less a character than

a personification of the haunting stately past she commemo-
rates in her chanted refrain: "My name is Millarca. I lived in the
past. I live now."

Le Fanu's intensity fades into remote and decorative effects.
Like *Vampyr, Blood and Roses* is made to be watched, not shared.
Its sleepy actors are there to display the director's gorgeous red-
and-white imagery: spreading bloodstains emphasize the bosoms under pristine white dresses; in a floral conceit that replaces contact with mortals, swollen roses wither under a vampire's touch. When Carmilla vampirizes Georgia at last, her visit
swells into a dream sequence so ornate that it obliterates any
potential affinity between the women. As in *Vampyr,* visual spectacle displaces the erotic plot. We are spectators of somnolent
women who (at least in the bowdlerized American version)
scarcely notice each other as they drift about erotically for our
delectation.

The Vampire Lovers (1970, dir. Roy Ward Baker), one of the
later, softer products of England's prolific Hammer Studios,[51]
learns its technique from Dreyer and Vadim, but this *Carmilla*
variation is giddily hostile to high art. Like all Hammer films, it
exudes a cheerful semi-pornographic opulence bold in its time;
but as in *Vampyr* and *Blood and Roses,* the predations of the vampire are dependent on the obsessions of a watching male, here
a famous vampire-killer who comes on at the beginning and the
end to control the action, framing the women's story in narrative voice-over. Primarily, though, that watcher is the drooling
adolescent in the audience.[52] Baker multiplies Le Fanu's two
women into five sexy vampires, victims, and intermediates: the
nameless Karnstein decapitated by a strapping Baron in the
opening sequence, Carmilla, Laura (whom Carmilla quickly
kills), Emma (the Laura figure), and Emma's German tutor, sinister because intellectual, who becomes, without being bitten,
Carmilla's slavish acolyte. For the body of the movie, these
women parade around in various combinations, displaying to
caressing close-ups blown-up breasts celestially echoed by a
swollen moon. Not only does this breast fetishism "reduce lesbian desire to an infantile, pre-Oedipal phase of development"
(Weiss, *Vampires and Violets,* p. 96); it muffles the vampire's
mouth, the dominant weapon in Hammer's *Dracula* series, not

only submerging her in maternal fleshiness, but silencing her. In both art and commercial film, Le Fanu's characters forfeit their story to become cinematic spectacles.

One would expect feminist chic to radicalize female vampires, and in one sense it has: they have become success symbols. In the iconoclastic *Daughters of Darkness* (1971, dir. Harry Kümel), where Delphine Seyrig's suave vampire does overcome the perverse sadism of the supposedly normal husband, this cool creature is a victor, but scarcely a friend: though Seyrig and the battered wife kill the husband and go off together, Seyrig's Countess Bathory is an imperious aristocrat like Dracula, not a sharer like Carmilla.

Miriam Blaylock in *The Hunger* (1983, dir. Tony Scott), the affluent Carmilla of the 1980s, has roots in the self-obsessed, almost airless cinematic art of the 1930s and the teasing spectacles of the 1960s and '70s. Neither Scott's film nor the Whitley Strieber novel on which it is based acknowledges Le Fanu directly. Strieber does allude to Keats's Lamia, who, like Miriam, specializes less in dreams and desire than in gorgeous decor, but Lamia enchants only men, while Miriam's seduction of Sarah, the scientist trying to study her, is at the center of *The Hunger.* Unlike the sleepwalkers in earlier movies, Miriam and Sarah almost manage to be friends; unlike most women in vampire movies, they do talk to each other; but in both film and novel, their creators' conventions come between them.

Whitley Strieber's novel is an exactingly intelligent myth of "another species, living right here all along. An identical twin" of humanity, but a twin glowingly superior, self-regenerating, attuned to the laws of history through surviving the repeated rise and decline of empires.[53] Strieber's Miriam is a dominant, superior consciousness who has survived centuries of arrogant imperial persecution. Tony Scott's film fractures Strieber's vivid imagination of higher organisms. Scott's Miriam is far from timeless. She epitomizes the glamour of the 1980s, subordinating history to seductive objects: jewelry, furniture, lavish houses in glamorous cities, leather clothes. Responding to the success stories of her consuming decade, Miriam lives through her things. She kills, not with her teeth, but with her jewelry, an ankh that hides a knife.[54] She preserves her desiccated former lovers, who age eternally once their vampirism wears off, as carefully as she does her paintings. These things, along with the music and the cityscapes over which she presides, make us envy Miriam's accoutrements instead of her immortality. Vampires in *The Hunger* are not their powers, but their assets.

The movie reduces Miriam not only by subordinating her to her props, but by appropriating the staccato visual techniques of MTV. The characters, like the look of the film, are fractured. Miriam loses not only the memories that, in Strieber's novel, take her back to the beginning of Western civilization, but her controlling consciousness. Originally a figure of lonely integrity throughout the waste of empires, Scott's Miriam becomes an icon of glamorous discontinuity.

Dreyer's and Vadim's vampire women shrank to stylized figments of a male artist's dream, Baker's into interchangeable stuffed breasts. Scott too turns his characters into parts of themselves. Mouths predominate, often crosscut with the giant grimace of a laboratory monkey, but Scott also cuts between disjointed eyes, hands, nipples, teeth, throats, blood, and (in the love scene between Miriam and Sarah) legs and breasts, fetishizing fragments until the audience scarcely knows what eye or hand belongs to which man or woman, or (in the love and murder scenes) who is doing what to whom. Although Catherine Deneuve's soft blond Miriam and Susan Sarandon's dark edgy Sarah are contrasting visual types whose rhythms evoke different centuries, Scott's slashing camera makes them effectively indistinguishable in key scenes.[55] Postmodern cinema aligns itself with 1930s high art and 1960s soft porn, creating a collusion between director and viewer that dwarfs personality and overpowers the chief gift of Victorian vampires: their friendship.

Moreover, while Le Fanu's Laura became Carmilla by remembering her at the end, Sarandon's Sarah becomes Miriam by dismembering her: after flexing her new vampirism by butchering her male lover, Sarah defies and displaces Miriam. In *Blood and Roses* and *Daughters of Darkness,* the seemingly dead vampire lived on in her female victim at the end, but Susan Sarandon is more conqueror than possession. *The Hunger* ends with an opaque shot of Sarah and a female lover looking down over another city; her distinctive style, her rhythm, her decor, all have turned into Miriam's. The vampirism that meant sharing in the 1870s adapts to the competitive business ethos that reigned over America in the 1980s. There is room for only one at the top.

Strieber's provocative novel features an omnipotent Miriam who continues to reign at the end, but in the novel too, the triumph of vampirism is the failure of sharing. *Carmilla*-like promises abound, only to be denied as wicked illusions: "[Sarah's] mother kept coming to mind. She had not felt this sense of intimate female friendship since she was a child" (p. 183). "Then she smiled and Sarah wanted to laugh with delight at the radiance of it. Her whole being seemed to rise to higher and higher levels as Miriam continued to look into her eyes. It was as if she could feel Miriam's feelings inside of herself, and those feelings were pure and loving and good" (p. 241).

The intimacy, the sharing, the maternal suffusion, were the essence, in the nineteenth century, of the vampire's allure. Le Fanu's Laura never stopped feeling Carmilla's feelings inside her, nor did she bother to question whether those feelings were good. Strieber, however, sunders the friendship with jarringly abrupt moralism. Once Sarah has killed her male lover, she suddenly sees Miriam in a higher heterosexual light: "You love only yourself! You're worse than a monster. Much worse! . . . You can't love me or anybody else. You're incapable of it!" (p. 295). Strieber hammers the diagnosis home by forcing even the victorious Miriam to acknowledge Sarah's sexual and spiritual superiority: "Miriam now realized that the gift she could confer was not above one such as Sarah, but beneath her" (p. 306). The vampire's uncharacteristic humility at the end disavows her earlier, exalted disrespect for human love: "Sarah had despaired of ever really being loved. She wanted Tom, enjoyed him sexually, but the old hollowness asserted itself, the reality once again emerging. Miriam could work in the forest of Sarah's emotions. She knew well her role in this age: the bringer of truth" (p. 141). But Miriam's cynical truth is never allowed to prevail: once Tom is dead, love conquers all. Strieber's sophisticated account of science, aesthetics, the tenacity of intelligence, and the fall of empires ends by capitulating to an emotional normalcy to which the Victorian Le Fanu was supremely indifferent. The journey into unknown countries is forbidden.

THE REAL TWENTIETH-CENTURY TALISMAN against vampires is not garlic or a crucifix, but Sarah's diagnostic cry: "You can't love me or anybody else. You're incapable of it!" Dracula, the father of our vampires, was vulnerable to the same accusation from a former lover: "You yourself never loved; you never love!"[56] The twentieth-century vampires Dracula spawned mean many things, but they have lost the love they brought to those they knew.

In the nineteenth century, vampires were vampires *because* they loved. They offered an intimacy, a homoerotic sharing, that threatened the hierarchical distance of sanctioned relationships. Generally contorted and vicarious, that love expressed itself most fully through men's imaginations of women, those licensed vehicles of intimacy. *The Hunger* grafts twentieth-century denials—formal and moral—to an essentially nineteenth-century vision of union. The vampires our own century creates are empire builders who repudiate the "intimacy, or friendship" of their sentimental predecessors.

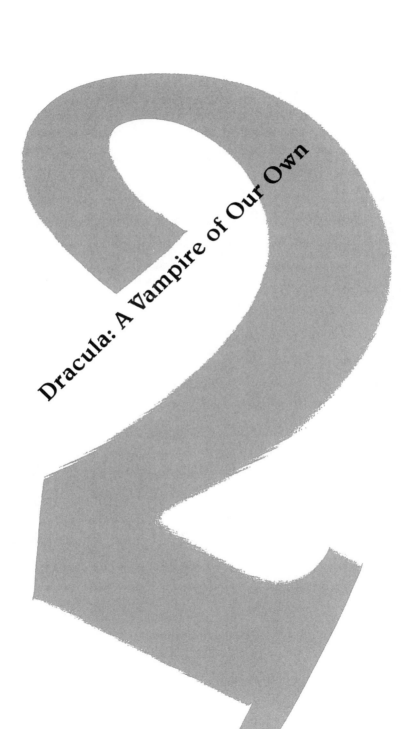

2

Dracula: A Vampire of Our Own

Dracula's New Order

DRACULA IS SO MUSTY AND FOUL-SMELLING, so encrusted with the corruption of ages, that it sounds perverse to call him "new." The up-to-date young people who hunt him dread his ancientness. To them, Dracula is not simply evil; he is an eruption from an evil antiquity that refuses to rest in its grave. The earnest Jonathan Harker, who visits Castle Dracula to his bane, fears that although his shorthand diary "is nineteenth century up-to-date with a vengeance," "the old centuries had, and have powers of their own which mere 'modernity' cannot kill."[1] Ruthven and Carmilla looked as young as their enthralled prey; Dracula flings his weight of ages against the acquired skills of a single generation. Surely this antediluvian leech has no role in their smart new century.

In his novel, Dracula awes because he is old, but within the vampire tradition, his very antiquity makes him new, detaching him from the progressive characters who track him. Ruthven was in some threatening sense a mirror of his schoolfellow Aubrey; Varney reflected his predatory society; Carmilla mirrored Laura's own lonely face. But in our first clue to Dracula's terrible nature, Jonathan Harker looks in his shaving mirror and sees no one beside him. In Jonathan's mirror, the vampire has no more face than does Dickens's Spirit of Christmas Future. In his blankness, his impersonality, his emphasis on sweeping new orders rather than insinuating intimacy, Dracula *is* the twentieth century he still haunts. Not until the twentieth century was he reproduced, fetishized, besequeled, and obsessed over, though many of his descendants deny his lovelessness—and perhaps their own as well. Dracula's disjunction from earlier, friendlier vampires makes him less a specter of an undead past than a harbinger of a world to come, a world that is our own.[2]

MOST CRITICS WHO BOTHER to study Dracula at all proceed on the lazy assumption that since all vampires are pretty much alike, his origins extend neatly back through the nineteenth century to Lord Ruthven, Varney, and, particularly, Carmilla.[3] Dracula, however, is less the culmination of a tradition than the destroyer of one. His indifference to the sort of intimacy Carmilla offered a lonely daughter is a curt denial of the chief vampire attribute up to his time.

Carmilla aspired to see herself in a friend. Dracula, in one of his few self-definitions, identifies only with a vanished conquering race whose token is not a mortal but an animal: "We Szekelys have a right to be proud, for in our veins flows the blood of many brave races who fought as the lion fights, for lordship" (p. 28). No human can share the mirror with a lord of lost races whose names Englishmen can't pronounce. Dracula's strangeness hurls to oblivion the Byronic vampire refrain, "Remember your oath." Earlier vampires insinuated themselves into a humanity Dracula reshapes, through magic and mesmerism, into his unrecognizable likeness.

Dracula's literary affinities lie less with vampires in earlier prose tales than with Keats's *Lamia* (1820), a poem that insists on the barriers between immortal predator and human prey. Lamia is a gorgeous serpent-woman whose influence flowers in vampire works of the 1890s; before that, she mattered less to vampire writers than did Geraldine, the serpent-woman of Coleridge's *Christabel,* who bequeathed human sympathies to the vampires she engendered.

Geraldine, we remember, diffused herself into Christabel's bleak household, exuding her identity into Christabel herself and half-becoming—as Le Fanu's Carmilla would do—the dead mother of her beloved female prey. Geraldine's potency rested in the breast that transfixed Christabel, a breast the reader never saw: the fountain of her expansive power was "a sight to dream of, not to tell."

Lamia dreams and tells; its serpent-woman is less sharer than spectacle. Like Lycius, the innocent young man she seduces, we watch Lamia's transformative gyrations from without. Some of us might have breasts, but none of us has Lamia's exotically endowed body, "Striped like a zebra, freckled like a pard, /

Eyes like a peacock, and all crimson barr'd."[4] Like Dracula with his Szekelys and lions, Lamia transfixes spectators because she belongs to a world only exotic animals share; no human body can emulate hers. Like Dracula's, Lamia's main vampiric attribute is not interpenetration, but transformation.

Keats's poem, like Stoker's novel, is a tale of metamorphoses. Lamia mutates continually (from serpent to goddess to mortal woman to nullity), confirming as she does so the barriers between life forms; over and over, she defines herself by what she is not. The world of Keats's gods, to which she belongs, is as distinct from that of mortals as is the world of Stoker's vampires: "Into the green-recessed woods they flew; / Nor grew they pale, as mortal lovers do" (ll. 144–45). In Coleridge's poem, Christabel's father understandably mistook Geraldine for his friend's daughter, but Keats's Lycius never thinks Lamia is human, even after her transformation into a maiden: like Stoker's seemingly mad Renfield, Lycius worships another order of being and knows he does. Christabel's household absorbed the vampire, while Lamia is segregated from the society she intoxicates: Lycius abandons his own home for Lamia's "purple-lined palace of sweet sin," a retreat as distinct from an ordinary residence as Stoker's Castle Dracula.

As with Dracula, to know Lamia is to destroy her. In the spirit of Stoker's interdisciplinary expert Van Helsing, Lycius's tutor Apollonius recognizes Lamia for what she is; he eyes her piercingly at her wedding feast, forcing her to vanish. The lore—scientific, superstitious, theological, criminological, legal, and geographic—with which Van Helsing comes equipped similarly allows Dracula to be defined and thus dissipated. For Keats and Stoker, vampires are so distinct from humanity that to know them is to dispel them; they can be cataloged, defined, and destroyed. Scientific expertise supplants the oath with which Polidori bound vampire to mortal.

Expertise had little relevance to Dracula's ancestors in English prose. Weaving in and out of their human prey, mysteriously incorporating their nature into our own, they were not remote spectacles, but congenial fellow travelers who were scarcely separable from their victim or from us, their victim/reader. Dracula is on a journey that is not ours. With his advent, vampires cease to be sharers; instead, they become mesmerists, transforming human consciousness rather than entering it. When he rejected Coleridge's Geraldine for Keats's gorgeous Lamia, Bram Stoker created an uncongenial vampire for an obscure future.

Dracula is defined by repudiations and new beginnings. Conventional wisdom assumes its derivation from *Carmilla,* but Stoker's most significant revision excised from his manuscript the shadow of Carmilla and everything she represented. In a canceled, posthumously published opening chapter, frequently anthologized as "Dracula's Guest," Jonathan Harker is trapped in a blizzard on his way to Castle Dracula. He stumbles into the tomb of

COUNTESS DOLINGEN OF GRATZ

IN STYRIA

Terrorized by her sleeping, then shrieking, specter, he is trapped until a great wolf, which may be Dracula himself, shelters him from the storm and saves him from this terrible woman.[5]

Since Carmilla is also a female vampire from Gratz, in Styria, scholars take Countess Dolingen as proof of Le Fanu's influence on Stoker.[6] Actually, though, the shadowy Countess personifies an influence rejected: the spectacle of a "beautiful woman with rounded cheeks and red lips, seemingly sleeping on a bier" (p. 170) has little to do with Le Fanu's insinuating guest, who, infiltrating the dreams of her hostess, is most dangerous when awake. Moreover, if this chapter was ever part of *Dracula,*[7] Stoker wisely deleted it, thereby exorcising an imperial female vampire who drives Dracula into an alliance with Jonathan. The women Stoker retained—Dracula's three lascivious sister-brides; the vampirized Lucy and Mina—may writhe and threaten, but all are finally animated and destroyed by masterful men. A ruling woman has no place in the patriarchal hierarchy *Dracula* affirms, a hierarchy that earlier, more playful and sinuous vampires subverted.

Dracula is in love less with death or sexuality than with hierarchies, erecting barriers hitherto foreign to vampire literature; the gulf between male and female, antiquity and newness, class and class, England and non-England, vampire and mortal, homoerotic and heterosexual love, infuses its genre with a new

fear: fear of the hated unknown. Earlier prey knew their vampires and often shared their gender: Carmilla introduces herself
to Laura in a childhood dream. But Dracula is barred from the
dream of Stoker's hero, which admits only three "ladies by their
dress and manner," one of whose faces Jonathan, like Laura,
"seemed somehow to know . . . and to know it in connection
with some dreamy fear" (p. 51). Jonathan's flash of recognition
remains unresolved, tempting later vampire hunters to identify
this fair predator with Lucy or Mina or both.[8] But whichever
woman arouses his dreamy fear, Jonathan surely does *not* recognize his own face in the vampire's as Le Fanu's Laura did. Like
the empty mirror, the face of the demon cannot reflect its prey,
nor can Dracula participate in Jonathan's exclusively heterosexual vision of three laughing chomping women who are not only
an alien species, but an alien gender. Stoker austerely expels
from his tale of terror the "intimacy, or friendship" that had,
since Byron's time, linked predator to prey.

Like Lord Ruthven, Dracula was a proud servant's offering
of friendship to a great man: the actor Henry Irving, whose
splendid Lyceum Theatre Stoker managed from its ascendancy
in 1878 to its fall out of Irving's control in 1898. Like Byron,
Irving became a hero for his age because he played damnation
with flair; his celebrated Mephistopheles gave Dracula his contours, just as Byron's sexual predations, in verse and out of it,
had flowed into Ruthven. Moreover, Irving, like Byron, could be
turned into a vampire by an underling not simply because he
posed as a demon, but because both men radiated the hero's
simulated transparency. Though they were known by all, they
were tantalizingly unattainable in private to the men they lured
into fellowship.

But friendship with Irving was a tribute to exalted distance,
not a spur to dreams of intimacy. Ellen Terry, Irving's partner at
the Lyceum, wrote shrewdly about his almost inhuman re-
moteness:

> H. I. is odd when he says he hates meeting the company and
> "shaking their greasy paws." I think it is not quite right that
> he does not care for anybody much. . . . Quiet, patient, toler-
> ant, impersonal, gentle, *close,* crafty! Crafty sounds unkind,

but it is H. I. 'Crafty' fits him. . . . For years he has accepted fa-
vours, obligations to, etc., *through* Bram Stoker! Never will he
acknowledge them himself, either by business-like receipt or
by any word or sign. He 'lays low' like Brer Rabbit better than
any one I have ever met.[9]

Accepting with pride the role of Irving's liaison with the
outside world, Stoker was no Polidori, fantasizing class equality
and impossible communion. Stoker knew his place, a mightier
one than Polidori's. As Byron's personal physician, Polidori was
hired to care for that famous body, but he ministered only to be
mocked. Stoker had no access to Irving's body but he did run
his empire, where his responsibilities were "heady and over-
whelming. He oversaw the artistic and administrative aspects of
the new theatre, and acted as Irving's buffer, goodwill ambassa-
dor, and hatchet man. He learned the pleasures of snobbery,"
admitting only the artistic and social elite to the glamorous
openings and even more theatrical banquets over which Irving
presided after the performance.[10] Like Jonathan in *Dracula,*
Stoker deftly manipulated the business of modern empire—particularly the intricacies of money, travel, and human contact—
that paralyzed his master. Onstage, Irving's power to mesmerize
crowds was as superhuman as the vampire's, but he relied, as
Byron never did, on the worldly dexterity of the servant who
made him immortal.

Byron's dismissal was Polidori's mortal wound, but Irving
never betrayed Stoker's faith in his master's protection. Even
when Irving's theatrical fortunes began to decline, shortly after
Dracula was published, Stoker continued to celebrate his master's benevolent omnipotence, writing glowingly about "the
close friendship between us which only terminated with his
life—if indeed friendship, like any other form of love, can ever
terminate."[11] One doubts whether the friendship was "close" in
Polidori's sense, but when that life did terminate, Stoker wrote
a two-volume official memoir, *Personal Reminiscences of Henry Irving* (1906), that consecrated his subject with a reverence
granted only to dignitaries and authors—never, until then, to
an actor. The Irving of *Personal Reminiscences* is as marmoreally
undead as the more animated Dracula.

Polidori never recovered from the humiliation of his service to Byron, writing truculently that "I am not accustomed to have a master, & there fore my conduct was not free & easy"; Stoker grew stately in his master's shadow, feeding on hero worship while paying extravagant lip service to heterosexual love.[12] Polidori's "free & easy" vampire who subsists on mortal affinities yielded at the end of the century to Stoker's master, an impenetrable creature hungering for control.

Jonathan's Master

Dracula's protracted intercourse with Lucy and Mina, whom he transforms in foreplay so elaborate that few readers notice its narrative incoherence, made him a star in the twentieth century. Jonathan Harker, the only man who is Dracula's potential prey, is overshadowed by bitten women who, in Lord Ruthven's time, were mere shadowy counters in the game between the men. Jonathan, however, is no player. His relation to Dracula is defined solely by power and status, with none of the sympathetic fluctuations that characterized the intercourse between Ruthven and Aubrey.

Polidori's Aubrey was a "young gentleman" flattered to travel with Lord Ruthven; Stoker's Jonathan Harker is not a gregarious youth on a grand tour, but a lonely tourist on a disorienting business trip who enters Castle Dracula as an employee. Dracula's ritual greeting—"Welcome to my house. Come freely. Go safely. And leave something of the happiness you bring" (p. 16)—sheds on his plodding solicitor the aura of an earlier age when travelers were gentlemen whose freedom of motion could be assumed. Fussing about his itinerary and his comfort, Jonathan is a coerced and reluctant tourist who is never his own man even before he becomes the vampire's prisoner. Encompassed by wonders and horrors, he relinquishes all responsibility for his journey with the querulous exclamation, "Was this a customary incident in the life of a solicitor's clerk sent out to explain the purchase of a London estate to a foreigner?" (p. 13).

In fact, as Jonathan goes on to remind himself, he is no longer a clerk, but a full-fledged solicitor. By the same standard, Count Dracula surely would prefer to be referred to by his title, and he is no foreigner in his own country. The edgy civil servant diminishes everything he describes; Dracula inspires in him neither wonder nor curiosity. Because Jonathan withdraws from communion into petty professionalism, employee and employer have nothing in common. Dracula's initial orations about his own heroism are a self-obsessed public presentation far from the intimate confessions of Carmilla, which demanded a response in kind. Like the Irving of Stoker's *Personal Reminiscences*, Dracula requires only an audience onto whom he can exude his construction of himself. Like the Stoker of the *Reminiscences*, Jonathan is merely the intoning man's scribe: "I wish I could put down all he said exactly as he said it, for to me it was most fascinating" (*Dracula*, p. 28).

Even when Jonathan, spying, realizes that since there are no servants in the castle, Dracula has been cooking and serving his meals, making his bed, and driving him in the coach, he feels no affinity with his host in this menial role: the servant's proficiency only reinforces the master's intimidating omnipotence. From the beginning to the end, this vampire monotonously plays the role he has assigned himself—"I have been so long master that I would be master still" (p. 20)—relinquishing the versatility of his kind.

There are no more companionable journeys, only Jonathan's uncommunicative voyeurism.[13] Instead of sharing with Dracula or feeding him, Jonathan spies on him from distant sites. Critical ingenuity can detect various subtle affinities between the horrified young man and the horrible old vampire[14]— Jonathan, does, for instance, crawl out of the castle in the same lizardlike fashion that appalled him when he watched Dracula do it—but finally, both assume the rigid roles of master and servant, spectacle and spectator, tyrant and victim, monster and human, making no attempt to bridge the distance. Caste, not kinship, determines their relationship. It is impossible to imagine Dracula admonishing Jonathan to remember his oath, for though Jonathan is a scrupulously obedient employee and even, for a while, a courteous guest, he is incapable of the voluntary— and lordly—fealty an oath demands. "Sent out" to the vampire, he quickly becomes the vampire's possession, though since he

is too pure and proper to be possessed, he fittingly remains un-
bitten.

According to Stoker's working notes, the heart of *Dracula*
was not blood, but an assertion of ownership. "One incident
and one alone remained constant [from 1890] right up to publication day [in 1897]": Dracula's occupation of Jonathan. One of
Stoker's editors unearths the claim at the heart of his novel:

> In March 1890 Bram Stoker wrote on a piece of scrap paper, in
> handwriting which he always called "an extremely bad
> hand": "young man goes out—sees girls one tries—to kiss
> him not on the lips but throat. Old Count interferes—rage
> and fury diabolical. This man belongs to me I want him."
> Again, in February 1892, in one of the many "structures he
> scribbled down: 'Bistritz—Borgo Pass—Castle—Sortes Virgil—
> Belongs to me.'" And in shorthand, again and again, over the
> next few years: "& the visitors—is it a dream—women stoop
> to kiss him, terror of death. Suddenly the Count turns her
> away—'this man belongs to me'"; "May 15 Monday Women
> kissing"; "Book I Ch 8 Belongs to me."[15]

Belongs to me. These words define the vampire the twentieth century cannot leave alone. The shared Romantic journey in which
nothing impedes two gentlemen's movements but the occult
ends with a servant immobilized and imprisoned in a castle he
never wanted to enter. Byron's "journey through countries not
hitherto much frequented by travellers" terminates in a mono-
maniac's refrain: "Belongs to me."

Jonathan's Progress

Dracula's possession of vampire literature was so unremit-
tingly bleak that his best-known progeny tried not to hear their
master's words. Whether they are moviemakers or literary critics, twentieth-century acolytes want to turn this account of appropriation into a love story, as if invoking "love" and "sex"
would save our culture from seeing its own unresponsive face in
the mirror.[16] It goes against the grain to recast Stoker's novel as
a love story, but the first (and still the best-known) film adapta-

tions tried to return to a pre-*Dracula* tradition by restoring, even intensifying, the homoerotic bond between predator and prey: both discard Stoker's Jonathan, a loyal employee to his bones, for a self-determined protagonist who willfully abandons domesticity to embrace undiscovered countries. But restoring the mutuality between victim and vampire does not restore the half-human vampire of an earlier tradition; instead, it forces us to question the possibility of human men.

F. W. Murnau's silent *Nosferatu* (1922) and Tod Browning's stagy *Dracula* (1931) feature the first male mortals in our tradition whom the vampire not only lures, but actually bites.[17] Both choose to go to his country; as penance for voluntarily crossing the border, both belong to the vampire not only in body, but in blood. The young traveler into the unknown is not an infatuated schoolmate, as Polidori's Aubrey was; he is not simply "sent out," like Stoker's Jonathan; he re-creates himself in his journey toward the vampire. These early cinematic pilgrims are infected by the vampire's hunger before they set off to meet him. Their restless willingness to abandon decorum adds psychological dimension to their relation with the vampire, but it softens Stoker's impersonal vision of dominion. Stoker's Dracula can subjugate the most stolidly reluctant mortal, while these movie Draculas cast their spell only over alienated, even tainted visitors.

Murnau's film features a sick city, not an invaded nation. Renfield,[18] Stoker's lone "zoophagous" madman who becomes Dracula's acolyte only after incarceration in Dr. Seward's asylum, is in *Nosferatu* Jonathan's mad employer, a secret enemy agent who chortles over the vampire's occult messages and gloats over his wish to buy a house "in our city."

Jonathan—who now represents only a real estate agency, not the lofty British law—is as receptive to the vampire's infection as is the city itself. Gustav von Wangenheim's performance is all preening and guffawing. He is delighted to abandon the embraces and mystic foreboding of Nina (not "Mina"; see n. 18 above)—to whom he is already married in Murnau's version—for a stint in the land of the phantoms. Cautionary expertise, here embodied in the *Book of Vampires* he finds at his inn, only makes him guffaw further; with his instinctive respect for authority, Stoker's Jonathan wore the cross the worried peasant gave him, while Murnau's Jonathan tosses the book, and all authorities, aside with a blasphemous self-delighted laugh.

Unlike Stoker's traveler, who waits with impatient helplessness for various and increasingly sinister vehicles, Murnau's *walks* across the border. His coachman refuses to pass over the bridge into the land of phantoms, and so Jonathan crosses it on foot, accompanied by the portentous title: "And when he had crossed the bridge, the phantoms came to meet him."

This momentous transition is far from the nervous docility of Stoker's Jonathan: "I feared to go very far from the station, as we had arrived late and would start as near the correct time as possible. The impression I had was that we were leaving the West and entering the East" (p. 1). In Murnau's film, at the moment of Jonathan's crossing, the world changes: beyond the bridge, the film is photographed in negative, reversing the phantasmal country to black-on-white rather than conventional white-on-black.

Max Schreck's Dracula is closer to the ghostly Ruthven of the Victorian stage than to the heavily material creatures of Stoker's novel. Murnau's looking-glass photography and Schreck's luminous makeup, with his radiantly obtruding bald dome, fingers, ears, nose, and ratlike teeth (which, unlike the familiar dripping canines, he never seems to use), function like the Victorian vampire trap to dematerialize the creature's hunger. Like those of the Victorian actor disembodied in the vampire trap, his movements are ostentatiously unnatural: on the ship, he doesn't climb out of his coffin, but is miraculously elevated from it; in Bremen, he dissolves (with his coffin!) through a solid door.

Moreover, while Stoker gets his first big effect by revealing that his corporeal Dracula has no soul and therefore casts no shadow, Schreck *becomes* his shadow in the climactic episodes when he stalks Jonathan and Nina, a shadow even more elongated than his body, its interminable fingers seeming to slide through matter as it glides toward his prey. This vampire is scarcely bounded by matter, expanding into the shadow, or looking-glass image, of the madly chortling community that courted him, of which Jonathan is the representative.

Murnau not only has Dracula bite Jonathan at least once (Nina's somnambulistic powers prevent a second attack); his crosscutting emphasizes the parallel rhythms of the vampire's and Jonathan's journeys back to Bremen—a suggestive convergence that Stoker's narrative chronology suppresses—so that when the invasion finally comes, we are never sure whether Dracula or Jonathan (or both in collusion) unleashes the rats that carry the plague that wastes the city.

Like his vulnerable agents (Renfield is lynched for his collaboration with the vampire, and Jonathan is ambiguously debilitated for the rest of the movie), Murnau's Dracula is more carrier than master. His ghostliness makes him as fragile as he is agile. Isolated by his clownlike makeup and by immobilizing compositions that confine him within closed spaces or behind bars, he is no more than a shadow of the community he infects. As the first vampire to be destroyed by the sun under which Stoker's Dracula paraded vigorously,[19] he inaugurates an important twentieth-century tradition; but when Nina sacrifices herself to family and community by keeping Dracula with her after daybreak, Schreck merely vanishes. Unlike the more seductive vampires of the 1960s and '70s, he is not fleshly enough to burn.

The final title—"as the shadow of the vampire vanishes with the morning sun"—presumably heals the stricken community and Jonathan as well, allowing us to forget the ominous fact that the sun usually *creates* shadows rather than dissipating them. But Bremen has already infected itself from within. It was Jonathan's wanton walk across the bridge that desecrated his family and city, thereby fusing the domestic and the foreign, the mortal and the monster, the victim and the tyrant, all of whom Stoker kept carefully apart. By making Dracula a shadow of the good men of Bremen, Murnau also crosses the bridge between men and women that Stoker scrupulously erects: Stoker's Dracula possesses only females, while Murnau's uses no lustful, animalistic women as his agents, but only respectable men. According to the *Book of Vampires* that Jonathan discovers, "Nosferatu drinks the blood of the young." Indifferent to gender, Nosferatu unleashes mass death, not individual sexuality. Anyone, under Murnau's rules, will satisfy a vampire.

But only a pure woman can destroy one. Nina accordingly

becomes the final, crucial bridge between town and invader, humanity and the monster. By luring the vampire to her bed so that he will vanish with daybreak, Nina both dies for humanity and, more knowingly than her husband, crosses the bridge beyond it. Nina's ambiguous sacrifice abolishes Stoker's polarization between pure and carnal women, for Nina is less a victim than a link between shadow and substance, life and death, corruption and respectability. She may dispel Max Schreck, but she also marries him to the civil domesticity she represents.[20]

Murnau's film is, of course, admonitory, not, as Stoker wanted to be, congratulatory: Stoker quarantined his vampire from British civilization, while Murnau's was a shadow of his own diseased Germany.[21] Thus, *Nosferatu* itself crosses the bridge between classes, genders, and orders of being that *Dracula* erected so carefully. But in bringing Jonathan and Dracula together, as sinister collaborators if not friends (Murnau's Dracula reads with silent disdain as Jonathan wolfs down his meals, while Stoker's declaims about himself at length as Jonathan nibbles delicately), Murnau does not restore the vampire's mortal sympathies; instead, he intensifies Stoker's vision of impersonal power. Max Schreck is dispelled, but he was only the city's shadow. *Nosferatu* seems to begin where *Dracula* might have ended, in a community that has been transformed into something savage and rampant. An image of the picturesque antihuman, Bremen survives its citizens, whether they are mortals or vampires.

Tod Browning's American *Dracula* is famous now only for Bela Lugosi's performance, but in one sense this commercial American movie, inexpertly adapted from a popular if quite un-Stokeresque Broadway play, is more daring than the masterpiece of German Expressionism serious audiences revere. Following Murnau's lead, Browning transforms Jonathan from a dutiful servant with corporate loyalties to an eccentric trespasser who courts transformation, but Browning's defiant explorer, the wild and maddened Renfield, is no prospective husband; he is scarcely even a man of business. Dracula's visitor is no longer Stoker's stolid, if fragile, emissary of Western civilization; as Dwight Frye plays him, Renfield is so effete and overbred that he is more bizarre than Lugosi's impeccably mannered vampire.[22]

Renfield has nothing of the employee about him: florid and faintly effeminate, he is a Hollywood version of a decadent English gentleman. Stoker's Jonathan was infallibly, if condescendingly, courteous to his Transylvanian hosts; Browning's Renfield orders them around like a stock American tourist, even calling imperiously to his unholy coachman, "Hi, Driver! What do you mean by going at this—." His disapproval is squelched only when he sees that his coach is being led by a bat (not, in this version, by Lugosi himself, whose Dracula is too stately to make a good servant). Renfield's white hat and cane make him an oddly dapper figure among the hefty Transylvanians; he floats through his coarse surroundings with a demeanor of dreamy rapture that anticipates Fred Astaire's until, to his horror, the ghostly vampire women swarm around him and he faints, only to be swooped upon by Dracula.

This Dracula never affirms "This man belongs to me," for Dwight Frye's Renfield belongs to nobody. He does claim that his journey is "a matter of business," later muttering something to Dracula about the lease on Carfax Abbey, but he represents no organization, nor is he tied to the domestic characters we will meet later. "I trust you have kept your coming here secret," Dracula intones. Renfield indicates that a secret journey posed no problem, thereby breaking the social web that bound Stoker's Jonathan to the mighty institutions of British law and marriage and implicated Murnau's Jonathan in civic corruption and domestic hypocrisy.

The doomed traveler in the American *Dracula* floats beyond ties, so it is safe for him to become Dracula's servant. Once bitten, he turns extravagantly mad, but unlike the women, he isn't quite a vampire. In the long, dull domestic portion of the film, Dwight Frye's pyrotechnics provide a counterpoint to the stolidity of humans and vampire alike, just as his character—the vampire's servant who can't shake off human sympathies—links human to inhuman by belonging to neither. Renfield is as alien and irritating to Dracula, who finally tosses him down a huge staircase, as he is to his mortal and supposedly sane caretakers. In the American 1930s, the corrupt traveler, not the vampire, is the movie's authentic alien. Sucking blood is less sinful than is Renfield's mercurial desire to leave home.

The Transylvanian beginning, the most compelling portion of the movie, hints at the old Byronic fellowship between dandy and vampire. Renfield is not Dracula's property as Stoker's Jonathan was, but neither is he Dracula's friend. The film establishes an identification between these two overdressed creatures—Lugosi wears cloak, tuxedo, and medals even indoors—that in 1931 America whispered of perversity. Bela Lugosi is not the phantom Max Schreck was; he is corpulent, clothes-conscious, and, in close-up, clearly wearing lipstick and eye makeup, the only male character who does. In the "dinner" scene that follows Jonathan's arrival, no food is served; this Dracula avoids the indignity of cooking for his guest and the awkwardness of watching him eat.[23] There is no coziness in this Castle Dracula, only the covertly titillating effect of two baroque men eyeing each other in a grotesque set freighted with cobwebs, candelabra, and suits of armor. Renfield gets only a glass of wine, and that only so Lugosi can intone his deathless "I never drink—*vine*," an archly self-aware aside that Browning's movie originates: Stoker's growling Count was no ironist.

The wine also allows Renfield to cut himself so that Dracula can eye him hungrily and then shy away from his crucifix. But even before he sees blood, Dracula has been leaning lewdly toward Renfield; when Renfield sucks the blood from his own finger, Dracula grins knowingly, presumably savoring their affinities. When, in a silent, gracefully choreographed sequence, he banishes the vampire women and stretches toward Renfield's throat, he communicates less pride of ownership than the embrace of kinship. Browning's Renfield is so clearly beyond the pale of any human community that the bond between vampire and mortal Stoker did his best to break is, however briefly and perversely, renewed.

But once they leave Transylvania and the domestic story begins, this faint communion of dandies is over: power and mastery prevail.[24] Renfield mutates from fop into madman who is always trying vainly to elude his many keepers; Lugosi also drops his foppishness, becoming so dependent on commanding attitudes and penetrating stares that he practically turns into a monument. His affinities are no longer with the mercurial Renfield, but with Edward Van Sloan's marmoreal Van Helsing, who is even more autocratic than the vampire. Whatever intensity the movie retains comes less from Dracula's predations among sketchily characterized women than from Van Helsing's and Dracula's battle of wills.

Humanity triumphs when Van Helsing becomes a more overbearing patriarch than the vampire. He disposes of the other human men almost as easily as he stakes Dracula, for Seward is a cipher and Jonathan a fool. Unable to imagine a heroic human lover, Browning's adaptation consigns Jonathan to romantic parody, breathing such lines as "My, what a big bat!" and (to Mina as she is manifesting vampiric tendencies) "You're so— like a changed girl. You look wonderful!" Such a silly man might become a husband when the vampire is dead, but he is no use to heroes. Browning drops the corporate ethos that makes the vampire hunt possible in Stoker's novel.[25] Van Helsing brooks no collaborators; he saves humanity by barking out the Dracula-like demand, "I must be master here or I can do nothing." The affinities of Transylvania fall away; the question of Browning's film is which is to be master. Once the movie concludes that humanity needs a leader, Dracula becomes surprisingly vulnerable, allowing himself to be staked with scarcely an offscreen grunt. Does he refuse to fight for his life because he misses home and Renfield?

Immediate descendants of Stoker's novel, Murnau's *Nosferatu* and Browning's *Dracula* struggle to reunite the vampire to his mortal friend. In both cases, though, apparent affinity yields to that more vulnerable bond, perversity.[26] Finally, both films acquiesce in the emphasis on power they inherit from Stoker: Murnau's stricken Jonathan languishes into the civic corruption both he and the vampire represent; Browning's Dracula abandons Renfield to his keepers to engage in an authoritarian duel with Van Helsing. Both movies finally succumb to the coldness at the heart of Stoker's novel, the requiem of a tradition of intimacy.

Dracula is a desolate inheritance for Murnau's *Nosferatu* and Browning's *Dracula,* which become more joyless as they proceed, concluding in images of ineffable loss. Both are more doleful than the novel they adapt because both banish Stoker's Lucy Westenra, whose kaleidoscopic transformations are Stoker's sub-

stitute for the affection that had been the primary vampire endowment. Lucy's transformations, the most memorable spectacles of the novel and of most movies after the 1960s, leaven
the heterosexual hierarchies that deform the creatures vampires
had been. By relegating Lucy to the role of an incidental offscreen victim, Murnau and Browning cast off Stoker's sadism as
well as his spectacle; by focusing instead on a restless man who
travels beyond boundaries toward the vampire, both apparently
look back with some yearning toward the homoerotic phase of
vampire literature. Finally, though, their stories are trapped in
the weary decorum with which Stoker made vampires palatable
in the 1890s.

Vampire Propriety

Critics unfamiliar with vampire evolution fail to notice the
relative respectability of Stoker's predators, especially his
women. Bram Dijkstra, for example, deplores *Dracula*'s legacy in
terms quite different from mine. Disapproving of vampires in
general rather than these particular vampires, he laments that
after Stoker, "Female vampires were now everywhere.... By
1900 the vampire had come to represent woman as the personification of everything negative that linked sex, ownership, and
money."[27] But Stoker cleaned up more than he degraded. Above
all, he gentrified female vampires, who, for the first time, are
monogamously heterosexual. Van Helsing even seems to doubt
whether Lucy can digest female blood, at least from the veins of
servants. According to his diagnosis, "A brave man's blood is the
best thing on this earth when a woman is in trouble" (p. 149),
and also, presumably, when she needs nourishment.

Not only do Lucy and the sister-brides in Castle Dracula
prowl exclusively at men;[28] Lucy, at least, becomes more virtuous after death than she was in life. Far from personifying a reversion to woman-hating in late Victorian men, Lucy raises the
tone of female vampirism by avoiding messy entanglements
with mortals, directing her "voluptuous wantonness" to her fiancé alone.

"Come to me, Arthur. Leave those others and come to me.
My arms are hungry for you. Come, and we can rest together.

Come, my husband, come!" (p. 257). As a vampire, Lucy the flirt is purified into Lucy the wife. The restless pet who had collected marriage proposals and complained, "Why can't they let a girl marry three men, or as many as want her, and save all this trouble?" (p. 78), the enticing invalid who had "married," through blood transfusions, those very three men (plus the smitten Van Helsing), ignores, as a vampire, "those others" who bled into her adoringly: for the first time she wants her prospective husband and no one else.

Vampirism in *Dracula* does not challenge marriage, as it did earlier; it inculcates the restraints of marriage in a reluctant girl. Even before Arthur celebrates their wedding night with hammer and stake, thumping away unfalteringly while her "body shook and quivered and twisted in wild contortions" (p. 262), Dracula had baptized Lucy into wifely fidelity.

Lucy is more monogamous than the promiscuous vampires she inspired. Two representative vampire women from 1900 have no loyalties left; both are indiscriminate incarnations of female hunger. Hume Nesbit's story "The Vampire Maid" reduces its Ariadne to a biting thing: "I had a ghastly dream this night. I thought I saw a monster bat, with the face and tresses of Ariadne, fly into the open window and fasten its white teeth and scarlet lips on my arm. I tried to beat the horror away, but could not, for I seemed chained down and thralled also with drowsy delight as the beast sucked my blood with a gruesome rapture."[29] When church restorers disinter an ancient demon in F. G. Loring's story "The Tomb of Sarah," scientific reality is more ghastly than any dream: "There lay the vampire, but how changed from the starved and shrunken corpse we saw two days ago for the first time! The wrinkles had almost disappeared, the flesh was firm and full, the crimson lips grinned horribly over the long pointed teeth, and a distinct smear of blood had trickled down one corner of the mouth."[30]

Lucy's progeny, Ariadne and Sarah, do not, like her, mature through vampirism into true womanhood: they are closer to the will-less killing machines who dominate later twentieth-century vampire literature. These dreadful female mouths that feed on popular culture at the turn of the century do personify unleashed female energy in the fear-mongering way Dijkstra suggests, but this energy is not as anarchic as it looks. Since these indiscriminate biters are heterosexual, their raging desire aggrandizes men as well as depleting them.

Moreover, their men are immune from female demonism: Ariadne and Sarah offer not Carmilla's dangerous empathy, but oblivion. Ariadne induces "drowsy delight"; Sarah lures a young man by murmuring, "I give sleep and peace—sleep and peace— sleep and peace" (p. 103). These fin-de-siècle vampires do not arouse unclassified sensations; they induce postcoital fatigue. Their horror springs from their propriety. As good women, they want only men; in approved motherly fashion, they do not stimulate, but lull. The vampires Lucy spawned may be more promiscuous than she, but they are, like her, sexually orthodox. A model of wifeliness, as much a true woman as a new one, Lucy infused womanliness into her kind. Her innovative propriety is a testament to the heterosexuality of her twin creators, Dracula and Bram Stoker.

Perhaps because he is so normal, Dracula is the most solitary vampire we have met. He is, as far as we see, the only male vampire in the world: there is no suggestion that the sailors he kills on his voyage to England will join the ranks of the Undead. Moreover, he can anticipate no companionship, for Stoker's rules allow only humans to unite. "We have on our side power of combination—a power denied to the vampire kind" (p. 238), Van Helsing assures his vigilant community. Ruthven, Varney, Carmilla, and their ilk flourished because of their "power of combination": gregariousness was their lethal talent.

Innovative in his isolation, Dracula can do nothing more than catalyze homoerotic friendship among the humans who hunt him. His story abounds in overwrought protestations of friendship among the men, who testify breathlessly to each other's manhood. In fact, Van Helsing should thank the vampire for introducing him to such lovable companions. Borrowing the idiom of Oscar Wilde's letters to Lord Alfred Douglas, he declares himself to Lucy's former fiancé: "I have grown to love you—yes, my dear boy, to love you—as Arthur" (p. 169). For Dracula and his acolyte Renfield, blood is the life, but the men who combine against him find life by drinking in each other's "stalwart manhood" (p. 168).

Dracula forges this male community of passionate mutual admiration, but he cannot join it. Only indirectly, by drinking Lucy's blood after the four men have "married" her (and each other) in a series of transfusions, can Dracula infiltrate the heroic brotherhood. Turning women into vampires does nothing to mitigate his solitude: his mindless creations have too little in common with him to be friends. Many twentieth-century adaptations soften Dracula's contempt for women by making him fall in love with Mina, aiming to promote her to his co-ruler, but in Stoker's original, Mina is only a pawn in his battle against the men. Stripped of his power of combination, catalyzing homoerotic friendships in which he cannot participate, this vampire loses his story, for he has no confidante willing to hear it.

Dracula begins the novel by telling an unresponsive Jonathan Harker his history in almost flawless English, but thereafter he is silent. In the massive, impeccably collated testimony that comprises the long English portion of the novel, Dracula has no voice: he leaps in and out to make occasional florid boasts, but his nature and aspirations are entirely constructed—and diminished—by others, especially Van Helsing.

As Van Helsing gains authority, Dracula's fluency evaporates into the dimensions of a case history. The lordly host who began the novel was, according to Jonathan, a master of civilized skills: "He would have made a wonderful solicitor, for there was nothing that he did not think of or foresee. For a man who was never in the country, and who did not evidently do much in the way of business, his knowledge and acumen were wonderful" (p. 44). In England, though, Jonathan and the rest turn their judgment over to Van Helsing, whose floundering English somehow confirms his authority, as that of psychiatrists will do in 1930s popular culture. Van Helsing assures his followers that the vampire is still precivilized, "a great child-brain" growing only slowly into the position of "the father or furtherer of a new order of beings" (pp. 302–3). Having devolved, under Van Helsing's authority, from magus to embryonic patriarch, Dracula is easily immobilized and trapped. As a presence, he is extinguished so early that at the end, a mere bowie knife kills him: his death requires neither Bible nor stake. Dracula is so easily, even inevitably, obliterated that all concerned forget the elaborate rituals needed to still the writhing Lucy.[31]

Dracula is dissipated less by science or the occult than by the clamor of experts that gave form to his decade. His responsiveness to his enemies' classifications sets him apart from the other great monsters of his century. Frankenstein's creature galvanized his book with an eloquent apologia halfway through. Even monsters who had not read Milton defined themselves with ease: Lord Ruthven in his various incarnations, Varney, Carmilla, all renewed themselves through compelling and compulsive self-presentations. Varney dissociated himself easily from the ignorant mob that pursued him, whose superstitious violence threw the vampire's superior humanity into relief. Dracula has no mob to tower over, but only the constraining categories of professional men. His relative silence has, of course, fed his life in the twentieth century: as we shall see, he is so suggestively amorphous in Stoker's novel that he is free to shift his shape with each new twentieth-century trend.[32] In 1897, though, Dracula was, despite his occult powers, so comparatively docile a vampire, so amenable to others' definitions, that he stifled the tradition that preceded him.

As the first vampire who conforms to social precepts, fading into experts' definitions rather than affirming his unnatural life, Dracula is a consummate creation of the late 1890s, dutifully transmitting its legacy to our own expert-hounded century. The British 1890s were haunted not only by the Undead, but by a monster of its own clinical making, the homosexual.[33] In constructing an absolute category that isolated "the homosexual" from "normal" men and women, medical theory confined sexuality as narrowly as Van Helsing does the vampire. More in conformity than in ferocity, Dracula takes definition from a decade shaped by medical experts.

I suspect that Dracula's primary progenitor is not Lord Ruthven, Varney, or Carmilla, but Oscar Wilde in the dock.[34] The Labouchère Amendment of 1885, which criminalized homosexuality among men, not only authorized Wilde's conviction: it restricted sexuality in the next decade "by shifting emphasis from sexual acts between men, especially sodomy, the traditional focus of legislation, to sexual sentiment or thought, and in this way to an abstract entity soon to be widely referred to as 'homosexuality'" (Dellamora, *Masculine Desire*, p. 200). The Wilde trials of 1895 put a judicial seal on the category the Labouchère Amendment had fostered. As a result of the trials, affinity between men lost its fluidity. Its tainted embodiment, the homosexual, was imprisoned in a fixed nature, re-created as a man alone, like Dracula, and, like Dracula, one hunted and immobilized by the "stalwart manliness" of normal citizens. Now unnatural and illegal, the oath that bound vampire to mortal was annulled.

Before the Wilde trials, vampires felt free to languish in overtly homoerotic adoration of their mortal prey: in "The True Story of a Vampire" by Eric, Count Stenbock, published the year before Wilde's incarceration, Count Vardalek madly plays Chopin to a faunlike young man, kisses him on the lips, and weeps over his "darling's" diminishing "superabundance of life."[35] Dracula was born in reaction to Vardalek's devouring love: new rules imposed on his alien kind forbid him to love anyone on earth. The only music that moves him is the music of the wolves, and he cannot participate even in that.

Dracula's silence recalls the silence forced on the voluble Wilde after his trials. The foreigner who had poured out irresistible words in flawless English tried vainly to speak after the judge had sentenced him to prison. "'And I?' he began. 'May I say nothing, my lord?' But Mr. Justice Wills made no reply beyond a wave of the hand to the warders in attendance, who touched the prisoners on the shoulder and hurried them out of sight to the cells below."[36] As in the London books of *Dracula*, the versatile and florid performer disappears under institutional regulation.

The ghostliness of earlier vampires had deflected improper intercourse with mortals: when a vampire walked through walls or turned for life to the moon, audiences remembered that he was another order of being, one whose body (as opposed to his teeth) could not quite penetrate a human's. Dracula, fully corporeal, has no sheltering spirituality, and so he is as vulnerable as Oscar Wilde to opprobrium and incarceration. Unlike Wilde, however, Dracula is careful.

His intensifying silence, his increasing acquiescence in what experts say he is, reflect the caution of Stoker's master, Henry Irving. In 1895, just after the Wilde trials—which subdued English manhood in general and the English theater in particular—Stoker began in earnest to write *Dracula*, which had haunted him for five years. Irving had spent 1895 lobbying for his knighthood (the first ever awarded to an actor) by petrifying himself and his Lyceum into attitudes of patriotic grandeur, although his imperial postures had been assaulted by two wicked Irishmen: Shaw, whose savage reviews exposed, in the person of Irving, all British heroes to terrible laughter; and the seductively rude Wilde, whose comedies mocked everything that was supposed to inspire Irving's audiences. Bram Stoker, a third Irishman but a loyal one, protected Irving against potentially lethal laughter. His *Dracula* was fed by Wilde's fall, but its taboos were those of his master, whose reward came on May 24, 1895: on that day Irving's knighthood and Wilde's conviction were announced, ending the comedy. As a martyr, though, Wilde had won, for he drained the vitality of Stoker's vampire as consummately as he had deflated Irving's heroics in his glory days.

When Irving died ten years later, the *Daily Telegraph* praised him for rescuing England from the "cult" of Oscar Wilde (quoted in Skal, *Hollywood Gothic*, p. 36). But he never rose again. Irving and all heroes were forced to define themselves in opposition to the devastating figure of Wilde, whose fate became an actual vampire that drained the vitality of future theatrical generations.[37] Irving held the stage for a few more years because of what he was not; he turned from player to exemplary façade. Oscar Wilde in prison constricted actors as well as vampires, forcing expansive figures into self-protecting silence. The Wilde trials, and the new taboos that made them possible, drained the generosity from vampires, forcing them to turn away from friendship and to expend their energies on becoming someone else.[38]

Transformations

Adhering to more taboos than he breaks, Dracula inhibits future vampires in major ways. Varney and his ilk reached outward to take their essential life from the moon; Dracula takes his from his coffin. His existence is hedged by absolute if arbitrary rules vampires fear to break even now. His need to travel with hampering boxes of native earth; his enfeebling inability to form alliances; his allergies to crucifixes, communion wafers, and garlic; his vulnerability to daylight—all defined vampires by the many things they could not do.

In Transylvania, his fixed role of master blocks his infiltration of human lives; in London, his helpless responsiveness to expert definition depletes him long before his actual death. The creature who insists on playing master is forced to take the shape of human fears. But despite these impediments, Dracula has one gift that inaugurates a new dispensation for vampires: his transforming powers, the sole compensation for his hedged-in life.

Before *Dracula,* vampires were incessantly, aggressively, themselves, though some, like Varney, had a predilection for disguise, while others, like the stage Ruthven, faded in and out of materiality. The midcentury moon, the source of their occult powers, turned them on and off like a light switch without altering their natures. Early film Draculas share these intact egos, scarcely evoking Stoker's mutable monster. Max Schreck's and Bela Lugosi's define themselves by florid, reiterated mannerisms and extravagant makeup that immobilizes their expressiveness. "I *am* Dracula," Lugosi announces with ponderous relish. Surely he will never be anyone else.

Stoker's Dracula, on the other hand, is many creatures, not all of whom have titles or even names. Not only does he go from a steely old man to a frisky young one in the course of his novel, stealing the youth from a Jonathan grown white-haired and tired; he becomes at need a wolf, a bat, a dog, as well as fog and mist. Animals flee Max Schreck's phantasmal Dracula, the enemy of vitality, but animals become Stoker's Dracula, who inaugurated the shape-shifting vampire we live with today. Barred from union with mortals or with other vampires, Dracula diffuses his solitary nature into other orders of being.

But his transformations are more convenient than spectacular. After reaching London, he is so indirect a presence in his story that his metamorphoses are muffled. We never see him changing shape; his ability to slide in and out of human form makes him a wily antagonist, not a source of awe. His changes are modestly presented compared to those of Lucy and Mina, his female victims. Once again, women perform on behalf of withheld males the extreme implications of vampirism. Just as Carmilla played out the erotic implications of Ruthven's forbidden friendship, Lucy and Mina exhibit the new metamorphic prowess of vampirism in the 1890s.

One of Stoker's great chills is Van Helsing's tolling line: "Madam Mina, our poor, dear, Madam Mina, is changing" (p. 382). The line is authentically frightening because it is uncharacteristically subtle, reminding us that we have no fixed idea what Mina is changing into. We know what Lucy, the pampered belle, became when she changed, but how can Mina become a fleshly predator, a "bloofer [beautiful] lady" who offers children dangerous kisses?

For Mina, unlike Lucy, is an earnest wife and unwavering motherly beacon inspiring brave men. Even before she is bitten, her almost occult secretarial competence endows her with the metamorphic potential of the New Woman; she repeatedly saves the day by knowing some bit of mystic lore about office work. Accordingly, once Mina begins to be a vampire, she is no bloofer lady, but a medium whose mind forces itself into Dracula's until, immobilized in his coffin, he virtually becomes her creature. Lucy is transformed into a ravenous animal, Mina into a clairvoyant; neither is like their progenitor Dracula (both lack his shape-shifting ability, hairy palms, red eyes, and veneer of civility), nor do they have the ironic tinkling laughs of Dracula's Transylvanian sister-brides. No vampire, it seems, is like any other. In fact, as vampires, Lucy and Mina have less in common with each other than they did when they were alive. The discrepancy between the women's transformations hints at the range of a vampire's possible selves.

Sexually, Stoker's vampires are dutifully conventional; personally, they lack flair, craving only power and possession. They are striking only in their transformative potential. Like all respectable creatures, they suggest more selves than they let us see. Most particularly, their animal affinities, which may seem the ultimate constraint in their already constrained lives, point toward an expanded being new to vampires.

> Hitherto I had noticed the backs of his hands as they lay on his knees in the firelight, and they had seemed rather white and fine; but seeing them now close to me, I could not but notice that they were rather coarse—broad, with squat fingers. Strange to say, there were hairs in the centre of the palm. The nails were long and fine, and cut to a sharp point. As the Count leaned over me and his hands touched me, I could not repress a shudder. It may have been that his breath was rank, but a horrible feeling of nausea came over me, which, do what I would, I could not conceal. (Pp. 25–26)

In Jonathan's first extended view of Dracula, he is fine (aristocratic) in dim light, coarse (animal) when he comes close. His civilized and his brutal sides seem as rigidly differentiated as were Dr. Jekyll and Mr. Hyde's. No one but Jonathan suggests that his breath may be rank; Lucy and Mina, who know his mouth, never admit to smelling it; thus it is likely that it is not his bad breath, but his hairy palm, or animal potential, that brings on Jonathan's "horrible feeling of nausea." On this first meeting, Dracula flaunts his animalism more than he will do later. His sly touch is a prelude to his lyrical response to the howling of the wolves: "Listen to them—the children of the night. What music they make!" (p. 26). His wolfish affinity repels Jonathan, but in this suggestive tribute, Dracula expands beyond hierarchical categories to appropriate an inhuman art that goes beyond the mere brutality of a Mr. Hyde.[39]

APART FROM HIS TRADEMARK BLOODY FANGS, Dracula loses his expansive animalism in most twentieth-century films. Actors like Lugosi, Christopher Lee, and Louis Jourdan may be sexier on the surface, but they are so self-consciously irresistible that it is hard to picture them howling with wolves. In most vampire films, animalism is less metamorphosis than coded eroticism, but in late Victorian England, animals were not represented as notably sexual. Instead, they generated a lonely awe human beings were too socialized to inspire.

"'I wonder,' [Seward asks Renfield, his zoophagous lunatic] reflectively, 'what an elephant's soul is like!'" (p. 324). The question torments Renfield, leading Seward to conclude that "he has assurance of some kind that he will acquire some higher life. He dreads the consequence—the burden of a soul" (p. 325). In his assumption that only "higher life" has a soul, Dr. Seward shrinks into humanity just as Jonathan Harker did when Dracula's hairy palm touched him. The zoophagous maniac knows better. The resonant question of animal souls, or some purely animal principle of existence, lends intimations of transfiguration to Stoker's bleak portrait of vampires.[40]

It is not Dracula rampant or Dracula in his coffin that inspires Jonathan's half-despairing, half-awed cry: "What manner of man is this, or what manner of creature is it in the semblance of man?" (p. 48). At the climax of his Transylvanian visit, Jonathan is stricken with holy terror at his host's elusive animalism: "What I saw was the Count's head coming out from the window. I did not see the face, but . . . I could not mistake the hands which I had had so many opportunities of studying. . . . But my very feelings changed to revulsion and terror when I saw the whole man slowly emerge from the window and begin to crawl down the castle wall over that dreadful abyss, *face down*, with his cloak spreading out around him like great wings" (pp. 47–48).

Since he can turn into a bat, Dracula has more efficient means of transportation than crawling down his castle walls; perhaps he does so here only for exercise, but his sport devastates Jonathan with a vision of otherness in human shape. It also teaches Jonathan his own metamorphic potential; with the deftness of Kipling's Mowgli picking up animal skills in the jungle, he will escape from the castle by similarly crawling down the wall: "Where his body has gone why may not another body go?" (p. 62). Jonathan's chaste emulation of his master's body is as close as he comes to turning into a vampire. He is never as hungry as Lucy or as clairvoyant as Mina, but when he emulates Dracula, he does briefly expand his awareness of his own potential elasticity.

In its time, Dracula's descent, not the three weird women who captivate Jonathan in the next scene, was the heart of the novel's horror; Skal (*Hollywood Gothic*, p. 39) reproduces the cover of the first paperback edition, in which Dracula, a dignified old man, crawls down his castle wall. His short cloak does not begin to cover his agile body; his sleeves and trousers are hiked up to emphasize the recognizably human hands and bare feet with which he propels his descent. This Dracula has no fangs, long nails, blazing eyes, or other vampire accoutrements familiar from later illustrations and films: his horror is his human body, a horror that lived beyond the turn of the century. In a draft of *The Waste Land*, T. S. Eliot amplifies his "bats with baby faces in the violet light" with the *Dracula*-derived line, "I saw him creep head downward down a wall."[41]

Attracted as our own century is to the three slavering sisters, with a relish we insist is Victorian, these lustful fiends decorate neither the original paperback nor T. S. Eliot's Modernist Gothic. In its time, *Dracula*'s most resonant image was that of a lone human body doing a supposedly nonhuman thing associated with neither sexuality nor predation. As in his paean to the music of the wolves, he is exhibiting, for no particular reason, his animal affinities.

Dracula was not the first Victorian monster to flaunt his transfiguring animal potential. In 1884, a young surgeon with some of the compassionate curiosity of Stoker's Dr. Seward was transfixed by a poster advertising the spectacle of an Elephant Man. The actual Joseph Merrick, whose patron Frederick Treves became, was a tragic example of false advertising: a small man weighted down by deforming epidermal growths, the frail Merrick had little in common with an elephant. Nevertheless, when Treves wrote his memoir forty years later, he described the poster more vividly than he did his patient:

> Painted on the canvas in primitive colours was a life-size portrait of the Elephant Man. This very crude production depicted a frightful creature that could only have been possible in a nightmare. It was the figure of a man with the characteristics of an elephant. The transfiguration was not far advanced. There was still more of the man than of the beast. This fact—that it was still human—was the most repellent attribute of the creature. There was nothing about it of the pitiableness of the misshapen or the deformed, nothing of the grotesqueness

of the freak, but merely the loathing insinuation of a man being changed into an animal. Some palm trees in the background of the picture suggested a jungle and might have led
the imaginative to assume that it was in this wild that the perverted object had roamed.[42]

Responding to the "transfiguration" of the poster rather than
the pathos of the man, Treves could be describing the crawling
Dracula: "There was still more of the man than of the beast. This
fact—that it was still human—was the most repellent attribute
of the creature." Like Dracula crawling down his battlements or
Kafka's Gregor Samsa waking from uneasy dreams, the poster of
the Elephant Man reveals the creaturely capacities of an apparent human whose "repellent" animalism may endow him with
holy terror: Leslie Fiedler associates the Elephant Man with such
un-Christian divinities as "the elephant-headed Ganesh from
the Great Temple at Karnak, awesome but somehow neither
loathsome nor grotesque."[43] The image of a monster who may
also be a god forces on Treves Dr. Seward's perplexed question:
"I wonder . . . what an elephant's soul is like!"

After Merrick died, Treves convinced himself that this elephant at least had a soul, one that cast off the beast to assume
a perfect manly body: "As a specimen of humanity, Merrick was
ignoble and repulsive; but the spirit of Merrick, if it could be
seen in the form of the living, would assume the figure of an
upstanding and heroic man, smooth browed and clean of limb,
and with eyes that flashed undaunted courage." Dracula brings
no such assurance to the professional men who study him. Dracula, like Merrick, is a dandy who lives without mirrors, an essential celibate with embarrassingly "amorous" proclivities,[44] a
charismatic isolate who is helpless before the human community. As with Merrick, his one source of stature is his propinquity
to animals.

The nineteenth-century Development Hypothesis, most fa-
mously demonstrated in Darwin's revelations of humanity's animal origins, revised Victorian faith in humanism—and thus in
heroism—in ways that involved both denial and abashed embrace. Throughout the century, guardians of powerful institutions affirmed their shaky humanity by cataloging and thus

controlling animals as Van Helsing does Dracula: as Harriet Ritvo demonstrates, "Animals were uniquely suitable subjects for a rhetoric that both celebrated human power and extended its sway, especially because they concealed this theme at the same time that they expressed it."[45] Accordingly, at midcentury, Tennyson became Poet Laureate after his *In Memoriam A. H.* exhorted struggling readers to evolve beyond their animal inheritance by "working out the beast, / And let the ape and tiger die."

But animals were not so easily killed: their new genealogical intimacy with humans raised them, in the eyes of compassionate reformers, to moral and spiritual exempli whose life shared human sacredness. In 1847, the *Christian Remembrancer* forbade pious readers to let apes and tigers die: "There is a growing feeling of reverence for the lower creation. . . . We regard them as sharers in one quality, and that the most tangible portion of our inheritance—they share in life, they are living creatures."[46] Like Renfield's biblical "the blood is the life," philanthropic reverence undermined human-centered hierarchies on behalf of a vital fellowship whose sacred essence was pagan. As literary rhetoric became increasingly weary and pessimistic, this fellowship became covert salvation: union with animals beatified a declining humanity. By the 1890s, man himself seemed so depleted that, in fiction at least, the ape and tiger might have been all that kept his vitality alive.

Kipling's *Jungle Books* (1894) feature a boy-hero fitting for a shrunken decade who, far from working out the beast, takes his power from beasts: raised by wolves and schooled by a wise panther and a tender bear, Mowgli relishes the ontological fluidity and heroic skill instilled by his jungle teachers. Though Kipling's narrator ranks the animals in incessant if arbitrary fashion, assuring us, like the guardian of culture he wants to be, that they all defer to Mowgli's human superiority, these hierarchical protestations fall away when Mowgli graduates into a human society more brutish than the jungle. In his first foray to his kind, he is banished for being a "wolf-child," "a sorcerer [like Dracula] who can turn himself into a beast at will."[47] When, indisputably a man, he leaves the jungle for the last time, his life as an Indian civil servant will surely lack the perpetual transfiguration of a jungle existence where he spoke every animal's language. Kip-

ling tempts us to picture a colonized Mowgli sighing nostalgi-
cally for the wolves and his wolf-self: "Listen to them—the children of the night. What music they make!"

Only his animal affinities make Mowgli worth writing about
at all. Like the Elephant Man who preceded him and the vampire that followed, Mowgli is a hero because he can become an
animal. The animals that glorify the boy have little to do with
eroticism, which, in the *Jungle Books,* is virtually a human trait:
Mowgli knows he must leave the jungle when he reaches pu-
berty and finds himself drawn to a woman. The loving and potent community he leaves behind—the snake Kaa, the bear Ba-
loo, the panther Bagheera, and his tutelary brother wolves—is
composed of aging male celibates. In most 1890s representations, animals are grand because they scarcely couple. Like that
of the Elephant Man, their allure is their singularity.

Dracula crawling down his castle walls is not as winsome as
the Elephant Man or Mowgli, but he is like these late-Victorian
hybrids in that his creaturely alienation from humanity makes
him the center of a cult, one that in Dracula's case is thriving
today. Monotonously asserting a dominion that isolates him
from humans and other vampires; so alone that, like most tyrants, he is vulnerable to anything that is said about him;
hedged by the arbitrary rules that have come to define his vam-
pireness: Dracula steals power from awe-inspiring animals.

This power is muted compared to Mowgli's; aside from a few
nostalgic remarks and his one solitary crawl, we never see him
changing. In England, his one gesture of animal kinship—apart
from commanding a swarm of rats to frighten the vampire-
hunters away—is his release of the wolf Bersicker from the zoo,
a perplexing gesture described so indirectly that we never see
Dracula and the wolf together. Does he need Bersicker to let him
into Lucy Westenra's bedroom, to which he always had access
before? Or does he, like Mowgli, come into his powers in the
company of wolves? Like his crawl, his release of the wolf makes
little narrative sense,[48] but it does provide this vampire with the
one bond his author does not taboo.

Though Stoker only sketches Dracula's animal metamorphoses, awe at animals underlies his story. Van Helsing demonstrates wonders to his skeptical hearers by summoning a pageant

of immortal beasts: "Can you tell me why, when other spiders die small and soon, that one great spider lived on for centuries in the tower of the old Spanish church and grew and grew, till, on descending, he could drink the oil of all the church lamps? . . . Can you tell me why the tortoise lives more long than generations of men; why the elephant goes on and on till he have seen dynasties; and why the parrot never die only of bite of cat or dog or other complaint?" (p. 237).

Dracula's association with these vigorous creatures gives him a subterranean vitality new to his kind: it is less his autocratic assertions than his unbounded identity and his ability to expand the identities of others beyond human limits that give Dracula the aura of power his plot, in fact, denies him. Succeeding Draculas would not know what to make of the metamorphic power that had such intensity in the 1890s. While Max Schreck's teeth are ratlike, he never turns into a rat, seeming most alive when he is half-disembodied or swelling into a shadow. Bela Lugosi is occasionally replaced with a rubbery bat, but Lugosi himself is so statuesque that one cannot imagine him changing into anything.[49] Wolf aficionados in the first half of the twentieth century took the more pathetic form of werewolves. I suspect, though, that without his furtive animalism, Dracula would never have survived to metamorphose on film. His empathy with "children of the night" rather than with humans released a dimension of fear: the fear, not of death and the dead, but of being alive.

The Blood Is the Life

Earlier vampires may not have been mortal, but they could pass as human. Despite his corpse-like pallor, Ruthven was a popular party guest, while even with his protruding teeth Varney was a far better neighbor than Dracula would be. Only his eyes reveal his malevolence, but there is nothing characteristically animal about "a lurking and suspicious look," which could characterize any number of human villains and paranoid heroes.

Carmilla appears to be winsomely human. She becomes an animal only fitfully and ambiguously, and only when she is feeding. Laura perceives "a sooty black animal that resembled a monstrous cat. It appeared to me about four or five feet long, for it measured fully the length of the hearth-rug as it passed over it; and it continued to-ing and fro-ing with the lithe sinister restlessness of a beast in a cage. . . . I felt it spring lightly on the bed," but in Laura's kaleidoscopic perception the cat quickly mutates into "a female figure standing at the foot of the bed, a little at the right side." When the General replaces her as narrator, he describes the feeding creature as less animal than thing, "a large black object, very ill-defined, crawl[ed], as it seemed to me, over the foot of the bed, and swiftly spread itself up to the poor girl's throat, where it swelled, in a moment, into a great, palpitating mass."[50] Compared to Dracula, whose first appearance reeks of animalism, Carmilla is at best "very ill-defined." We know her only as a passionate friend who in her hunger becomes something else.

Dracula's blatant animal affinities are new to vampires; they alone lend vitality to this constricted, life-denying tyrant. Dracula is not only unprecedentedly animal-like; he is the first vampire we have met who is not visibly a corpse. Like the vampires he makes, he is alive even in his coffin: "It seemed as if the whole awful creature were simply gorged with blood; he lay like a filthy leech, exhausted with his repletion" (p. 67). Ruthven was notable for "the deadly hue of his face, which never gained a warmer tint" (Polidori, *The Vampyre,* in *Penguin,* p. 7), but Dracula is hideously ruddy. Ruthven was dead; Dracula, in Stoker's suggestive coinage, is *un*dead.

This coinage was central to Stoker's image of his book, which, as late as a month before publication, was titled not *Dracula* but *The Un-Dead* (Frayling, *Vampyres,* p. 300). The original title may be less striking than the weird name, but it points toward the essential gift of Stoker's vampires to the twentieth century: a reminder, not of the dreadfulness of death, but of the innate horror of vitality.

"The blood is the life! The blood is the life!" Renfield cries for them all (p. 181). But this paean to bodily fluids entered our imaginations only with Bram Stoker's Undead. Earlier vampires enfeebled their prey; Dracula energizes his, reminding his victims—and us—that they have life in them. Just as he makes

Jonathan aware of his animal potential, he executes transformations that are less purely erotic, in the sense of something
shared, than they are sensory: the women he transforms come
to apprehend the vibrancy of their world. Le Fanu's Laura was
aware under Carmilla's ministrations only of Carmilla and her
own sensations, but Stoker's Lucy describes her initiation as a
breathtaking awareness of newly vivid surroundings. Despite
our own critical infatuation with Dracula's sexuality, Lucy's awe
at her expanded world is as solitary as Jonathan's crawl down
the castle:

> I remember, though I suppose I was asleep, passing through
> the streets and over the bridge. A fish leaped as I went by, and
> I leaned over to look at it, and I heard a lot of dogs howling—
> the whole town seemed as if it must be full of dogs all howl-
> ing at once—as I went up the steps. Then I have a vague mem-
> ory of something long and dark with red eyes, just as we saw
> in the sunset, and something very sweet and very bitter all
> around me at once; and then I seemed sinking into deep
> green water, and there was a singing in my ears, as I have
> heard there is to drowning men; and then everything seemed
> passing away from me; my soul seemed to go out from my
> body and float about the air. I seemed to remember that once
> the West Lighthouse was right under me, and then there was
> a sort of agonising feeling, as if I were in an earthquake, and I
> came back and found you shaking my body. I saw you do it
> before I felt you. (P. 130)

Stoker's Undead do not drain vitality; they bestow it. Anne Rice
will glorify this sensory reincarnation as quasi-angelic "vampire
sight," but in the 1890s Stoker associates it with the unabashed
blood-awareness only animals enjoy.

A pageant of wounded women illustrates vampires' progress, at the turn of the twentieth century, from death to heightened life. In Polidori's *Vampyre*, Aubrey is entranced by the "life-
less corpse" of his beloved, on whom Ruthven has fed: "He shut
his eyes, hoping that it was but a vision arising from his dis-
turbed imagination; but he again saw the same form, when he
unclosed them, stretched by his side. There was no colour upon
her cheek, not even upon her lips; yet there was a stillness about

her face that seemed almost as attaching as the life that once dwelt there" (*Penguin*, p. 15). Aubrey's Ianthe is doubly still because there is no suggestion that Ruthven has transformed her; the vampire's animating powers affect no one but his splendid self. Like Wordsworth's mountains or Keats's urn, Ianthe lures the poetic viewer because she is utterly without life. The vampire bestows a stillness no mortal can emulate.

Varney's supine Flora is more ambiguous. As a potential vampire, she is "more beautiful than death" not because she is livelier—like Ianthe, she is irresistibly immobile—but because death's proximity turns her into art.

> She looked almost the shadow of what she had been a few weeks before. She was beautiful, but she almost realized the poet's description of one who had suffered much, and was sinking into an early grave, the victim of a broken heart:
>
> "She was more beautiful than death,
> And yet as sad to look upon."
>
> Her face was of a marble paleness, and as she clasped her hands, and glanced from face to face . . . she might have been taken for some exquisite statue of despair. (Rymer, *Varney*, p. 134)

Death clings to Flora while she lives, making her desirable. When Stoker's Lucy is a corpse, she is desirable because she is not dead at all: "There lay Lucy, seemingly just as we had seen her the night before her funeral. She was, if possible, more radiantly beautiful than ever; and I could not believe that she was dead. The lips were red, nay redder than before; and on the cheeks was a delicate bloom" (p. 245).

Once again, women display the powers male vampires are too respectable to release.[51] "She was more beautiful than death"; "I could not believe that she was dead." It is not only that Lucy changes; she embodies the change in the vampire's powers. Earlier female victims were seductive because stilled. Through them, death immobilized life, while in *Dracula*, life engorges death. Lucy enthralls spectators because she is *not* stilled. After death, she continues to writhe and foam, prowl and shriek, turning not to marble, but to blood.

It is easy and obvious to condemn out of hand the sexist sexuality of her staking, in which her fiancé "looked like a figure of Thor as his untrembling arm rose and fell, driving deeper and deeper the mercy-bearing stake, while the blood from the pierced heart welled and spurted up around it" (p. 262), but its erotic vitalism is, for better or worse, vampires' new medium. The parallel scene of Clara's staking in *Varney* is all bloodless, loveless horror. The blacksmith, a more efficient executor than the vampire's stricken fiancé, does the staking with dispatch, after which Clara's father goes mad and the family collapses. We last see the benevolent patriarch Sir George Crofton gibbering about his own transformation: "I am a vampyre, and this is my tomb—you should see me in the rays of the cold moon gliding 'twixt earth and heaven, and panting for a victim. I am a vampyre" (p. 839).

When Clara is staked, her father's authority dissolves into vampiric babble, while Lucy's staking confirms the authority of an armed community of fathers. Granted that her wedding is a rape; vampires who appreciate only power and possession participate only in ceremonies of coercion. But for all the violence she ignites, Lucy is the first dead girl we have met who is in her heart alive. Inflexibly conventional, recoiling from intimacy, she and her bloody kind have survived decades of disapproval because they have no love of death and no sympathy with stillness. We may not like these vampires, but we continue to believe in them. Perhaps our century has made it impossible for us to believe in wiser fiends or better friends.

5

Our Vampire, Our Leader: Twentieth-Century Undeaths

Vampires and Vampires

"There are vampires and vampires, and not
all of them suck blood."
Fritz Leiber, "The Girl with the Hungry Eyes" (1949)

WHEN HE OFFERED HIS REPULSIVE SELF for our worship,
Dracula gave us more than a smell, an accent,
and bloodlust: he propagated "vampires and
vampires" whose tastes were less specialized than
their master's. Before Dracula, vampires embodied forbidden ideals of intimacy; after Dracula, they moved to
America and turned into rulers. Just as Victorian patriarchal precepts officially forbade citizens to long for
friendship, so American democracy forbade us to long
for monarchs. Vampires, however, reigned and continue
to do so. Whether their leadership is a dangerous threat
or (as it becomes in the 1970s) a poignant wish,
twentieth-century vampires entangle themselves in the
sources of power.

Later on this chapter will follow the Draculas who
stalk and shape-shift through the twentieth century,
adapting to changing romantic ideals. It seems truer,
though, to the scope of the revulsion Dracula unleashed
to begin with his legatees, the psychic vampires who
look so ordinary that we can scarcely extract them from
our lives. Technically, psychic vampires are a breed
apart; instead of merely drinking blood, they sap energy; but all twentieth-century vampires suck identity
from the psychic vampires who infiltrate the eroticism,
the ambition, and the power determinants of ordinary
life.

FASHIONS DETERMINE DRACULAS; the psychic vampires so
persistent in horror literature from the Edwardian age
to the present change their styles but keep their essence.
As a species, they predate Dracula,[1] but their power fed

on his. More absorbent than their rigid master, they drink energy, emotional generosity, self-control, creativity, talent, memories, even (in a recent story) as mundane a life fluid as writing time.[2] They relish intensity and joy. In Alice and Claude Askew's "Aylmer Vance and the Vampire" (1914), a "vampire detective" defines his prey as less the enemy of life than life itself:

> I suppose . . . that there is such a thing as vampirism even in these days of advanced civilization? I can understand the evil influence that a very old person may have upon a young one if they happen to be in constant intercourse—the worn-out tissue sapping healthy vitality for their own support. And there are certain people—I could think of several myself—who seem to depress one and undermine one's energies, quite unconsciously, of course, but one feels somehow that vitality has passed from oneself to them.[3]

Psychic vampires can be anybody one knows: their defining characteristic is familiarity. *The Vampire Encyclopedia* claims evasively that the first psychic vampires were "young humans and animals" (p. 215)—probably because children and animals are by definition dependent—but in literature, at least, psychic vampires lurk at the sophisticated center of adult society. Though they might be animals or children, they are as likely to be powerful men; those licensed parasites, women; or those urbane outcasts, homosexuals.

Edwardian vampires were, as a rule, more perverse than their later counterparts. The most flamboyant embodied the attraction of undomesticated desires. Homosexuality clung to them in the sickeningly sinister form it assumed after the imprisonment of Oscar Wilde. Dracula was one particularly debased incarnation of the fallen Wilde, a monster of silence and exile, vulnerable to a legalistic series of arcane rules. Reginald Clark in George Sylvester Viereck's American novel *The House of the Vampire* (1907) is Wilde inflated into cosmic world-brain, "an embodiment of the same force of which Alexander, Caesar, Confucius and the Christos were also embodiments."[4] As Dracula, Wilde could be isolated by diagnoses and paralyzed by rules, but as the psychic vampire Reginald Clarke, Wilde's image, ungovernable and cosmic, rules the world.

A paragon of brilliance, wit, and "world-embracing intellect," Reginald Clarke is the center of a dazzling New York salon. Like the curdled Lord Henry Wotton, that pernicious influence in Wilde's *Picture of Dorian Gray,* Reginald entices beautiful young men into a rarefied environment whose "seemingly most harmless books may secretly possess the power of scattering in young minds the seed of corruption" (p. 30). By some mystic process, Reginald absorbs the genius of his protégés, so that their works of art seep into his own. After imbibing their talent, he discards them. His sinful gift is plagiarism on a cosmic scale: this psychic vampire is a repository of others' creativity.

The House of the Vampire is steeped in echoes of Wilde. The two young men consumed by Reginald's influence are Ernest and Jack, best friends and budding geniuses. These fugitives from *The Importance of Being Earnest* breathe poetry at each other while "twitching with a strange ascetic passion" (p. 42), but even when they form an alliance with the "motherly" Ethel Brandenbourg, a painter whose talent for subtle pigmentation Reginald has captured, these tender heroes cannot preserve themselves from the vampire's "demoniacal influence": after Reginald absorbs a play from Ernest that abounds in echoes of Wilde's *Salomé,* he leaves our hero "a gibbering idiot." But in an unmistakable hint of the Wilde trials, retribution waits beyond the novel: "Many years later, when the vultures of misfortune had swooped down upon [Reginald], and his name was no longer mentioned without a sneer, he was still remembered in New York drawing rooms as the man who had brought to perfection the art of talking" (p. 4). As psychic vampire, Reginald is unconquerable; as homosexual, he, like Dracula, is vulnerable to the rules his enemies invent.

Viereck is so eager to divorce himself from homoeroticism that he concocts a doomed love affair between Ernest and the sophisticated Ethel, wherein Ernest briefly and implausibly grows up: "The child in him had made room for the man" (p. 149). But unlike the Catholic paraphernalia of Van Helsing, this gesture toward emotional normality withers in the face of the vampire's power, which is not only perverse, but progressive. Stoker's vampires were atavistic enemies of progress; Viereck's psychic vampires are the engines of human advance.

In a long self-justification that nothing in the novel contradicts, Reginald aligns himself, not with animals or demons, but with a pantheon of culture heroes. The psychic vampire is the analogue, not the enemy, of Christ.

> They are the chosen. Carpenter's sons they are, who have laid down the Law of a World for millenniums to come; or simple Corsicans, before whose eagle eye have quaked the kingdoms of the earth. But to accomplish their mission they need a will of iron and the wit of a hundred men. And from the iron they take the strength, and from a hundred men's brains they absorb their wisdom. . . . Homer and Shakespeare, Hugo and Balzac—they concentrate the dispersed rays of a thousand lesser luminaries in one singing flame that, like a giant's torch, lights up humanity's path. (P. 118)

Reginald is part of a visionary company. The community of vampire hunters, not the monster, is the obsolete obstruction, for Reginald is not the sole, nor even the primary, predator in his novel: his own epic of the French Revolution is absorbed into a great sculptor's "lost conception of Narcissus" (pp. 27–28). Conventional vampires like Dracula can be immured in coffins and purged from domestic life; a psychic vampire like Reginald creates his own domestic center—most of the action takes place in his "stately apartment-house overlooking Riverside Drive" (p. 13)—so that he can orchestrate the march of Western culture.

Ernest's cry to Ethel—"Your vampires suck blood; but Reginald, if vampire he be, preys upon the soul!" (p. 147)—anticipates the comprehensive vampirism of a later story set in a less refined American city: Fritz Leiber's "The Girl with the Hungry Eyes" (1949). Reginald embodies high culture; forty-two years later, Fritz Leiber's Girl personifies popular culture. In both works, psychic vampires are the essence of cherished social images and beliefs.

"The Girl with the Hungry Eyes" abandons Viereck's perfumed pretensions; its racy language is that of a tougher, more indigenously American urban life, one steeped in the abusive manliness of Mickey Spillane, not the rich verbosity of Oscar Wilde. Moreover, Leiber's America discards the cult of the genius to embrace the cult of the star. In the course of the story, an enigmatic billboard girl captivates America; like other imperial commodities, her face is exported around the world. Midcentury America's classic psychic vampire, Leiber's nameless Girl is not the poisonous cultural influence Reginald was, but her society's poisonous norm. Reginald was all brain; the Girl is all face. She exists as sheer display, devoid of name, home, and life. The tough-talking photographer who discovers her fears, not a monster, but femaleness itself:

> There are vampires and vampires, and the ones that suck blood aren't the worst. . . . I realized that wherever she came from, whatever shaped her, she's the quintessence of the horror behind the bright billboard. She's the eyes that lead you on and on, and then show you death. She's the creature you give everything for and never really get. She's the being that takes everything you've got and gives you nothing in return. When you yearn toward her face on the billboards, remember that. She's the lure. She's the bait. She's the Girl.

By definition, "you" are a male reader, as vulnerable to draining desire as Stoker's women were. As sheer personification who engulfs direct experience but has no role in it, the Girl drains more than blood. Reginald needed genius. The Girl needs, more simply, a life: "'I want you. I want your high spots. I want everything that's made you happy and everything that's hurt you bad. I want that shiny bicycle. I want that licking. I want that pinhole camera. I want Betty's legs. I want the blue sky filled with stars. I want your mother's death. I want your blood on the cobblestones. I want Mildred's mouth. I want the first picture you sold. I want the lights of Chicago. I want the gin. I want Gwen's hands. I want your wanting me. I want your life. Feed me, baby, feed me.'"[5]

This streetwise incantation is more inclusive than *Dracula's* sonorous "the blood is the life." Stoker's vampires are locked in symbols; the tastes of psychic vampires are as varied as any reader's ordinary day. Trapped in self-enclosed rituals, Stoker's vampires blend with mortals only at intervals, by the ungainly process of biting their necks. Their soullessness bars them from human space: they cast no shadows, they transmit no reflected image. The Girl lives as her own photographic shadow. No ta-boos bar her from the reader's frame of reference.

For the girl with no life—who in this America is all girls—blood fades before the memories, the feelings, the interiority, of the men whose devotion creates her. Her murderousness is the reflection of their adoration: "Imagine her knowing the hid-denmost hungers of millions of men. Imagine her seeing deeper into those hungers than the people that had them, *seeing the hatred and the wish for death behind the lust.* Imagine her shaping herself in that complete image, keeping herself as aloof as mar-ble. Yet imagine the hunger she must feel in answer to their hunger" (p. 343; my italics).

Leiber's tough-guy photographer denounces the Girl—and all girls—but his life breeds psychic vampires. In a city of men who talk only to each other, this shadow of a face is the *only* girl we see. Dracula was, as far as we knew, the only male vampire in the world; whether she is human or vampire or both, the girl with the hungry eyes is the only identifiable female. The horror of Leiber's story is the realization that all adored girls exist as shadows hungering after the vivid lives of men.

Stoker's vampires were trapped in their own knowability. Their clearly defined abilities and disabilities assured us that if we studied hard we could conquer the unknown and kill un-death. Psychic vampires infiltrate so much that their victims can only telegraph warnings to each other, for killing psychic vam-pires means killing social life itself. *The House of the Vampire's* turn-of-the-century New York strained to be a European palace of art; post–World War II America lived among photographic images of its native supremacy and wealth. MGM films and *Life* magazine flourished by showing a victorious country pictures of its own incessant happiness; whether they were giggling movie stars or wives grinning in photographs on successful men's desks, women reinforced the achievements of American men by looking blissful in pictures. The "poisonous half-smile" of the girl with the hungry eyes, the girl who strikes all her assigned poses, the girl who is always and only seen, is one of twentieth-century America's commonplace urban landmarks. Leiber's psy-chic vampire is so familiar in her time and place that she seems worlds away from those weird Victorian women in foreign castles who infected only one victim at a time.

Dracula's comparatively modest sister-brides wanted only to bite their prey, not to become him. Most female vampires at the turn of the nineteenth century were, like those sister-brides, characterless and compulsive appetites. Leiber's quintessentially American Girl does, nevertheless, have nineteenth-century ancestors who, like her, suck more than blood. Arthur Conan Doyle's "The Parasite" (1894) and Mary E. Wilkins-Freeman's "Luella Miller" (1903) add a lethal dimension to the most widely circulated Victorian stereotypes of controllable women: the old maid and the wife.

In these superb stories, psychic vampirism is inseparable from womanly dependence. Miss Penelosa, the mesmerist in Doyle's "The Parasite," is an aging spinster, foreign and lame, who falls pathetically in love with Professor Gilroy, the self-satisfied narrator. In an ordinary story, the man would have all the advantages—"She is far older than myself and a cripple," Professor Gilroy fumes. "It is monstrous, odious"[6]—but this old maid is a mesmerist more potent than Svengali. Under her influence, the professor cuts clownish capers during his lectures, robs a bank, and, having lost his profession and position, is about to murder his exemplary fiancée when Miss Penelosa dies providentially and releases him, having consumed, not his blood, but his identity.

This love-starved spinster is not the butt of the jokes that comic writers like Dickens and W. S. Gilbert had made. Her pathetic clinging is her power: "She can project herself into my body and take command of it. She has a parasite soul; yes, she is a parasite, a monstrous parasite. She creeps into my frame as the hermit crab does into the whelk's shell. I am powerless" (p. 127). Doyle makes literal and occult the parasitism inherent in the yearning old maid of countless Victorian jokes.

Wilkins-Freeman's "Luella Miller" has a sharper social edge than "The Parasite." An adored inhabitant of her New England village, the babylike Luella, with her "blue eyes full of soft pleading, little slender, clinging hands, and a wonderful grace of motion and attitude,"[7] is far from the chomping viragos of most fin-de-siècle British Gothic. Unlike Doyle's Miss Penelosa, Luella manifests no monomaniacal passion; she has no occult powers; she is no dangerously empowered New Woman. Her allure is her helplessness, which entices strapping men and women to do her housework until they wane and die. The vital fluid in "Luella Miller" is not blood, but work. A perfectly idle Victorian lady who exists to be helped, Luella is the exemplar of her class and time, the epitome of her age, not an outcast in it.

"The Parasite" and "Luella Miller" feature women so stereo-typical that they become Everywoman; each suggests that all women, or at least all proper women, are psychic vampires. It is the horror of *Dracula* that Lucy and Mina might decompose into the fetid women in the vampire's castle; it is the horror of "Lu-ella Miller" that a loved woman and a ghoul are one. Psychic vampire stories discard transformation scenes and vitiate benign assurances like Jonathan Harker's "Faugh! Mina is a woman and there is naught in common. They are devils of the Pit!"[8]

All compliant women may be psychic vampires, but not all psychic vampires are women—or homosexuals, or artists. In 1914, we remember, Alice and Claude Askew's vampire detective evoked "the evil influence that a very old person may have upon a young one." In 1914, that "very old person" was, historically at least, likely to be a commanding male; the First World War erupted to ravage the young out of territorial rivalries among ruling men, "the worn-out tissue sapping healthy vitality for their own support."[9] By implication, catastrophic history itself is a process of psychic vampirism.

But the Askews' vampire detective does not stop at genera-tional predators, broadening his definition still further to in-clude "certain people—I could think of several myself—who seem to depress one and undermine one's energies, quite uncon-sciously, of course, but one feels somehow that vitality has passed from oneself to them." This resonant category implicates us all. Psychic vampirism taints not only romantic love and the sacrifices of war, but ordinary talk. It encompasses men and women, old and young, dullness and brilliance, banality and strangeness, wholesomeness and perversity.[10]

The psychic vampires of twentieth-century horror might be antidotes to *Dracula*'s constraints. Dracula is marginal; they are mainstream. They evade the restrictions Stoker constructs. They are not foreigners; they can go anywhere; their coffin, if it is one, is as large as Western culture. But insofar as they poison friendship and turn love into death, psychic vampires are Dracula's brood. Unlike the expansive vampires of the early and middle nineteenth century, psychic vampires thrive on revulsion—their own, their victims', and their readers'. Viereck's Reginald exposes the cannibalistic violation within Carlylean myths of heroic individualism; Leiber's Girl feeds on (and is swallowed by) advertising's version of courtly love. Both expose the predatory underside of inspirational idealism.

Dracula was the first vampire vulnerable to the accusation: "You yourself never loved; you never love!" Despite twentieth-century efforts to romanticize him, revulsion is Dracula's essence; it is also the essence of the more mobile psychic vampires he legitimized. Dracula preys on the normal, turning its most stalwart adherents into his snarling image; psychic vampires *are* normal. No sentiment is too noble to accommodate them.

At the beginning of the nineteenth century, Byron's generous Augustus Darvell offered his adoring schoolmate "intimacy, or friendship." At the end of that century, Dracula nullified both, bequeathing us a brood of psychic vampires who feast on the horror inherent in friendship and intimacy. They refuse blood, but they grow fat on human fellowship.

THROUGHOUT THE TWENTIETH CENTURY psychic vampires have unobtrusively infiltrated horror literature—no doubt because they adapt so well in less bizarre environments. More pervasive and less obviously monstrous than their progenitors, they take the color of their times so well that they make their stagy originator Dracula appear quaintly obsolete.[11] Unlike Dracula, whose condition is confinement, psychic vampires in the late twentieth century can shrink to a whisper or expand to fill contemporary history. Dan Simmons's stunning novel *Carrion Comfort* (1989) is an epic about elegant racists who are so skilled at psychic vampirism (or, as they delicately call it, their Ability) that they implant racial hate in nations. The German Willi inspires Nazism and thrives on concentration camps; Nina and Melanie, purring southern belles, manipulate racial hatred in the United States.

Along the way, for exercise, they foment such apparently isolated catastrophes as the murders of John Kennedy and John
Lennon. Their primary motive is neither sex nor violence: they
find nothing erotic beyond the simple act of controlling others.

Throughout their massive novel, they indulge in languid
"Feedings" on the rage they instill. For the hero, Saul, a concentration camp survivor, they are the epitomes and creators of
"this entire century," which is "a miserable melodrama written
by third-rate minds at the expense of other people's souls and
lives. We can't stop it. Even if we put an end to these . . . these
aberrations, it would only shift the spotlight to some other
carrion-eating actor in this violent farce."[12] Less cloistered than
Viereck's Reginald, but genii of history like him, Willi, Nina, and
Melanie are the courteous spirits of a savage age.

But Simmons's vampires belong only fortuitously to the
twentieth century; their Ability was formed by gentler times.
They are not only epic agents, but creatures of romance who
learned vampirism from the conventions of love. Melanie reminisces fondly about the antebellum summer when she and Nina
incited their lovers to a duel.

> It would have been harmless except for our Ability. We had
> been so successful in our manipulation of male behavior—a
> manipulation which was both expected and encouraged in
> those days—that neither of us had yet suspected that there
> lay anything beyond the ordinary in the way we could trans-
> late our whims into other people's actions. The field of para-
> psychology did not exist then: or rather, it existed only in the
> rappings and knockings of parlor game séances. At any rate,
> we amused ourselves with whispered fantasies for several
> weeks and then one of us—or perhaps both of us—used the
> Ability to translate the fantasy into reality.
> In a sense it was our first Feeding. (P. 12)

Simmons's vampires feed on history's hatreds, but the origin of
Feeding—and its only mundane approximation—is love. "We
love being in love because it is as close as humans can come to
feeling this psychic addiction," Melanie muses (p. 296). Love
offers no salvation from vampires; instead, it summons them.

Freed from blood-drinking and other specialized needs, psychic vampires can go anywhere, but in general they are bred in intimacy. Ellen Datlow's two powerful anthologies, *Blood Is Not Enough* (1989) and *A Whisper of Blood* (1991), feature psychic vampires who are lovers and intimates before they are political prime movers. Stealthily, though, these denizens of privacy acquire cultural control. Datlow's introduction to her first collection insists that psychic vampires are too inclusive to be monsters: "In traditional vampire fiction, blood is the essence. When I talk about vampirism I mean the draining of energy, the sucking of the will, the life force itself. . . . And it seems that vampirism becomes one of the main themes of our culture in this century."[13] By 1989, Datlow's dismissal of "traditional vampire fiction" adheres to a literary convention of its own, one that relegates bloodsucking to embarrassing cliché and canonizes the psychic vampire. The typical material of these collections is mundane: seduction, empathy, sympathy, romance, religious awe, art, and parental love.[14] Their moral is summarized by the consuming "empath" in Pat Cadigan's "Dirty Work": "Every relationship is something like this. . . . People feed on each other whether it's lover to lover, friend to friend, audience to artist. We consume, we are consumed. You couldn't live otherwise" (p. 301).[15]

"You couldn't live otherwise": in an ultimate feeding, victim and vampire, horror and health, narrator and reader, merge, implicating everything that is supposed to bring us together. The operative word in psychic vampire fiction is no longer *blood,* but the more inclusive *feed.* The noun *feeding* weaves through *Carrion Comfort;* the verb *feed* is the hypnotic refrain of Ellen Datlow's collections. Leiber's Girl croons "feed me, baby, feed me" for them all: stealing her metaphor from the lullaby language of motherhood, she drinks from the baby she is apparently nourishing, just as she drains the experiences of the voyeuristic men she obeys. Her sinister lullaby replaces Renfield's more specialized (and, in a culture of AIDS, dubious) "the blood is the life." Few readers, after all, drink blood; not all of us have seen it; but even at our most spiritual, we feed. We couldn't live otherwise.

Sophisticated psychic vampires disown their parent Dracula as a gauche anachronism, but his compulsions have been their primary food. Dracula's dominance in our century allows us to imagine our relationships, intimate and political, as entangled in psychic vampirism. Vampires and vampires live with us today because, throughout the twentieth century, we have embraced Draculas and Draculas.

Draculas and Draculas

In the United States especially, Dracula has been one constant in the volatile twentieth century. He changes, but imperceptibly. Unlike the psychic vampires who are indistinguishable from their surroundings, Dracula stands apart, an alternative to mass society, a cultivated remnant of a stately past our country never had, a forbidden lover in times that claim to forbid nothing, the king Americans are not supposed to want.

Stolid persistence has given Dracula authority in a century whose monsters, actual and imagined, are as vulnerable to trends as their victims are to them. The Blob, the Thing, Jason, Freddie, vanish into nostalgia like once-popular songs, while—perhaps because he himself is steeped in nostalgia—Dracula is, at least apparently, not limited to an age. By appearing immutable, he has survived this most fickle of centuries.

Of course, Dracula does change, all the time. Stoker's rabid animal has virtually nothing in common with Gary Oldman's whimpering costume-changer in Francis Ford Coppola's 1992 adaptation; but his mutations seem as glacial as the changes in ourselves over the years, changes we perceive only when we see our earlier selves in photographs. In the same manner, Dracula's changes are manifest in his movies. Four popular *Dracula*s from 1931 to 1979—starring Bela Lugosi, Christopher Lee, Jack Palance, and Frank Langella—say as much about America as they do about vampires. More than our heroes or pundits, our Draculas tell us who we were.[16]

Belligerently, even comically foreign though he is, Bela Lugosi's Dracula is the first authentic transplantation of Stoker's character to America. Paradoxically, Dracula was not notably foreign until he became American. Stoker's Count struggled to pass, perfecting his English accent and idioms, filling his library with British books, newspapers, magazines, reference works, and even, as Jonathan Harker notes admiringly, railway timetables.

Once in England, he blends into Piccadilly so well, if so lewdly, that not even Mina notices him. No Englishman, he vows, will say of him, "'Ha, ha! a stranger!'" (p. 28).

Bela Lugosi revels in being a stranger—even a comic stranger to whom we might say "Ha, ha!" His succulently foreign intonations inspired the legend that he learned his lines phonetically, scarcely understanding the dialogue of his fellow actors.[17] Whether or not Lugosi knew the language he made his own, his accent *became* Dracula, expelling Stoker's adaptable invader. After his American transplantation, to be Dracula meant speaking in a different voice.

Lugosi's clothes are similarly alienating, not only from America, but from human standards of comfort: he wears his tuxedo, cape, and medals not only indoors, but in his coffin. Stoker's Dracula was in no way sartorially distinguished; in *Nosferatu*, the vampire is set apart by nature, not dress. Max Schreck's costumes generally resemble Jonathan's, but his pallor, tentacle-like ears and fingers, and rodent teeth define this vampire as a different species.

Bela Lugosi's Dracula is the first who bears no monstrous marks: he is fangless, solid, and elegantly human. But he is also the first to separate himself by his costumes and mannerisms from the actors who encompass him. His singularity became so indelible a vampiric attribute that it created a new order of fear in the twentieth century: fear not only of otherness, but eventually, and more subtly, of kinship. Psychic vampires infiltrate human lives so well because they neither look nor sound like Bela Lugosi. In the manner of Henry Higgins, Lugosi taught us to identify a vampire by his accent, making us too quick to trust those who talk and dress as we do.

Lugosi's Dracula is not only an alien; he flaunts his alienation as an aesthetic style. In this he owes nothing to his conscientiously conformist Victorian namesake, but a great deal to a more cultured ancestor: Gaston Leroux's Erik, or, as he is variously called, the Angel of Music and the Opera Ghost. Film and theater audiences know this possessive, plaintive monster as the Phantom of the Opera.

Like Lugosi's Dracula, Erik is striking in his formality: "He was wearing his dress-clothes in broad daylight?" asks an incred-

ulous opera-dancer.[18] Like him, too, Erik captivates his women
by dangling before them erotic visions of death. Abducted into
his underground lair, Christine describes his bedroom with awe:
"I felt as though I were entering the room of a dead person. The
walls were all hung with black, but instead of the white trim-
mings that usually set off that funereal upholstery, there was an
enormous stave of music with the notes of the *Dies Irae,* many
times repeated. In the middle of the room was a canopy, from
which hung curtains of red brocaded stuff, and, under the canopy, an open coffin. 'That is where I sleep,' said Erik. 'One has
to get used to everything in life, even to eternity'" (pp. 168–69).
Mimicking Sarah Bernhardt, whose coffin-bed was one of her
best props, Erik makes death an erotic invitation.

Lugosi's Dracula woos Lucy with the same entrancing pros-
pect of dying. Before he flaps into her bedroom, he insinuates
himself into her box at the symphony, where he joins her in a
toast to the dead. "To die—to be really dead—that must be—
glorious," he intones. Lucy responds and vanishes from the
movie. Had she been given more lines, she would surely have
echoed Leroux's Christine: "That is the terrible thing about it.
He fills me with horror and I do not hate him" (p. 166), words
any number of bitten ingenues could use to describe their Dracula. Like Erik, Lugosi makes no appeal to vitality; he entices his
women with promises of death.

Stoker's Dracula was too single-minded to bother with seductive rituals. He was fundamentally a rapist, but one with no
lust for death, injecting into his victims incessant, frightening
life. Lugosi's affinity with the Phantom of the Opera throws him
back to mid-Victorian vampires like Varney, whose Clara
achieves full beauty as a prospective corpse: "Her face was of a
marble paleness, and as she clasped her hands, and glanced from
face to face . . . she might have been taken for some exquisite
statue of despair."[19] These romantic aesthetes kill more effectively than Stoker's autocratic animal.

Above all, like the stage-struck Erik, Lugosi's Dracula is a
creature of the playhouse, not the wild.[20] His florid self-
revelations are inspired by their setting in a theater, not, like
those of Stoker's Dracula, by his own castle and native earth. His
authentic theme is not the music of the wolves, but Tchaikov-

sky's *Swan Lake,* whose second act opening plays piercingly under the opening credits.[21] *Swan Lake* evokes not a smelly or a
bloody animal, but a stylized one. No fly-eating Renfield could
invade *Swan Lake;* its hybrid star is no cannibal, nor is the wizard
who bifurcates her; though the same ballerina dances its tragically enchanted Odette and its malevolent enchantress Odile,
Odette and Odile are equally decorative and equally eager to
please their prince and their audience. They do not devour love;
like good performers, they solicit it.

This musical equation with Tchaikovsky's Swan-Queen refines Dracula's bestiality into a theatrical trope. Stoker's Dracula
infiltrated English households only furtively, as animal or mist;
Lugosi's makes stagy, self-delighted entrances into his adversar-
ies' drawing-rooms. As alien, artist, social being, and sexy personification of death, Bela Lugosi is the first Dracula who demands our love. In fact, like Odette/Odile, he lives on our
applause.

Lugosi takes his aesthetic allure not only from the Phantom
of the Opera and the wizardry that refines itself into Swan Maidens, but from Rudolph Valentino, whose exotically dressed sheik
became the delectably foreign sovereign of 1920s Hollywood.
Lugosi's vampire, like Valentino, wears elaborate makeup obvious in close-up. He is, as Skal calls him, "a Valentino gone
slightly rancid," but unlike Valentino, he is sartorially masculine: his cloak is a mere dashing shadow of Valentino's flamboyant Arabian robes.[22] Shaped less by Stoker's horrid animal
than by the art and erotic gestures of lusher decades, Lugosi's
Count is a sexually coded figure no matter what his script makes
him do. Dracula is not essentially lovable, nor, in Stoker's novel,
is he especially erotic—repulsive in himself, he catalyzes spectacular changes in women—but Lugosi's artful re-creation
allows the twentieth century to steep him in desire.

Because of Lugosi's performance, contemporary critics celebrate *Dracula*'s supposedly Victorian sexuality as George Stade
does: "Bram Stoker's Dracula, in short, is an apparition of what
we repress, traditional eros. To be bitten by Dracula is to become
a slave to a kind of lust, abandoned to unlawful hungers, a projection of the beholder's desire and dread. . . . Dracula is the
symptom of a wish, largely sexual, that we wish we did not

have."[23] Entangled in "our" sexual wishes and fears, Lugosi's Dracula authorized the psychic vampires who nestle in twentieth-century love.

Lugosi's Dracula is so singular that he is impossible to emulate; the transformations he induces are muted and muddled compared to their kaleidoscopic prominence in Stoker's novel. He can be killed only by his double, Edward Van Sloan's Van Helsing. With his ceremonial line readings and foreign accent, Van Sloan is a pale parody of Lugosi, even, like him, shunning daylight: at the end, he stays in the crypt with the dead Dracula, directing the young lovers as they walk somnambulistically up a huge staircase toward the light.

Van Helsing is not a vampire, but he is the sole possible vampire-killer: only another ponderous foreigner can fulfill Dracula's need to die. This Van Helsing is less hero than magus, orchestrating the action, for unlike Stoker's Dracula, Lugosi's poses no threat to the nation or the human race, limiting his predations to a single household. But benign as he is in his movie, evoking death, art, and sexuality rather than conquest and metamorphosis, this soft-seeming foreigner possessed his century. He did so by giving the bleak decade of the 1930s a romantic past it had never had.

For most commentators, Bela Lugosi's Dracula is neither romantic nor Victorian; he is herald and epitome of the American Depression. According to Skal, Lugosi's vampire is "the first monster, the fear that preceded fear, that shadowy harbinger of the Depression that was now at every throat."[24] He was also the harbinger of a community of movie monsters who diverted and defined a newly fearful America in the 1930s. John Barrymore's Svengali and Boris Karloff's Frankenstein monster appeared in the same year, 1931. King Kong followed two years later, an eruption of the animalism Lugosi disowned, breeding, in the '40s, such relatively humane hybrids as Lon Chaney Jr.'s Wolf Man and Simone Simon's Cat Woman. In his sexy self and in the monsters he licensed, Dracula, like Walt Disney, gave bereft America new, hybrid objects of faith. According to one of his current chroniclers, "Dracula evidently appeals to nations in crisis."[25]

But how can even Dracula identify a national crisis? It has

been difficult for this century to distinguish times of *non*-crisis. Two world wars, for example, were surely rich in the rhetoric of Armageddon, but they were sparse in monsters; so were the American 1960s, despite political assassinations and violent division over civil rights and the Vietnam War. Monsters in the 1960s were, for the most part, tired shadows, while the 1970s— a decade of relative political consolidation in America, in which the Vietnam War ended at last, and, domestically, the political system held—generated a robust horror cycle.[26] Perhaps, in twentieth-century America, monsters are shadows, not symbols, of crises; or perhaps we live in a continuing crisis—fanned by rabid journalism and seemingly incessant change—that sometimes takes the shape of vampires.

The three captivating monsters of the 1930s—Bela Lugosi, Boris Karloff, and King Kong—evoke the Depression only subliminally, but their very distinctiveness defines '30s hopes and fears.[27] As we have seen, Lugosi is the first fully human Dracula: despite his occasional bestial protestations and some awkward insertions of a limp bat, he has nothing animal about him. He fastidiously refused fangs; he uses his cape as Victorian ladies were supposed to use their fans, as a discreet screen for illicit kisses, but he never tries to fly with it. His distinctiveness is his *willed* difference of accent, costume, and rhythm. His stately, hypnotic cadences, the long close-ups that make him seem more statuesque than alive, the old-fashioned theatricality with which he confronts shrill American actors, differentiate him absolutely from his human company.

The same is true of Karloff's monster, who, compared to his prototype in Mary Shelley's novel—a "creature," like humans, not a "monster," like no one—is opaque and anomalous. James Whale's movie throws primary responsibility for his monstrosity not on Frankenstein but on his inept assistant Fritz, who mistakenly gives the creature a criminal and thus "abnormal" brain, then goes on to brutalize him with fire. Fritz guarantees Karloff's monstrosity before the viewer can define him. Moreover, unlike Mary Shelley's compulsive self-explainer, Karloff is silent, miming his emotions graciously among a voluble human company. Mary Shelley's creature was utterly malleable; he killed only in response to his creator's murderous abandonment. Karloff's creature is labeled "abnormal" even before he is made.

Like Lugosi's Dracula, Karloff's monster has nothing in common with the rest of the cast, or, by implication, with his audience. Both are creatures of the 1920s unleashed into the littler, more frantic '30s: Lugosi wears the costume of the Phantom of the Opera in the style of Valentino, while Karloff's carefully choreographed miming is a shadow of the cinematic conventions talkies had killed. These anachronistic acting styles, fruitlessly resurrecting a dead decade, affirm by negation the reality of the present.

Not to be Dracula, foreign and formal; not to be Karloff's monster, abnormal and speechless; is to be American in 1931. The monsters' eccentricity confirms American authority. Today, Lugosi may look like a capitalist, or Karloff like a proletarian, but in their time they were antithetical to native fears about money and work. Outlandish, aberrant, they buttressed Americans' commitment to the devils they knew. Ironically, these creatures of lean times are less hungry than the monsters who gnaw their way through movies made in wealthier decades, like *Jaws* or *The Hunger*. They care less about appetite than about flaunting themselves so eccentrically that they startle American moviegoers out of nostalgia, back to grim native reality.

The sheer strangeness of Karloff and Lugosi protects humans from their lewd embrace. Despite Karloff's yearning and Lugosi's heavy eroticism, both monsters are as asexual as Dorothy's Scarecrow of Oz. Dracula's brides, more spectral than their counterparts in the novel, scarcely appear in the same frame with Lugosi before vanishing from the movie, and Karloff's marriage in *The Bride of Frankenstein* (1935) exists to be unconsummated. Their grotesqueness, along with scrupulous directorial censorship, deposits an aura of obscenity around monsters' intercourse with mortals.[28] Lugosi in particular is scarcely touchable. His vampire, like Barrymore's Svengali, is more mesmerist than biter, effecting with his staring eyes the penetration from which the rest of his body abstains.

This withheld relation of monster to mortals speaks for its time. American movies refrained from showing any embrace that smacked of miscegenation, and besides, a singular, physically aloof monster is more easily relegated to anachronistic fantasy than an expansive or gregarious one.[29] But the barrier that separates monster from mortal perpetuates Stoker's legacy in America. The first vampire who did not move fluidly in and out of human society, Dracula was barricaded from mortals by the diagnostic hunger of the British 1890s. To breach that barrier was obscenity. Victorian phobias adapted easily to self-protective American Puritanism.

Like his austere namesake, Bela Lugosi's Dracula was alone in his world, essentially unmateable, the only creature of his kind. He was as distinctive as the quartet of Western masters—Franklin Roosevelt, Churchill, Mussolini, and Hitler—who would dominate international affairs until the end of the Second World War. Like each of them, Lugosi incarnated the rituals of a lost world, posing as the last representative of his nation's aristocracy. After the war enthroned democracy, the future seemed bright, in America at least. So, in a short time, were its Draculas.

ONE COULD ALMOST SEE the '60s dawning in *Horror of Dracula* (1958; dir. Terence Fisher), the first and most startling of the Christopher Lee *Dracula*s that swarmed out of England's Hammer Studios between 1958 and 1970. As the series progressed, Lee was reduced to snarls and stares, but in this inaugural appearance he is brisk and entrepreneurial, more up-to-date than the little men who scurry around to protect their strapping, sexy women.

Even before the story begins, the postcredit sequence announces a brave new world for vampires, one that dispels Lugosi's gloom. Lugosi made his famous first entrance in a crypt furnished with rats, coffins, cobwebs, and other inhospitable props. His hand creeps out of his battered coffin, but we never see his body move: in the next shot he stands cloaked and still "while the camera moves toward him like a supplicant."[30] He never climbs out of his coffin: he is prone and then he is erect; his power is his immobility. His formal attire makes him a statuesque and rather sad discord in his ghastly home.

By contrast, Christopher Lee's coffin, on which DRACULA is elegantly carved on a gleaming surface, is, like his castle, immac-

ulate. The credits roll as we admire his taste and care in main-
taining a coffin so handsome. Suddenly, bright red blood, the
Hammer trademark, splashes on his white name from some indeterminate source, making a pattern as stylishly vivid as a
painting by Jackson Pollock. Is Christopher Lee splashing his
own coffin as he comes home from a kill? Or does his presence
inside his coffin magically attract any blood around? Logic is
nonexistent. It doesn't finally matter whose blood we are watching, since it looks so good. Christopher Lee's taste does not desert him on his travels: when he goes off to prey on Lucy and
Mina, he brings a white portable traveling coffin that will be an
important prop in the story. These tasteful accoutrements define
a vampire who spurns decay and cobwebs. His element is modernity, speed, and above all, color.

The bright colors of Hammer movies were their exhilarating
innovation. Hammer vampires and other monsters are not segregated in the black-and-white gloom of 1930s America. In vibrant color, they are substance, not shadows. They are not primarily costumes and makeup, like Lugosi and Karloff: they are
bodies.[31] Technically they remain children of the night—
though Christopher Lee wastes no time with this or any lugubri-
ous self-definition in *Horror of Dracula*—but the vampires we see
are children of the light.

In these vivid spectacles, blood is beautiful, but it is no
longer the life. Appropriately for movies shockingly bathed in
light, the sun becomes for the first time the primary vampire-
killer: stronger than Catholic ritual, modern technology, or even
Van Helsing, the sun displaces all these as Dracula's preeminent
adversary and double. Stoker's Dracula, we remember, could not
shape-shift in daylight, but he walked around in it freely. Max
Schreck in *Nosferatu* is technically the first vampire destroyed by
the sun: when Nina detains him past dawn, he dissolves.[32] Tod
Browning's Mina claims Dracula failed to kill her because "the
daylight stopped him," but Lugosi must be staked before even
nominally dying. He and Max Schreck fade in sunlight, but they
never burn. As a shadow, Schreck simply dissipates, while Lugosi
is enervated but alive. Neither endures the scorching inflicted
on Christopher Lee when Van Helsing pulls down his draper-

ies—a scorching that has become our primary image of vampire destruction.

The closing sequence of *Horror of Dracula* is as innovative as its beginning, helping us forget the florid incoherence that dominates the middle. Confronted by dawn, Dracula retreats to the library of his gorgeous castle. He is pursued by Peter Cushing's athletic Van Helsing, who is less an occultist or sonorous patriarch than a shrewd fighter who, like his double Dracula, exists above all as a body.[33] Outmatched after a bravura fight, Cushing throws down the lush draperies and floods the room with sunlight, sending the vampire into balletic paroxysms of anguish.

Cushing does pay lip service to the supernatural by making a cross out of Dracula's elegant candlesticks and advancing on the vampire with this unconsecrated artifact, a strategy more ingenious than reverent, but this pseudo-cross only reinforces the potency of the sun that quickly reduces Dracula to a pile of ashes—at least until he rises in the next Lee movie, *Dracula, Prince of Darkness,* whose precredit sequence replays this ravishing burning.

This "death" frees Dracula from the old metaphysics, steeping him in a physical empiricism that will define him throughout the century. Stoker's Van Helsing needed carefully consecrated weapons: presumably nothing without clerical sanction would work against the vampire. For the Hammer Dracula, symbol becomes body; he recoils from the mere shape of a cross. Hammer's rules insist on this loss of metaphysical signification. Van Helsing, solitary rule-giver, listens solemnly to his own recorded voice, reminding himself that Dracula is *allergic* to light—not repelled by its goodness.[34]

Stoker's Dracula was vulnerable to time, not light: no matter where he was, sunrise enervated him and sunset invigorated him. The Hammer Dracula is disconnected from time. Indoors in day, he is as strong as ever, but his body is vulnerable to a stronger body, the sun's.[35] Like twentieth-century mortals dependent on mechanized gadgets, this Dracula has severed his tie to the universe. He is bounded by senses and flesh.

For better or worse, the vampires that follow Christopher

Lee are shorn of their occult identities. They may yearn for them, as do Anne Rice's spirit-haunted seducers, but they live in their own sensations, not in the cosmos. Vibrant and lethal at once, the Hammer sun struck a new kind of vampire. This creature was invented in the late 1950s, but anatomists of horror exalted him as mythic and timeless: "A single beam of the sun falling upon [the vampire's] body will bring instant, complete and absolute disintegration," Drake Douglas's compendium of horror assured readers.[36] Decades after Christopher Lee, the sun can destroy even such refined, self-healing predators as Frank Langella's Dracula, Chelsea Quinn Yarbro's Count Saint-Germain, Fred Saberhagen's Vlad, Anne Rice's Lestat, Jewelle Gomez's Gilda, and Patrick Whale's Braille (in *Night Thirst*, 1991). In novels like George R. Martin's *Fevre Dream* (1982) and movies like Kathryn Bigelow's *Near Dark* (1987), the primary sensory experience is neither biting nor bloodsucking, but the sun's rending of tender vampire flesh. The lethal Hammer sun inspired as extensive a vampire paradigm-shift in 1958 as Planché's moon did in 1820, when Polidori's elliptical tale became the spectacular melodrama, *The Vampire*.[37]

But what the early nineteenth-century moon bestowed, the mid-twentieth-century sun destroys. Planché's Ruthven quivers to life under the full moon; the Hammer Dracula writhes and twitches into dissolution when the sun strikes him. Until Stoker changed the rules, Planché's moon spiritualized nineteenth-century vampires; it diluted their dependence on blood and obscured their addiction to human intercourse, refining them into clean and pure communion. Hammer's sun, and the great welts it caused for decades after *Horror of Dracula*, throws vampires into the pain of physical existence. But at the same time as the sun aligns vampires with mortals, it limits their access to mortal society. For all their style and charm, photophobic vampires are too weak to belong to the devil, too delicate to live in human company.

"Listen to them—the children of the night. What music they make!" Child of nobody, Stoker's vampire listened from his castle, but because of their tender skin, Christopher Lee and his progeny became the mid-twentieth-century's children of the night. We now gaze at vampires with the admiration Stoker's

Dracula reserved for wolves.[38] For as twentieth-century vampires became more material and thus more human, they acquired an allergy that forbade them to live human lives. They exchanged crypts for stylish homes, but they could not leave those homes at will. Planché's moon and the Hammer sun elevate vampires but isolate them from mortal life. The moon revives and the sun kills, but neither quarantines the vampire completely.

THE CHANGING INFLUENCE of heavenly bodies is an index of restlessness on earth. For the British working-class audiences and American students who devoured Hammer films in the 1960s, even sun-struck vampires carried subliminal messages about their own societies.[39] The early Christopher Lee is a freeing alternative to Lugosi. There is nothing foreign in his line readings: he rattles through the familiar speeches with brisk, British efficiency, making them as suitable for a London corporation as for a Transylvanian fortress. Lee's castle is spacious and modern, full of expensive furniture, abounding in sinuous columns and candelabra. Its colorful rooms have just been painted; even its crypt is sparkling. Anyone in the Hammer target audience would covet this art deco home, a pointed contrast to Lugosi's unlivable mausoleum. Lee's decor announces his allegiance to a sleek future, not a dusty past; his Castle Dracula is a streamlined respite from the suffocating clutter of the virtuous family's Victorian home. Before Van Helsing throws his curtains open, Lee himself has let the light in on a timid, claustrophobic domesticity.

One of the more enticing incoherences in *Horror of Dracula* is its bizarre handling of space. There is no dislocating journey from London to Transylvania and back. Jonathan, a disguised vampire-hunter in this one, does have to take some sort of trip to Dracula's castle, but in the course of the movie, the characters scurry back and forth so easily that Dracula's castle seems to creep next door to the cluttered Victorian home. The distance between vampire and family is so inconstant that Dracula manages to hide his sparkling coffin in Arthur Holmwood's own cellar: while protective men are waiting for him to invade the house, he rises from within it. Some sort of Van Helsing–like logic has evaporated from this *Dracula,* leaving a presence who is the emanation, not the enemy, of the family.

This family is itself a scrambled version of Stoker's clearly differentiated international community of vampire hunters. *Horror of Dracula* shuffles Stoker's good characters around for no discernible reason, thereby draining integrity from the vampire-hunters more effectively than Dracula does: in a world where Lucy and Mina, Arthur and Jonathan, change places with impunity, the only constant is Dracula himself. In *Horror of Dracula,* the Western alliance shrinks to a household in which everyone is related to everyone else: screenwriter Jimmy Sangster replaces Stoker's elite, carefully selected vigilante community, the cream of Western civilization, with a series of ingrown relations. This Lucy is the fiancée of the dead Jonathan and the sister of Arthur, who is married to Mina. A little girl, Tania, floats around with no clear antecedents: a vampire she calls *"Aunt* Lucy" abducts her, though she is not Arthur and Mina's child, but the daughter of the housekeeper. All relationships in this movie are literally or essentially familial, with the exception of Van Helsing, who hovers alone, austere and above the circle, and Dracula, its devouring potential.

The heart and the horror of *Horror of Dracula* is the family. As Waller puts it, "The vampire's assault/seduction of Lucy and Mina becomes an attack on the patriarchal family, which relies on strictly defined female sexual roles, and on the home, which provides neither privacy nor protection for the family" (p. 115). In this family-bounded environment, women rise. Lucy and Mina are under the control of a slew of interchangeable paternalistic men—until Dracula comes. But as Terence Fisher directs these scenes, Dracula is scarcely there. This vampire is too elusive to be another overbearing male; he is an emanation of the anger, pride, and sexuality that lie dormant in the women themselves. Stoker's nightmare of violation becomes a dream of female self-possession.

A docile Lucy is bustled over in bed, childish in braids and demure blue nightgown. Once left alone, she undergoes an inward change with no vampire catalyst. Deliberately, she rises and listens at the door, then opens the window; we see a woman's body within the suddenly sheer little-girl nightgown. She removes her crucifix, lies down, and, in a tender rhythm of auto-eroticism, fondles the vampire bites on her neck. We never see Christopher Lee enter her room; the sequence fades out on the open window. The scene suggests vampirism, but we see, instead, a woman alone, claiming herself. This sequence is all the more suggestive because the screenplay gives us no "normal," pre-bitten Lucy: we see only an infantilized girl shutting out her keepers and opening the window to her adult self.

The bitten Mina repeats this gleeful autoeroticism. Throughout the movie, Mina has been a leaden, matronly presence, sitting dully while the men plan futile attacks on Dracula. When the vampire lures her into his power, we never see him touch her. She simply returns home sparkling, clutching the fur collar around her neck. In a witty close-up, she smiles deliciously and snuggles into the fur, seeming to caress her animal self. The close-up is not only postcoital; like Lucy's fondling of her bites, Mina's grin is, as far as we see, an infusion of self-delight, not delight in Dracula.

Of course, Lucy is staked and Mina is purified. These glimpses of exhilarated women, aroused by neither husband nor vampire, are only interludes in a traditional script, but though Terence Fisher's men always kill their vampire and reappropriate their women, *Horror of Dracula* exposes women, teenagers, and other restless spectators to a future more colorful than the restrictive 1950s. Postwar America had celebrated its victory over fascism by targeting enemies within. Self-canonized authorities—medical, moral, and patriotic—proliferated, all preaching the health of domesticity (national and familial) and the horror of the world beyond. With a ferocity alien even to most Victorians, they implanted in women family values and no others. Popular psychiatry insisted that not only women's lives, but our dreams and desires, were limited to endless reiterations of the patriarchal family plot. *Horror of Dracula* provided an image of disobedience, showing us two women opening windows beyond the family and, in the guise of vampire victims, surging into themselves.

Stoker's Lucy is the only character who crosses the border from human to vampire: she accomplishes the metamorphosis that threatens Jonathan, Renfield, Mina, and, by extension, England. The long middle of Stoker's novel is a voyeuristic account of Lucy's protracted transformation. Until the Hammer *Dracula* series, this transforming woman was relegated to the margins of the story. *Horror of Dracula* places her at its heart: the next thirty years would play sophisticated ideological variations on her unstable form. In the 1970s, women would write new vampire conventions, but the Hammer series provided tantalizing images of transformation that later, flagrantly unorthodox films would develop into structural principles.[40]

For most of the young women who, like me, loved Hammer films in the 1960s and weren't sure why, these grins of aroused discovery were subliminal surprises in a waste of staked bimbos. Hammer films never explicitly challenged the status quo, becoming more authoritarian as they became more popular.[41] As the films became increasingly pious (at least on the surface), Hammer women grew more swollen and soporific: tiny crucifixes swung enticingly in the crevasse between their mountainous breasts, but their faces had little energy. The *Dracula* series hinted only intermittently at the delights of awakening; its primary effect was an almost hypnotic insistence on the eroticism of repression. The brightly colored Victorian decor was a plush evocation of barely contained sexiness. For young people in the 1960s, who, as Walter Kendrick shrewdly notes, were "the first generation . . . that had probably never met a Victorian," Victorian England oozed out of Hammer movies as a psychedelic goofy glow—though the ostensible setting was Switzerland![42]

Children of a tasteless American suburbia, which was invaded in the 1950s only by the Blob, the Thing, giant ants, and other preconscious monsters with which it was impossible to identify, loved the ripe, somewhat sickly innocence of Hammer England. Like the Beatles, those similarly seductive Edwardian revenants, Hammer films led Americans on a mythic return to their glamorous British origin. The lyrical Hammer wood, where in movie after movie someone falls out of a coach and is attacked; those enormous Hammer beds with their puffy comforters and infinite pillows, where women writhe delicately as they wait for the vampire; those cluttered Hammer drawing-rooms whose inhabitants are so languid that we can't tell whether they've been bitten or not; all created a picture of Victorian England as a sadistic fairyland, a respite from too-knowing times. In Stoker's *Dracula,* 1897 is the model of sophisticated technology on which vampires intrude from prehistoric antiquity; Hammer films generated nostalgia for a magically remote Victorian past where vampires were at home. The 1960s was a decade whose young Americans were haunted by utopias of sweet, pseudo-childish sexuality. The Hammer Victorian England was one of the silliest and the sweetest.

For young women, though, its violence was strangely contemporary, or, as we used to say, "relevant." Hammer films courted the youth market, but not with wars and political protests. *Taste the Blood of Dracula* (1970; dir. Peter Sasdy) does show a group of giggling teenage girls killing their debauched, hypocritical fathers under Dracula's influence, but a fatherly fiancé quickly places Alice, their leader, under his solemn control. For the most part, the violence of Hammer films involved the staking of female vampires, an activity so overtly sexual that in those days, when politics was associated only with war, it did not seem political.

Vampirism threatens to spread among women in Hammer films. Perhaps for that reason, only female vampires are staked; their male leaders generally earn more ingenious deaths. In *Horror of Dracula,* "Aunt" Lucy, smiling and fanged, leads little Tania through that wonderful Hammer wood. The sequence bristles with suggestions of witchcraft, with forbidden knowledge passed down through generations of women, suggestions more potent because Tania is a new character: Stoker's Lucy abducted a little Cockney *boy* who learned nothing from her, but only burbled about her beauty as the men did. The Hammer Lucy is not an antimaternal seductress of men, but a subverter of women. Tania returns intact—but what did they talk about in the forest?—and Lucy is staked, but in *Dracula, Prince of Darkness* (1966; dir. Terence Fisher), there is a more explicit interchange between a female vampire and a mortal woman.

Helen (Barbara Shelley) is the starchiest member of two British couples sightseeing in Carlsbad (the Hammer substitute for Transylvania). They ignore warnings and visit Castle Dracula, which in this movie is so spiffy that it does duty as a luxury hotel. Clove, the sinister servant of the supposedly dead Dracula, serves them a scrumptious meal. Only Helen is afraid, and Helen is right, for Clove murders her silly prowling husband in the night and hangs him by his feet. The blood that drips from his throat resuscitates the ashes of Dracula, who promptly vampirizes Helen as she prowls after her husband.

The vampire Helen is as intelligent as the mortal, but she is no longer prim and fearful. As a sign of her condition, she wears a new, low-cut nightgown when Diana, the other English-woman, comes upon her while searching for her husband. "Come sister," Helen replies, baring her fangs and opening her arms. "*You don't need Charles.*" This resonant sentence has none of the insinuating intimacy of Le Fanu's Carmilla and the loving lesbian vampires she inspired: Helen infiltrates Diana's social conditioning, not her dreams. Helen's wicked remark is as shrewd as her earlier insistence that they get out of the castle and back to England, but it brings down the fury of humans and vampires alike: Dracula enters, snarling, blocking her access to Diana; Charles runs in and flings her to the floor, then escapes with Diana. Helen tries to embrace Dracula, who flings her back to the floor. The forces of darkness and light converge against the vampire who told the woman that she didn't need her man.

Helen's staking by a coven of faceless, chanting monks is the most authentically frightening sequence in the Hammer series. There is no masterful Van Helsing, no sobbing Arthur, no other familiar men who throb sympathetically as they kill for eternity the woman they claim to love, but only a faintly sadistic priest named Father Sandor directing his efficient, anonymous monks.

This Helen is not encased in her coffin as Stoker's Lucy was: the monks heft her up, twisting in terror, onto a raised slab that looks like an operating table. Moreover, we do not *watch* Helen as Stoker's Van Helsing and his crew watched the writhing Lucy, filtering her agony through their own convictions. The point of view in the sequence is that of the terrified woman. As her pow-erful body is held down, arranged, and finally staked, we experi-ence through her eyes the impersonality of her destruction. Bar-bara Shelley is large and strong. The central image of the scene is not her fangs or even the blood that wells from her, but the strapping arm the little monks hold down as they prepare to stake her.

For many of us,[43] the scene was close to home. Only a fanatic could believe that Helen, the film's central authority, is saved for heaven. The sequence is closer to gang rape, or to gynecological surgery, or to any of the collective violations women were and are prone to, than to the sacred marriage Stoker's reverent narrators made readers accept. Stripped of the sensibility of loving, maiming men, seen instead from her own point of view, the staking of the female vampire is less a rite of purification than the licensed torture of a woman who knew women didn't need men.[44]

Despite these resonant sequences that seemed at the time to leap out of the movies and whisper warnings to the young female viewer, and despite their increasingly calculated appeal to a self-conscious youth market, the Hammer series rarely broke new ground; it hinted at new possibilities in old plots. Its vampires were defined largely by fangs, not (as they were in the 1930s) by eyes. The first movie vampires to be associated with mouths rather than mesmeric powers, they turned vampirism into an immediate bodily experience rather than an esoteric endowment. It was fun at first to see those penile eruptions popping out of the mouths of women as well as men, but as the series ground on, the makeup lost its sting: the fangs seemed not so much new organs as uncomfortable clutter in the actors' mouths.

Christopher Lee's Dracula became more limited and less broadly menacing over the years. Increasingly inarticulate, he became more animal and less chic; when he did talk he abandoned his brisk authority for lingering chants in the manner of Lugosi. No longer a stylish young man who might be power-brokering in London, Lee's Dracula turned primitive as he aged.[45] When Lee dropped the idioms that made the vampire a pervasive social presence, the forces of society, headed by Peter Cushing's concentrated Van Helsing, combined easily against him.

As Lee reverted to a force of anticivilization, Cushing's Van Helsing or his churchy surrogates acquired such easy omnipotence that it was only a matter of which ingenious method of vampire destruction they would choose. As the series progressed through the 1960s, the student revolution evolved into a potent organization: militant young people had gone beyond Hammer vampires. Consequently, nervous moviemakers lost touch with these intractable student audiences. As youth became increasingly defiant, especially in America, Hammer films turned almost respectable. For vampires, at least, authority triumphed over cheekiness—not only the authority of Van Helsing, but that of Bram Stoker himself.

By the end of the 1960s, the authentic vampire tyrant was neither Christopher Lee nor Peter Cushing, but Bram Stoker's plot. For sixty years, Stoker's characters, his situations, his rules, were wearily, ritually repeated in vampire literature until they acquired scriptural authority. The first Hammer *Dracula* jolted viewers out of familiar expectations by scrambling Stoker's characters, but by the end of the '60s, scrambled names had ceased to matter: under whatever name, Van Helsing was Van Helsing, Mina was Mina, and Dracula, Dracula: there was no other vampire before him.

The King-Vampire fed a doomed quest for permanence among the decade's seers. Intellectuals in the 1960s were transfixed by the supposed immutability of Jungian psychic archetypes. Perhaps because the '60s abounded in radical social blueprints that seemed, in that visionary decade, on the verge of implementation, literary typologies like Northrop Frye's *Anatomy of Criticism* (1957) acquired the authoritative power once attributed to the Bible. For Frye, social changes were mere repetitive cycles. Our minds, and the literature that welled almost unconsciously from them, were and would always be repositories of mighty (because changeless) imaginative structures. Vampires in the '60s partook of this majestic immutability. Hazy memories of Stoker's novel collaborated with the insistent repetitions of Hammer movies to turn Dracula, originally a highly particularized, even innovative creature, into a weighty archetype, The Vampire.

"One cannot imagine a man-made monster or a werewolf creating a panic in the garish world of Times Square; more than likely he would be looked upon as a further interesting example of the native product. Dracula would simply not stir up much of a commotion in the bloodsucking centers of Wall Street or Madison Avenue. These creatures belong to the dimly lit, foggy

back alleys of Victorian London."[46] Drake Douglas's 1966 anatomy of horror is closer to Northrop Frye than to actual vampires. Grafting Stoker's character to Hammer's mythic Victorian-
land, Douglas is so committed to timelessness that he can
neither conceive nor foresee the garish native vampires of
America.

For writers like Douglas, there are no vampires, only The
Vampire. He is always male, always Dracula, and always emanat-
ing from untouchable dark places in our minds. "There may well
be . . . in the still-little-understood labyrinths of the human
mind, deeper and more ominous reasons for horror's continued
fascination. . . . Perhaps, in some small way, the imaginative, often violent, world of horror provides us with a psychological
safety valve, a mental expression of the hostilities and the urge
to violence which we must subdue within ourselves" (pp.
12–13).

Such archetypal descriptions of horror are covertly reassur-
ing: if there are no vampires, but only The Vampire, our minds
are bedrocks of eternal repose, and the world holds no frightening surprises. Dracula becomes an angel of reason and a bulwark
against change. By the end of the 1960s, he was so fixed a figure
that, like all authorities, he existed to be shattered. In reaction
to his seeming perpetuity, the 1970s bred a wealth of new vampires, creatures so varied and unprecedented that they decom-
posed the archetype of The Vampire and even, with a hint from
history, constructed a new and supple Dracula.

THE 1970S WAS A HALCYON DECADE for vampires, one in which they
not only flourished, but reinvented themselves. Hammer vampires, young and swollen with desire, had teased pompous authorities before retreating into solemnity and the old roles. Vampires in the 1970s *become* authorities. Hovering between animal
and angel, they are paragons of emotional complexity and dis-
cernment, stealing from Van Helsing the role of knower but adding a tenderness and ineffable sorrow human beings have become too monstrous to comprehend.

In 1975, Fred Saberhagen's *The Dracula Tape* allowed a witty
and humane Dracula to tell his own story, one that exposed the
sadistic idiocy of the vampire-hunting men and the profundity

of his love for Mina. Saberhagen's sophisticate is an acute critic of Stoker's ambiguities and contradictions, but his rich sympathy, his keen awareness, could never come from the "child-brain" of the original Dracula. Saberhagen's Dracula—or Vlad, as he prefers to be called—is not a variation on Stoker's, but a different character altogether. As a new being with an old name, he is the type of the new vampires who, for the first time, belong in the age that bred them.

The sophistication and variety of the 1970s horror cycle is easy to appreciate, but difficult to explain. After a decade of violent social division and political upheaval, monsters sank into American self-perceptions. At the time, the few critics who cared about them explained their insurgence in terms of a national Armageddon of the spirit. With an urgency that now seems endearing, Robin Wood argued that the horror film "is currently the most important of all American genres and perhaps the most progressive, even in its overt nihilism—in a period of extreme cultural crisis and disintegration, which alone offers the possibility of radical change and rebuilding."[47]

More than twenty traumatic years later, the "extreme cultural crisis and disintegration" of the 1970s seems difficult to discern, particularly for a woman. In retrospect, the 1970s seem, to me at least, a decade of reintegration, full of hope for new beginnings. The Vietnam War ended, and so did Nixon's presidency. With an assurance that seemed to me miraculous, women were moving into the public world, not as isolated anomalies, but on our terms. Vampire literature, however, like my own frame of mind, was more reintegrative and less nihilistic than the horror films Wood was seeing: *The Texas Chainsaw Massacre* was doom-ier than the two *Dracula*s that appeared in that decade. Like women, vampires were assuming an authority unprecedented in their history. No doubt they were able to do so because, in the 1960s and '70s, so many official authorities had fallen.

The assassinations that peppered and created the 1960s—not only John Kennedy's, but those of Malcolm X, Robert Kennedy, and Martin Luther King, Jr.—were eerily replayed in the two American presidencies that followed Kennedy's. In 1968, Lyndon Johnson was forced out of the presidency by broad re-

pudiation of the officially nonexistent Vietnam War, and also
(as I remember it) by an orgy of popular hate. In 1974, the more
official and sedate Watergate investigation forced Richard Nixon
to resign. Leaders fell like extras in movies. As I remember it, the
ease with which they crumbled into death or disgrace aroused
as much glee as anxiety, but whether Americans feared cultural
crisis and disintegration or relished the new beginnings they
promised, authority in the 1970s was, before all things, mortal.
Vampires rushed in to fill the vacuum.

Scholarship ennobled Dracula, not just in dreams, but in
history. Raymond McNally and Radu Florescu's *In Search of Dracula* (1972) reincarnated Stoker's solitary devourer as patriot and
leader. Their claims for the eminence of Vlad Tepes, his regal
source, were sober and sweeping: "Using dozens of ancient
chronicles and maps of European provenance, documents contemporary with Dracula, and nineteenth- and twentieth-
century philological and historical works, and drawing on folklore and peasant traditions, we have pieced together a dual
history: an account not only of the real fifteenth-century Dracula, or Vlad Tepes, who came from Transylvania and ruled in
Wallachia, but also of the vampire who existed in the legends of
these same regions."[48]

The association of Stoker's monster with Vlad Tepes, or Vlad
the Impaler, is probably more a matter of appellation than of
substance. "Dracula," a title rather than a name, means simply
"child of the dragon" or the "devil"; probably because it
sounded better, Stoker ended his vampire's name with the feminine suffix *-a*. Nevertheless, *In Search of Dracula,* which claimed
to give Stoker's character historical authenticity, in fact inspired
a new Dracula myth for the late twentieth century.

Vlad Tepes was a military hero who protected Romania from
engorgement by the Ottoman Empire, then went on to become
a sadistic Wallachian ruler. Vlad, who tortured his subjects for
sport, not sustenance, was, on the face of it, far more monstrous
than Stoker's solitary predator. Moreover, since the stake was his
weapon, not his bane, he was more vampire-hunter than vampire. He impaled his many enemies, foreign and domestic, en
masse in public spectacles, sometimes eating dinner while ob-
serving their torments:

This torture was often a matter of several hours, sometimes a matter of days. There were various forms of impalement depending on age, rank, or sex. . . . There were also various geometric patterns in which the impaled were displayed. Usually the victims were arranged in concentric circles, and in the outskirts of cities where they could be viewed by all. There were high spears and low spears, according to rank. There was impalement from above—feet upwards; and impalement from below—head upwards; or through the heart or navel. There were nails in people's heads, maiming of limbs, binding, strangulation, burning, the cutting of noses and ears, and of sexual organs in the case of women, scalping and skinning, exposure to the elements or to the wild animals, and boiling alive. (Pp. 45–46)

This theater of cruelty has little in common with the cloistered eroticism of the staking rituals in *Dracula*. Since McNally and Florescu's Vlad sometimes forces his victims to drink blood or eat flesh while abstaining himself (p. 123), he seems more a voyeuristic director than an actor. His addiction to the stake makes him resemble a Van Helsing stripped of his holy mission; his addiction to watching aligns him with the audiences at horror movies who chew popcorn during dismemberments. Vlad Tepes is an interesting tyrant, but he seems far from Stoker's withheld refugee who avoids stakes at any cost.

As McNally and Florescu admit, Stoker's working notes show little awareness of Vlad, his supposed inspiration. *Dracula* was a late change of title; until just before publication, the novel was to be called *The Un-Dead* or *The Dead Un-Dead*. Stoker's notes on Wallachian history do mention Voivode Dracula's defeat of the Turks, adding, however, that the battle brought "only momentarily success"—a sardonic modification of Dracula's boasting speech to Jonathan at the beginning of the novel. Stoker's notes show no profound study of Transylvanian history; like Irving's Lyceum productions, they treat leaders and battles as a picturesque background to a melodrama about individuals. Stoker is concerned less with the historical origins of the name than with its resonance as a tag for generic evil: "DRACULA in Wallachian language means DEVIL. Wallachians were accustomed to give it as a surname to any person who rendered himself conspicuous by courage, cruel actions or cunning."[49]

The relation between Vlad Tepes and Stoker's King-Vampire is tenuous at best. Like Vlad, Dracula has imperial ambitions, but unlike Vlad's they are thwarted: he dies a monarch with no dominion. He drinks blood, and compels his women to do so, because of his inhuman need; he is always watched, but he watches no one. His enemies use impalement to consolidate their power; he has no lust for stakes. Vlad Tepes is far more arbitrary and aesthetic in his sadism than Stoker's single-minded Dracula, who has no time to play. Despite these essential differences, Vlad's influence on fiction and film somehow transformed Stoker's character from his mid-twentieth-century incarnation as ponderous archetype. McNally and Florescu describe an insane ruler with no emotional allegiances. Perhaps because America needed a leader, popular culture transformed their Vlad into a faithful lover whose name happens to be Dracula.

Jack Palance in the TV movie *Bram Stoker's Dracula* (1973; dir. Dan Curtis) was the first cinematic Dracula to flaunt his authenticity rather than his deadness or his lust. The title's reverent invocation of authority, the heroic portrait of Vlad Tepes that dominates and controls the action, and, above all, the recreation of Dracula as lover rather than tyrant, all resurrect not so much a monster as a leader.[50]

Bram Stoker's Dracula opens with an evocation of lovely inhumanity: assuming the vampire's point of view, the camera sweeps around a misty lake to a pack of wolves running to a huge castle. This tracking shot from the killer's point of view would become the trademark of 1970s slasher films, particularly John Carpenter's *Halloween* (1978) and its sequels, but in *Halloween* the eye of the killer tracks his potential victims, while Dracula's eye tracks his home, his land, and his wolf-children. His gaze sanctions domesticity, not, as in *Halloween,* an impulse to stray and kill.

No intrusive Jonathan Harker imposes British fears on an alien landscape; the alien is Jonathan. When he does enter the movie, he is a sketchy character who sees nothing because he sleeps through his ride to the castle. He is too flimsy even to arouse Dracula's bloodlust: when he cuts himself shaving, Dracula merely turns away sadly, without bothering to snatch at his throat, recoil at his crucifix, or smash his mirror. No curiosity leads this Jonathan to the three vampire women; when he is imprisoned in their crypt, he is their helpless prey, screaming inelegantly, "No, no, no!" This Jonathan is too inconsequential even to be corrupt: he is there, not to define the horror of Dracula, but to be killed after leading the vampire to Lucy. Until this *Dracula,* Jonathan's was the dominant perspective, but now, the only consciousness is the vampire's.

Stoker's vampire was too self-imprisoned to reflect in a mirror, but Palance's Dracula is grand enough to project himself into an epic image: the large portrait of Vlad Tepes that dominates his study. A scroll over the final titles gives us some vague historical information, but our first sight of the portrait shows us only a vigorous warrior on horseback with a lovely little queen standing by him. The queen's face is that of Jonathan's fiancée, Lucy. Though the queen is painted on a diminutive and subordinate scale proper for the wife of a great man, her reincarnation as Lucy is Dracula's sole concern. He buys Carfax Abbey, not as a base of operations, but because it is near his restored beloved. This Dracula is not an arouser of suppressed women as Christopher Lee was, but a paragon of married love. He is no longer a destroyer of households, but a perfect husband. In accordance with the revised romantic imagery of the 1970s, the vampire's distinction is his exemplary monogamy.

We learn in flashbacks that Vlad's adored queen was brutally murdered by the Turkish army. Van Helsing repeats this traumatic butchery when he slaughters the transformed Lucy. Palance flings open her coffin, embraces her mutilated corpse, and weeps—an uncharacteristic vampire activity up to the 1970s, but one in which Jack Palance indulges copiously. Like the sensitized new men wishful feminists of the 1970s constructed, vampires are reborn in their own tears. In this decade, sanctioned male authorities like husbands and priests take over vampires' traditional role as rapists, while the lone loving vampire is a well of tenderness.[51]

The romantic reincarnation that inflames this vampire transfigures the past that had loomed menacingly over earlier *Draculas.* Stoker's Dracula personified the unburied past in all its smelly menace, embodying a devouring potential no timetables or Dictaphones could suppress. At the end of the nineteenth century, technological progress was a bulwark, if a fragile one, against bestial regression. The best of the Hammer *Dracula*s attributed progress to the vampire, by implication at least: chic young Christopher Lee lured his prey beyond the oppressive domestic clutter of father-ruled tradition. Though Jack Palance inherits his predecessor's good taste—his homes are as streamlined and colorful as Christopher Lee's were—his Dracula never looks forward. Consumed by nostalgia for a lost marriage, he is the first vampire to consecrate the past rather than making us dread it. This weeping lover/leader teaches us all to look back and mourn. As with America itself, a country still mourning in 1973, Dracula's best has already been.

Bram Stoker's Dracula authenticates itself by invoking authorities—Bram Stoker and, through their discovery of Vlad Tepes, McNally and Florescu—but these authorities are empty names used to license a topical new myth. McNally and Florescu's catalog of horrors contains no exemption for married love. Dracula's first queen may have committed suicide by jumping off a tower to escape the Turks, but McNally and Florescu offer no evidence that her husband cared: "From the native Romanian Dracula tales, it would seem that their marriage was not a happy one, for the prince was often seen wandering alone at night on the outskirts of the city, usually in disguise, seeking the company of the beautiful but humble woman who in time became his mistress" (p. 63). The exigencies of 1973, not of the fifteenth century, turn Vlad from impaler to lover.

The reincarnation plot probably has a more ephemeral source than McNally and Florescu's study: the poignant fantasy of the vampire Barnabas Collins in the popular Gothic soap opera *Dark Shadows* (1966–1971). Barnabas is enthralled by the fixed idea that Maggie Evans, a New England town girl, is a resurrection of his adored cousin Josette, who in the previous century had jumped over a cliff to escape, not the Turks, but Barnabas himself. Poor hulking Barnabas was a culture hero for disaffected young intellectuals in the late 1960s. Lost in the modern world, paralyzed by romantic nostalgia for his nineteenth-century life in the "old" Collins mansion, which he reconstructs in fond, obsessive detail, Barnabas was the first popular vampire to escape the Dracula plot into which Hammer movies were locked. Free to construct his own story, he embraced no brave new world: anticipating Anne Rice's beautiful young males, he yearned only for the lost century in which he was mortal.

Barnabas was pitiful in his fantasy, not, like Palance, noble in his faith. When he kidnaps Maggie Evans and tries vainly to remake her as Josette, he becomes as forlorn a psychopath as the heroes of such contemporary thrillers as *Vertigo* (1958) and *The Collector* (1965). For these doomed dreamers, the restoration of a perfect past is as dangerous a delusion as possession of the perfect woman: Barnabas's backward quest is, by definition, a lost cause. In the 1960s, even in vampires' dream worlds, life's value lies in the future. In the 1970s, the restorative mission that doomed Barnabas becomes the highest vampire creed. The vision of reincarnation that marked Barnabas as a lost soul is elevated into a hero's hope.

Richard Matheson, author of the screenplay, was a significant if obliquely acknowledged inspiration for the revised vampires of the 1970s. Matheson is a prolific horror writer—though, as Stephen King points out,[52] the smug pretense of the 1950s that horror had been safely domesticated led to his misclassification as a science fiction writer—but his novel *I Am Legend* (1954) has been a particular breeder of vampires. *I Am Legend* is a futuristic account of the solitary human survivor in a postnuclear world where only various mutant species of vampire survive. Human society was destroyed before the novel began; vampires are now the norm.

I Am Legend blurred the demarcation between its vampires and its singular, nasty hero too ruthlessly to be widely popular in the '50s, but later horror fed on its unsparing reversals. Some years after its publication, it inspired two heroic movies—*The Last Man on Earth,* with Vincent Price (1964), and *The Omega Man,* with Charlton Heston (1971)—but neither captures the dry, hate-filled pragmatism of Matheson's Robert Neville, whose lone murderous forays against his neighbors make him the vampires' vampire. Jack Palance's Dracula is ostensibly far from human, but he is closer to Matheson's Robert Neville than the sniffling Vincent Price or the square-jawed Charlton Heston. Like Neville, Palance is alone in an unfamiliar society of killers, consumed by memories of fulfillment. His lost wife is the emblem of a lost, fully human world. The man forced into a vampire's role in 1954 mutates, in 1973, into the humane vampire weeping for his past.[53]

The screenplay's fixation on this sympathetic Dracula must have intrigued viewers used to Christopher Lee's incessant snarls in the late Hammer movies, but if Jack Palance is less predictable than Lee, he is also less potent. He is far from the Hammer figure who permeates stuffy Victorian families to rouse their bored women. In fact, Palance's Dracula is so obdurately faithful a husband that he obscures the women around him, even the vampires. His sister-brides abjure tinkling laughs and teasing foreplay; unlike their richly complex master, they are mere avid animals, growling at Jonathan, pouncing on him, and eventually, enthusiastically, killing him. Seductive women never perturb this chivalrous adaptation.

Even Lucy, the vampire's reincarnated beloved, is refreshingly unsexy. She says nothing about marrying three men, nor do three men want to marry her. There is no community of adorers to pour manly blood into her; instead, Van Helsing crisply performs a blood transfusion with her maid, a potent taboo in Stoker's novel, whose strictly male-to-female transfusions reflected the phobic hierarchies of the 1890s. Dead, Lucy is not Stoker's sleeping beauty, but an ungainly, mangled horror. Except for the obligatory fangs, being a vampire scarcely affects her. She enters Arthur's room and begins to bite him with the same bland briskness that characterized her alive. Since Arthur is thoroughly unseduced, he has no need to stake her: Van Helsing performs the businesslike ritual without sanctifying marriage metaphors. Mina, who expresses no curiosity about the fate of her lost fiancé, Jonathan, is still more insignificant. Dracula pursues her solely in revenge for the loss of Lucy; the movie doesn't bother to include her purification after he dies. Its focus is Dracula and Dracula alone.

Like Matheson's Robert Neville, this Dracula puzzled his first audience, but he set the pattern for vampires to come. As time went on, Dracula's absorption into a Vlad who had nothing in common with McNally and Florescu's mad monarch made him not only the leader of a vanished kingdom, but a Christlike commentator on human sin and folly. Saberhagen's *Dracula Tape* takes the leap *Bram Stoker's Dracula* avoids: its human authorities, in their smug stupidity, become more dangerous than the vampire. Moreover, Saberhagen's reincarnated feminist Mina gives Vlad/Dracula a mate worth his salt, not a little woman in a painting. No longer a social predator, the mourning Dracula of 1973 authorized Saberhagen's biting social anatomist. His authority reached its pinnacle in the last Dracula of the 1970s, the most emancipated of them all.

Frank Langella's Byronic savior in John Badham's ambitious *Dracula* (1979) consummates the reversals that dominate 1970s vampire literature. In this breathtaking if confusing movie, Stoker's good men are villains; Stoker's vampire is a hero; the women, victims no more, embrace vampirism with rapture as the sole available escape from patriarchy. W. D. Richter's screenplay never bothers to tell the familiar story; it retells it for its age. Badham's unapologetic revisionism assumes that Stoker's novel has passed into folklore, becoming a gauge of the present, not an anchor to the past.

Badham's *Dracula* makes radical claims, turning the old story into a vehicle for twentieth-century social critiques, especially feminist critiques. Stoker's brave and good men become overbearing fathers and paternalistic doctors whose sole mission is to control women: Seward is now Lucy's father and Van Helsing is Mina's. Both are monuments of medical malpractice. When Jonathan, Lucy's grumpy and sleazy fiancé, is not destroying the landscape with his car,[54] he sours every scene in which he appears. For Lucy and Mina, the transfiguring embrace of the vampire is a glorious evasion of patriarchal control.[55] The movie's lush emphasis on transfiguration converges with the feminist vampire plots of novelists like Tanith Lee, Jody Scott, Suzy McKee Charnas, and especially Chelsea Quinn Yarbro, whose sartorially splendid and sadly wise Count Saint-Germain is scarcely distinguishable from Frank Langella.

But the heart of this radicalism is restoration. Badham does not expel past vampires as Stoker tried to do; he restores the suppressed significance of forgotten stories. Like the so-called minority studies that burgeoned in universities in the 1970s, Badham's *Dracula* aims to reclaim a past arrogant power has debased.

Not only does Badham restore the old play; he transforms it. When Langella starred in the Balderston-Deane *Dracula* on Broadway, it was the same confined drawing-room melodrama it had been in 1927. Badham opens it out, not only to sweeping shots of the English landscape, but to unstable depths of sea and sky. The movie is full of overhead shots and rapid, destabilizing pans; it begins and ends on a turbulent sea. Motion and space demolish the play's four walls, its monotonous interior set. In the same spirit, the immobility of Bela Lugosi, star of the original play and film, dissolves in the incessant motion of Frank Langella, who is always touching, moving, dancing, climbing, or riding horses. Langella's graceful hands replace Lugosi's transfixing eyes. Lugosi was anomalous and unmateable; the sympathetic Langella flows into mortal women. He and Lucy first explore their attraction by dancing together, a communion unimaginable in 1931. Langella's hands, like those of Yarbro's Count Saint-Germain, free the vampire to absorb everyone and everything he touches. Lugosi was an estranged and estranging Dracula; Langella is a Dracula of fusion.

Badham also restores the ingrown Hammer family, an impeccably virtuous unit that houses its own vampires. In the 1979 *Dracula,* however, there are no paternal husbands, only obstructive, incompetent fathers; the target is no longer bourgeois marriage, but patriarchy itself. Thus, rather than the cluttered respectability of the Hammer household, Badham's family inhabits the brutal chaos of Dr. Seward's madhouse.[56] The movie opens in incoherence: the chaos of the shipwreck that brings Dracula to England is crosscut with Seward's screaming lunatics. Authorities are not only ineffectual, but inaudible: the sailors shouting incomprehensible orders are the equivalent of Dr. Seward (Donald Pleasence, fresh from playing an ineffectual psychiatrist in *Halloween*) drifting helplessly through his asylum. Nature, madhouse, and family are part of a single upheaval. The movie's first audible line belongs to its women: Lucy and Mina, shut away from the noise in their bedroom, chant in giggling unison, "We are not chattel." Authority is overwhelmed from the beginning; only the women's voices are clear.

The madhouse/family brings Renfield back to the story. We have not seen Renfield since 1931, when, substituting for Jonathan Harker, he played Dracula's dandified double in Transylvania and went floridly mad in England. The 1931 film made some attempt to implicate the patriarchs in his madness; "Isn't this a strange conversation for men who *aren't* crazy?" he snickered at the vampire-hunters; but Dwight Frye was too extravagant to incriminate either vampire or mortals, and was finally simply dispatched. Renfield was excluded from the Hammer series and the Palance *Dracula,* whose vampires themselves were touchstones of civilized madness. Renfield is usually a bridge from supernatural to clinical cannibalism, embodying a hunger society can label and contain, but society exists only by implication in the confined stories of the '60s and early '70s.[57] In 1979, vampire stories have become political barometers, and Renfield returns to catalyze inept abuses of power.

This Renfield is a whistle-blower, silenced (as Lucy will be before Dracula saves her) by incarceration in Seward's asylum. He opens the movie by exposing Jonathan as a crooked lawyer who cheated not only Renfield himself, but Dracula, whom he duped into buying the dilapidated Carfax Abbey. When he insists later on that Dracula is a vampire, Jonathan hands him over to Seward, who ignores his warnings as an inmate's ravings. This Renfield is the truth-telling victim of authority's apparent sanity, not an embodiment of its potential madness: he has moved from id to commentator. Like other post-1960s culture heroes who vanished after giving fragmentary warnings—the Black Panthers, Karen Silkwood—Renfield becomes a silenced seer.[58]

Like Renfield, Mina (who plays the role of Stoker's Lucy) is authority's scapegoat; she dies to illuminate the necessity of escape. As in *Horror of Dracula,* the names of Stoker's familiar characters are scrambled: the old death-haunted Lucy becomes Mina, "frail all her life," while Stoker's mighty Mina, supreme mother and stenographer, becomes the Lucy, powerfully played by Kate Nelligan, whom Dracula singles out with a praise peculiar to the 1970s: "She is stronger than most women, isn't she?" This seemingly wanton reversal of the old names unmoors those of us who think we know the story. It may also remind us that the weak woman who dies and the strong woman who escapes are part of each other. The women's movement of the 1970s insisted that there were no "strong" exceptions to general subordination; women are part of a cohesive social category whereby each of us is implicated in the fate of all. This activist premise infiltrates a politically sophisticated *Dracula* that aims to destabilize the rigid categories of the old story.

There is nothing pretty about Mina's death or undeath. If the Jack Palance movie made her an ungainly corpse, Badham's makes her a horrible one, as if to suggest that even when their killer is a sexy vampire, murdered women are dreadful spectacles. Mina doesn't fade into robust new life: she chokes graphically to a death made more painful by the laudanum Dr. Seward idiotically gives her, afterward muttering apologetically, "It's been so long since I've practiced real medicine." Mina isn't killed by inept blood transfusions, like Saberhagen's Lucy, but paternalistic psychiatry mangles her death, as it mangles the lives of the asylum inmates. The collaboration of medicine, especially psychiatry, with patriarchy, a frequent concern of feminism in the 1970s and beyond, makes Dr. Seward, not the vampire, the murderer the movie indicts.

There is nothing seductive about the Mina who rises: she is no swollen Hammer sexpot, but a decomposing corpse with broken, bloody teeth. This Mina is contrary to literary vampire mythology, where undead corpses, like saints, remain in a state of perpetual preservation, but she is true to the vampires of folklore, who are not transfigurations, but actual corpses who leave their graves to devour their families.[59] Like these folklore vampires, Mina advances on the man closest to her: her terrified father, Van Helsing (Laurence Olivier, in a performance so flustered and overwrought that it seems designed to strip both character and actor of all the authority the years had given). She offers no ripe conjugal embrace. Instead, she croons disgustingly and repeatedly, "Papa, come." Since the movie's world is run by incompetent fathers, it is appropriate that the "frail" Mina becomes a folklore vampire, licensed by definition to kill her family. The clumsy, keening Van Helsing stakes her not ritually, but by accident.[60]

Lucy has no folklore rot about her; she is everything a feminist vampire should be. Her romance with Frank Langella could be one of the swoonier inserts of *Ms.* magazine. He loves her strength and self-assertion: she asks him to dance, she declares herself to him, while he responds to her unfemininity with delight. Most wonderful of all, in the 1970s at least, he invites her to dinner at Carfax Abbey.

Stoker's dinner scene, where the vampire plays servant to an unknowing Jonathan in order to become his master, undergoes its most baroque movie mutation in this meal. In the Lugosi *Dracula,* the never-served dinner was an ineffably decadent homoerotic tease between the stiffly amused vampire and the effete Renfield. In 1979, a dangerous flirtation modulates into enlightened heterosexual romance. Lucy goes eagerly to a Carfax that is nothing like Lugosi's barren castle. Though Jonathan bilked him into buying it, Dracula has decorated it in a striking candle-and-cobweb motif: Carfax is no longer dark and gloomy, but a heaven of refracted light. Like a perfect '70s man, Dracula does not sit back to be served; he entertains Lucy in his lovely home, and, presumably, cooks her a gourmet dinner—though alas, when they commune affectionately over the long table, the camera never shows us Lucy's plate.

Like a good assertive feminist, Lucy declares herself passionately, while Dracula, open and honest, tries to discourage her by telling her of the loneliness of vampire life. As the ardent heterosexual replacement for the Jonathan who, in Stoker's novel, "belonged" to Dracula, Lucy is a sympathetic repository of his confidences, which are no longer boastful, but openly vulnerable. Listening to the wolves, he adds a resonant word to Stoker's famous line: "What *sad* music they make," he ruminates softly. But Lucy is supportive: "Do you think it's sad? I think it's a wonderful sound. I really love the night; it's so exciting." After she persuades a reluctant Dracula that he is not a rapist—she came of her own accord—Lucy's transformation into vampirism takes place in a languorous red-tinted sex scene. As with Miriam's transformation of Sarah in *The Hunger* (1983), vampirism is all erotic tenderness. There are no blood, no fangs, no penetration or violence, simply a merging of bodies. When Lucy drinks from the vein in his chest, this Dracula is not coercive, but tender and enfeebled-looking, an ideal nonphallic man who relishes his passive role.

After many disappointing years, this vampire romance of the 1970s may seem merely, in that deadening phrase, "politically correct."[61] Frank Langella may be as laughable a love object now as Bela Lugosi was when I was growing up. But the rapidity with which our Draculas become dated tells us only that every age embraces the vampire it needs. In 1979, one image of a magical leader was Frank Langella, sad and wise and far-seeing, erotically easy in his animal self (for the most part Badham avoids artificial transformations; instead, at intervals, Langella *plays* himself as bat and wolf). Positioned constantly on heights, looking down at the scurrying little mortals—as opposed to Lugosi, who was always rising from depths—Langella was an enticing image of gentle power in a postwar decade that seemed to have evaded political revolution. Many progressives believed, in 1979, that power could be transformed or surmounted; feminists wrote of gender polarities reconciled in an androgynous union of opposites. Probably, though, such a consummation is possible only for an angel or a vampire.

The horror cycle of the 1970s no longer required Dracula to justify himself historically by being Vlad. Langella's origins are vague; he has only a history long enough to make him sad. Lucy is no reincarnation of a lost little queen, but a defiant woman of the present. Unlike Jack Palance, Langella neither weeps nor looks back, but like Palance, he is an aristocrat in a reduced world. He may win Lucy, but we know that Jonathan's car will supersede his gorgeous horses. Though this Dracula is not nostalgic himself, he is a symptom of the nostalgia for a chosen elite that suffused (and still suffuses) ostensibly radical works. This Dracula is not the tyrant Lugosi was; he is an elect being. As such, in a democratic age, he will always be hunted.

Both Palance's and Langella's Dracula are scorched to death in approved Hammer fashion, thus institutionalizing the sun as weapon of choice against vampires. Palance's death is a virtual reprise of Christopher Lee's: Van Helsing once more throws open the curtains so that the sun can do its burning work, though this Van Helsing finishes off Dracula with a spear, not a makeshift cross. The former warrior dies by a violence he doesn't understand. At the end, though, the camera, accompanied by ghostly voices of cheering troops, moves from Palance's cruciform corpse to his heroic portrait, and a tribute to his fifteenth-century ferocity scrolls over the final credits.

Langella dies exalted. Cornered with Lucy on a ship to Romania, he stakes Van Helsing, thus completing their role reversal; the dying Van Helsing, ever an inadvertent killer, accidentally impales the vampire on a great hook that sends him soaring skyward. From Dracula's stricken perspective, we see an assaultive sun so powerful that it could never rise on England: it would be more at home in *The Rime of the Ancient Mariner* or in such celestial science fiction films as *2001: A Space Odyssey* or *Star Wars*. The camera moves through the colors of the spectrum as the vampire's dying vision transfigures the object that is killing it.

The final sequence is less an opening for a sequel than a paean to resurrection. Dracula's cloak flies off and soars through the sky; as a wolf howls, the cloak assumes the shape of a great bat. Lucy watches rapturously, enduring sullen Jonathan because she knows Dracula lives and will return for her. The crypt that had enclosed Lugosi opens out to space and sky.

The heroic conclusions of both *Dracula*s are far from Lugosi's ignominious offscreen staking. The entrance of the sun in *Horror of Dracula* seemed originally to isolate the vampire from the dominant rhythms of sleeping and waking life, but in the 1970s, when ordinariness shrinks into perfidy, the sun becomes a medium of romantic consecration. It no longer shrivels Dracula, but shares with him its celestial dominance. Like the burning boy in Blake's *Glad Day* who steps joyfully out of an encompassing sun, the vampire vulnerable to solar death becomes a kind of sun-king. Neither Jack Palance nor Frank Langella shrivels to dust, as Christopher Lee did; each, instead, dies into his own heroic image. Palance swells into his noble portrait; Langella soars straight upward, like Shelley's skylark, beyond common sights and sounds.

Evolving from the self-imprisoned Bela Lugosi to the Promethean Frank Langella, Dracula progresses from death-bringing foreigner to angelic harbinger of better times. But as he casts off crypt and coffin for erotic enlightenment, he looks to the past, not the future, for a society beyond taboos. These adaptations that so wantonly defy their source move backward, away from the 1970s as well as forward to them, returning the viewer to an age when vampires were not scum, but authentic aristocrats. These blazing Draculas strive to restore the stories Stoker's rules and taboos forbade.

The 1970s: Feminist Oligarchies and Kingly Democracy

"No, amica mia, I am not the ravenous thing you think me. You could fill the ruby cup I gave to Laurenzo with what I take from the living. But just the blood is not enough. It will keep me . . . alive . . . but it is not enough. So when it is possible, I have intimacy as well. It is not only the blood that nourishes me. It is nearness, pleasure, all intense emotions. Only those who come to me knowingly are . . . tainted by me. Only those who accept me as I am will be like me."[62] Chelsea Quinn Yarbro's Count Saint-Germain, who at this writing is still thriving in a seemingly inexhaustible series of historical horror novels, epitomizes the highly evolved vampire of the late 1970s, whose refinement is an implicit reproach to humanity. Like that of his nineteenth-century predecessor Carmilla, the vampirism of Yarbro's Count flows from a thirst for intimacy—the romantic intimacy Stoker's Dracula destroyed in his estranged rage for dominance. Unlike Carmilla's, though, Saint-Germain's thirst is the symptom of a despairing social critique.

Tender vampires like Saint-Germain are more plausible when they hunt and love beyond Stoker's boundaries: when they call themselves Dracula as Frank Langella does, they spend an inordinate amount of energy fighting their preordained script. Saint-Germain's life creates its own history, as do his cohorts in vampire fiction by women: Suzy McKee Charnas's Weyland, Anne Rice's Louis and Lestat, and Tanith Lee's Sabella are superior beings whose lives the mortal reader is too ensnared to emulate.[63] Saint-Germain is more socially committed than Weyland and the rest, but the history he experiences always tells the same story: from pre-Christian Egypt through Nazi Germany, Saint-Germain watches with helpless anguish as mass brutality snuffs out frail enlightenment.

In virtually every novel, Saint-Germain tries to rescue a grand woman in thrall to a sadistic patriarchal system by transforming her into a vampire. Sometimes the saving transformation succeeds: Madelaine de Montalio in *Hôtel Transylvania,* a brilliant girl trapped in the degenerate intrigues of pre-Revolutionary France, and Olivia Clemens in *Blood Games,* whose sadistic husband Justus epitomizes the sick abuse of power in Nero's Rome, are saved from lethal marriages to become wise, tender, erotically knowing vampire companions. More often, though, the woman is disheartened or dismembered before she can turn. No matter when they live, civilization offers Yarbro's women no recourse but transformation or destruction.

Yarbro claims that she is more interested in history than horror, but since horror fiction is more marketable, she included a vampire.[64] Her vampire, however, is the only character strong enough—because he has learned from the tragic centuries he has lived in, because it is difficult though not impossible for him to die—to provide a humane perspective on the mass carnage that finds its domestic epitome in the degradation of women. Her mortal characters are too corrupt or too weak to appreciate the human tragedy. In Yarbro's long Saint-Germain series, history and horror are inseparable, a dark union that distinguishes her Count from some of the sweet-natured vampires that followed him.[65]

The xenophobic fear that inspired Stoker's *Dracula* was the vision of a racially alien foreigner ruling and transforming England. The fear that inspires Yarbro's historical horror series is the impossibility of such rule. Saint-Germain, who is scathingly nicknamed "Foreigner" in all countries and times, is a perennially wise and learned counselor who is always forced into exile. The reader is allowed to imagine an egalitarian triumvirate governing the world—Saint-Germain and the two brilliant women he has saved into vampire life—but the world will never be ready for them. The superior species, which understands not only government, but healing, sexuality, and art, will always be expelled.

A supreme artist and scientist, Saint-Germain excels at everything. Schooled in ancient medical arts, an alchemist who adapts the principles of transmutation from jewels to the human body, he is an artful healer. But the societies he tries to live in never accept his cures: his medical artistry makes him vulnerable to accusations of witchcraft. The antithesis of the disease-bringing vampire of *Nosferatu,* Saint-Germain has the wisdom and skill to heal the societies that cast him out.

No matter how barbarous his circumstances, his clothes proclaim his artistry. Even in the Dark Ages of Saxony, he is a monument to the luxury of earlier, more advanced civilizations: "He had changed from the bliaut he had been wearing to the dark wool roc he had persuaded Enolda to make for him four months earlier: like the Roman tunica circula he had worn six hundred years before, the shoulders were pleated to take up the fabric, and the sleeves of his heavy woolen chemise were revealed, and his dark braies below the knees."[66]

Christopher Lee's flamboyant taste in castles hinted at a stylish, post-Victorian future—lived on Carnabay Street perhaps. Saint-Germain's gorgeous clothes are monuments to the forgotten artistry of the lost past. Christopher Lee looked toward modernity; Saint-Germain looks back. Worshiped by those few who know him as the spirit of civilization and culture, Saint-Germain is a yardstick by which to measure society's recurrent falls. The horror of Yarbro's history is humanity's rage to persecute chosen spirits.

Though he is an erotic virtuoso, Saint-Germain is scarcely a body. He needs blood to live, a fact that embarrasses him, but animal blood will do for a time: his primary satisfaction lies in giving women pleasure in intimately nonphallic ways that suit his peculiar artistry, for since vampirism has dried up his bodily fluids, he has no penile life. Yarbro's many sex scenes make vampirism a celebration, not only of nonviolence, but of a sexuality richer and more variable than penetration. Feminists in the 1970s were discovering, just as the vampire's lovers do, the multiorgasmic versatility of women's eroticism, which, despite the admonitions of male experts, requires no penis for arousal. Vampire and alchemist, Saint-Germain knows the erotic secrets patriarchs withhold.

Artist though he is, Saint-Germain is scarcely an animal; his body doesn't extend beyond his clothes and his small, deft hands. Moreover, this master of centuries of erotica is doomed by his nature to frustration, for sexual communion between vampires is impossible. Once Saint-Germain's love for a mortal is consummated in her transformation, these chosen spirits can be lovers no longer. The erotic intimacy for which Saint-Germain longs is, by the laws of his being, eternally withheld. This vampire is by nature a denial of animality.

To his own eternal sadness, Yarbro's vampire has evolved beyond his body. The aloof, scholarly Edward Weyland in Suzy McKee Charnas's contemporaneous *The Vampire Tapestry* is Saint-Germain's complementary opposite: wryly ironic and brilliant, Weyland is nevertheless essentially animal. Saint-Germain turned Dracula's foiled sovereignty over mortals into a tragic loss of authentic leadership; Weyland turns Dracula's animalism into a token of a similar loss. By the late twentieth century, animals are no longer the evolutionary menace they had been a hundred years earlier; they are reminders of lost integrity, just as Saint-Germain's clothes are monuments to lost arts. One of Weyland's few acolytes, a lonely teenage boy, knows animals only as endangered species: "The documentary film . . . first lovingly detailed the cleverness of the coyote, his beauty and his place as part of nature, and then settled into a barrage of hideous images: poisoned coyotes, trapped coyotes, burned coyotes, and coyotes mangled by ranchers' dogs. Mark didn't think he would ever be cool enough to stand that kind of stuff."[67] An animal is by definition a sacrificial victim.

Weyland has none of Saint-Germain's grace; he shuns eroticism, art, and empathy as dangerous human invasions of his predator's integrity. Saint-Germain is all memory; Weyland preserves himself by forgetting. Renewing himself by periodic hibernations, he retains when he wakes only the survival skills acquired in his many past lives. Intercourse with him is scarcely transfiguring. His sole approach to love—the night he spends with his therapist, Floria, at her own urging—is, for both, more perplexing than enhancing. Floria may or may not be renewed, but her troubling abandonment of professional ethics erodes her hard-won independent identity.[68] For Weyland, as for the unicorn in the tapestry, nonviolent intercourse with a trusting mortal is a dangerous loss of autonomy from which he can recover only by the long sleep of forgetfulness. Charnas refuses to turn her tapestry into a Yarbro-like romance. No savior, her predator leaves behind an untransfigured city: "Same jammed-up traffic down there, same dusty summer park stretching away uptown—yet not the same city, because Weyland no longer hunted there. Nothing like him moved now in those deep, grumbling streets" (p. 180).

Charnas evokes myths of salvation she refuses to believe in. Male writers of the '70s also dreamed of a superior species among us, even feeding on us, but their New York does not grumble with desolation. Whitley Strieber, a more visionary, less ironic fantasist than Charnas, finds a consolation she refuses in the image of a beast hunting in New York. The climax of *The Hunger* (1981) is Sarah's ravenous prowl around New York's east side, a neighborhood vitalized by her metamorphosis. Perhaps because Strieber's master vampire is a woman, *The Hunger* and Sarah repudiate her at the end, but *The Wild* celebrates its hero's change as he stalks through New York as a wolf: "He was a generous man, and at that moment his heart burst with one wish, that all human beings everywhere could just for one instant experience the old world in this new way. He had not known it was like this, had never dreamed what a difference really powerful senses could make. Human eyes were strong, but not so strong as wolf ears, not nearly so discriminating as a wolf's nose."[69] Strieber's central saving myth of intercourse with a higher species crystallizes in *Communion: A True Story* (1987), an account of his own gradual transformation by extraterrestrial mentors. Moving from Gothicism to beast fable to scientific revelation, Strieber increasingly celebrates the interspecial communion whose impossibility women fantasists—tougher, perhaps, and more socially aware—lament.[70]

Despite the differences in their vampires (the disengaged Weyland sometimes turns into a sardonic commentary on Saint-Germain), Yarbro and Charnas both use fantasy to survey social

loss. It is easy to dismiss their vampire romances as, by definition, escapist, but both use their vampire as a yardstick by which
they measure American society in the late 1970s. Unlike
Strieber, whose wolves, vampires, and extraterrestrials are virtually omnipotent, Yarbro and Charnas carefully limit the saving
powers of their vampires. Even Saint-Germain manages to transform only a remnant of mortals who, like him, can become only
horrified spectators of power abused. Male authors give far more
power to their vampires, although, in their imaginative exuber-
ance, they pay less attention to the untransfigured majority.

The corporate corruption revealed by the Watergate investi-
gations seems to have been decisive in the transformation
of vampires into potential saviors. Not only Nixon's duplicity,
but his self-revelations on tape, might well inspire dreams of
extrahuman majesty: the witty and literate self-justifications via
cassette tape of Fred Saberhagen's Dracula in 1975 and of Anne
Rice's Louis in 1976 are more edifying than nasty Nixonian mutterings. Even the vampires of Yarbro and Charnas, Strieber and
Talbot, who are too preoccupied to define themselves on tape,
are survivors from an aristocratic age. They have dignity, man-
ners, sensuous intensity, in all of which the Watergate conspira-
tors were deficient. The past that threatened late Victorian England with savage reversion became, for late-twentieth-century
Americans, the fantasized source of a finer nation, a more authentic civilization.

THE BEST-KNOWN VAMPIRES of the 1970s are those of Anne Rice and
Stephen King. Neither species is paralyzed by social awareness.
Weyland, Saint-Germain, and their peers are vampires' vampires: they fascinate their admirers, arousing a longing for national as well as personal transformation, but their audience is
relatively specialized. These vampires may live in our houses,
but they are not household words. Anne Rice's Lestat, the vampire who is, is more beautiful than Saint-Germain, more self-
absorbed than Weyland. He has cosmic longings, but these
concern the discovery of his own origin, not the salvation of
mortals; he yearns after humanity en masse, but individually
humans are too dull for him to worry about. Saint-Germain and

Weyland were trapped in human history; Lestat inhabits a spectacular universe of his own.

When we first see him refracted through Louis's gloomy eyes in *Interview with the Vampire* (1976), he shatters all the old smelly stereotypes at once: "Of course, you must realize that all this time the vampire Lestat was extraordinary. He was no more human to me than a biblical angel."[71] Neither as wise as Saint-Germain nor as animal as Weyland, Lestat and his company are a species apart. They scarcely participate in history, even as an oppressed race. When Louis and, later in *The Vampire Chronicles*, Lestat seek the origin of vampires, that origin is unrecognizable to the human reader: these vampires live without reference to us, composing a mythic landscape of their own. Nevertheless, the fraught ménage of Louis and Lestat is a return to vampire beginnings. Their irritable mutual obsession recovers literary vampires' lost origin: the homoerotic bond between Byron and Polidori.

Our midcentury Draculas were free to subvert patriarchy, but all were hygienically heterosexual. They released chosen women from sadistic husbands, but oppressed men had to look out for themselves. The early Saint-Germain romances seem startlingly homophobic today: wicked husbands are often degenerate homosexuals who abandon to vampires the intricate responsiveness of a woman's body. Charnas's Weyland finds cruising men an outcast group on whom it is conveniently easy to prey, but the novel never suggests that they, like Floria, might be aroused by Weyland's animal touch. The taboos that Stoker institutionalized in the 1890s held for almost a hundred years of vampire fiction. Saint-Germain tries vainly to drink an earlier, lost intimacy, but only Louis and Lestat can admonish each other with the old assurance of affinity: "Remember your oath."

But this oath has become too momentous for mortals: only vampires can tolerate its intensity.[72] Putatively a new species with its own alternate history and mythology, the vampires of Anne Rice reclaim their literary origin, if not their prehistoric source, by limiting their feverish admiration to each other. The homoeroticism that infuses vampire life—imagined by a woman writer who finds male homosexuality as glamorous as vampirism is to the smitten (and finally bitten) boy who tapes

Louis's confession in *Interview*—restores a lost birthright. Rice's infraction of this final Stoker-instigated taboo brings a special electricity to *Interview with the Vampire,* giving its predators a glamour more socially engaged vampires lack.

The insularity of *Interview* was profoundly appealing in the leaderless 1970s.[73] Its vampirism is a select club, a fraternity of beauty and death whose members are expected to be handsome and refined enough not to irritate each other throughout eternity. They do little, but they are superb spectators. When they are not killing, they flex their highly developed vampire sight: "It was as if I had only just been able to see colors and shapes for the first time," Louis reminisces. Though the entire world is the vampire's spectacle, the most satisfying sight is each other: "I was so enthralled with the buttons on Lestat's black coat that I looked at nothing else for a long time. Then Lestat began to laugh, and I heard his laughter as I had never heard anything before" (p. 20).

This self-reflexive gaze is far from Saint-Germain's horrified fixation on human history. Amoral aesthetes, Rice's vampires are beautifully devoid of social consciousness, another major attraction for disaffected readers. Claudia, the little girl Louis and Lestat transform and adopt, is, in her enforced perennial childhood, bristling with feminist significance, but unlike Yarbro's Madelaine and Olivia, she scarcely articulates her complaint: like Hawthorne's Pearl, she is a visual icon of arrested development.

This lovely little vampire, worshiped and controlled by two fatherly lovers, reminds us of the Hammer Lucy *before* Dracula bit her into brief adulthood. For the Claudia who will always look like a doll, vampirism is no release from patriarchy, but a perpetuation of it until the end of time. Her only alternative is her futile attempt to kill Lestat; immolation for this treachery is her only respite from undeath. So suggestively angry and still that she is almost an allegorical figure, Claudia, like Stoker's Dracula, tells no story: we see her as a refraction of Louis's self-love and self-hate. "Claudia was mystery," he concludes. "It was not possible to know what she knew or did not know. And to watch her kill was chilling" (p. 101). Rice's vampires are compulsive storytellers, but Claudia, the ultimate spectacle, is unable to break free of paternal narrative. Instead of being released by vampirism, she is trapped in a mock-family as self-enclosed and strangling as was the Holmwood household in *Horror of Dracula* before it admitted Christopher Lee.

Louis and Lestat may be patriarchs, but they are dreadful fathers. Far from subverting paternal tyranny, Louis bemoans paternal ineffectiveness. His story is his futile search for an adequate mentor, but there is no one to initiate him into the permutations of undeath. Lestat, the fetid folklore predators of Varna, even Armand and the Parisian precision of his Théâtre des Vampires, all provide spectacle, but not authority. The final irony of Louis's account of abandonment is his own assumption of paternity at the end: he bites the pleading boy to become that boy's Lestat. Even though his last words to his swooning acolyte are "I don't know" (p. 345), Louis has become the spectacle of authority, and for these vampires, spectacle is the only credible substance.

The ornamental self-enclosure of Rice's select society saves her vampires from the excessive virtue that threatened their species in the 1970s. The visionary novelists who resurrected and remade vampires know that there are social forces more frightening than Dracula: tyranny, dullness, brutality, unbelief, mass self-deception and self-destruction. Deliberately, they drain fear from their vampires, admonishing thrill-seeking readers to look closer to home. These vampires who are more frightened than frightening become, at their worst, edifying, Superman-like rescuers—as, for instance, Saberhagen's Vlad does in the novels that follow his *Dracula Tape*, in which Dracula, under a variety of names, uses his powers to save friends persecuted by villains. The vampire who is a symptom of lost authority becomes, too often, too nice.

But the most famous vampires of the 1970s are not nice: Stephen King's down-home hordes in *'Salem's Lot* (1975). Deader than the finer spirits who followed them—*Interview with the Vampire* was published the year after *'Salem's Lot, Hôtel Transylvania* three years later—King's vampires are so horrible that they may look retrograde.[74] They are surely unsympathetic. No one could call them chosen spirits or leaders manqué. For women writers like Anne Rice and Chelsea Quinn Yarbro, new vampires must undergo a selection process as hairsplitting and fastidious as academic tenure; so must the recruits in later feminist novels like Jewelle Gomez's *The Gilda Stories* (1991). Even Stoker's Dracula chose his prey thoughtfully: his predations were power strategies through which he gained primacy over the charmed circle of hunters, the heart of the West. But vampirism in *'Salem's Lot* is open to all.

There are no elect spirits in *'Salem's Lot.* Anyone can become a vampire, and almost everyone does. It scarcely matters whether the citizens of the Lot have turned or not; even at their most human, the embittered Father Callahan smells in his flock "a mindless, moronic evil from which there was no mercy or reprieve."[75] Since evil is stupid, victimization is random; anyone exposed in the night can become a vampire. Vampires multiply so quickly that it scarcely matters who begins the chain. Metamorphosis is not a discipline, but an epidemic as indiscriminate as fire, as majority-ridden as democracy. Stephen King's vampires may not inspire sophisticated moral probing, but they are as iconoclastic as those of Anne Rice, for they too thrive without authority or rules.

One principle that does direct vampirism in 'Salem's Lot is an abyss of which we heard much in the 1970s: the generation gap, which takes on sinister new import when vampires invade the mean little town. Though anyone, young or old, can become a vampire, only the young expect them. Mark Petrie, one of those charmed Stephen King children born with apprehension of evil, understands the invasion because he has learned life from the random grue of horror comics. He is polite enough to love the parents who discuss him in temperate clichés, but he is scarcely surprised when Barlow knocks their heads together "with a grinding, sickening crack" (p. 351), for in comic books death is neither logical nor sacramental: "Understand death? Sure. That was when the monsters got you" (p. 139).

Mark is not cute; he is right. King has often claimed that Stoker's *Dracula* is the source of *'Salem's Lot,*[76] but his is a *Dracula* without pattern or rationale or rule-giving elders. Not only is there no viable Van Helsing;[77] vampires are so abundant that there is virtually no Dracula. Somehow, though, the young have access to terror their rationalist parents are denied. They are not guides or seers; they are seismographs. The generation gap becomes an almost visible abyss in *'Salem's Lot,* one from which Hiroshima, the violent lives of the Kennedys, and Vietnam peep out to divide the growing generation from its conventional parents.

Watergate is a silent but essential collaborator. According to Stephen King, its climate of lies shaped *'Salem's Lot:*

> I know that, for instance, in my novel *'Salem's Lot,* the thing that really scared me was not vampires, but the town in the daytime, the town that was empty, knowing that there were things in closets, that there were people tucked under beds, under the concrete pilings of all those trailers. And all the time I was writing that, the Watergate hearings were pouring out of the TV. There were people saying "at that point in time." They were saying, "I can't recall." There was money showing up in bags. Howard Baker kept asking, "What I want to know is, what did you know and when did you know it?" That line haunts me, it stays in my mind. It may be *the* classic line of the twentieth century: what did he know and when did he know it. During that time I was thinking about secrets, things that have been hidden and were being dragged out into the light.[78]

Bred on these buried horrors, the young people in *'Salem's Lot* seem always to have known that life was inhuman. If the monster-bred Mark Petrie—who finally knows only enough to get out of town—is the book's closest approximation to Van Helsing, his friend Danny Glick is the Lot's most memorable vampire. Danny's attack on a sick man inspires the novel's most quoted line:

> And in the awful heavy silence of the house, as [Matt] sat impotently on his bed with his face in his hands, he heard the high, sweet, evil laugh of a child—
> —and then the sucking sounds. (P. 165)

Danny is one of the more ravenous demon children who proliferate in popular horror of the 1970s,[79] but unlike *Rosemary's baby, The Omen's* Damien, and the toothsome babies of *It's Alive* (1974) and *It Lives Again* (1978), Danny, in this scene at least, is neither possessed nor a mutant. "The high, sweet, evil laugh of a child," the ensuing "sucking sounds," might, in any other context, be naturalistic descriptions; the adjective "evil" could simply characterize a cranky observer. The vampire Danny is Danny the child. Tobe Hooper's TV movie (1979) gives the transformed Glick boys clownish white makeup and rubbery fangs, but in the novel there is little distinction between child and vampire—or vampire-knower. Even when Danny first peers out of his coffin, there is nothing unnatural about him: "There was no death pallor in that face; the cheeks seemed rosy, almost juicy with vitality" (p. 135).

Whether they are vampires like Danny or vampire-knowers like Mark—whose toy cross is a more effective vampire repellent than Father Callahan's "real" one—boys are the heart, though not the cause, of the vampire epidemic in 'Salem's Lot. They are not, like other demon-children of the '70s, occult invaders of a benevolent adult society; they are the essence of that society. Danny Glick is a different sort of child from Claudia in *Interview with the Vampire,* for Claudia is an adult male construction, a stunted woman with no identity apart from the obsessions of the fatherly lovers who made her.

For Anne Rice, childhood is a monstrous imposition on an adult consciousness. For Stephen King, childhood is the essence of experience, one so haunted and frightening that adulthood is evasion. The degradation of Claudia's undeath is her enforced existence as a doll. At the end of *'Salem's Lot,* a forgotten doll is a mute truth-teller: "And perched in one corner of the sandbox, a floppy arm trailing on the grass, was some child's forgotten Raggedy Andy doll. Its shoe-button eyes seemed to reflect a black, vapid horror, as if it had seen all the secrets of darkness during its long stay in the sandbox. Perhaps it had" (p. 425).

Significantly, Anne Rice's resistant child/vampire/doll is female, while Stephen King's oracular Raggedy Andy is male. As is so often true, the woman writer wants to free herself from the childhood the male writer exalts. For both King and Rice, however, vampirism becomes for the first time inextricably attached to childhood, not an imposition by oppressive elders, as it was in the 1930s, or a strategy through which sexy young people evaded stuffy old ones, as it was in Hammer films. Children's innate affinity with horror means that vampirism is, for the first time, symptomatic of fear of the future, not the past. The horrors on youth's side of the generational abyss—which King calls by the names Hiroshima, Vietnam, the Kennedy lives and deaths, Watergate—are not tokens of a savage past that refuses to die, but portents of a dreadful new nation.

In the 1980s, horror will belong to the young. Vampire movies like *Fright Night* and *The Lost Boys,* as well as horror cycles like *Friday the Thirteenth* and *Nightmare on Elm Street,* make monstrosity a teenage phenomenon, not an invasion from antiquity. Stephen King, with his passionate allegiance to pre-adulthood, helped shift the axis of horror, but only *'Salem's Lot* depicts the appropriation of horror by the young as a historical event. *Fright Night, Nightmare on Elm Street,* and the rest are set in timeless American small towns closer to movies than to life. *'Salem's Lot* sees a small town evolve through American history to a point where vampires are known before they arrive. Heavy, slovenly, unrefined, Stephen King could not on the face of it be farther from Chelsea Quinn Yarbro, but like her—and like so many other writers of the 1970s—he writes historical horror. Their urgent political vision generates conventions that will become routine and unexamined in the 1980s, a decade when history seems to disappear.[80]

'Salem's Lot produces no Van Helsings, not even travesties like Laurence Olivier in John Badham's movie; the best knowledge one can have is the assurance that something is wrong. No authentic leaders emerge because there are no clear vampire rules. The townsfolk dredge up memories of Stoker's novel and Hammer movies, then hunt frantically for crucifixes none of them owns, but the rules that were once so reliable splutter and sometimes stop working altogether in 'Salem's Lot.

Mark's toy cross repels Danny Glick because Mark believes; so does the good doctor Jimmy Cody, who makes a functional cross out of two tongue depressors (though it saves neither Jimmy's neck nor his life). Jimmy's tongue depressors are more potent than the candlestick cross Peter Cushing held up to Christopher Lee in *Horror of Dracula,* which needed scalding reinforcement by the sun, but when Father Callahan, the only character whose crucifix is authentic, tries to repel Barlow's invasion of the Petrie kitchen, the cross fails embarrassingly.[81] Barlow's diagnosis seems to make smooth sense: "Without faith, the cross is only wood. . . . The boy makes ten of you, false priest" (p. 355).

But nothing in 'Salem's Lot is comprehensible except its plausible vampires. Father Callahan's cross may fail to work for the same nonreason that my computer could give out as I write this, or your car could stop dead on the freeway, or the predictable universe itself could (as our bodies will) lose a gear. In a seminar at the University of Pennsylvania, Stephen King described in a burst of eloquence, seeming to scare himself, a potential vampire story in which "the garlic doesn't work, the cross doesn't work, the running water doesn't work, the stake doesn't work, *nothing works:* and basically you're fucked. There's nothing you can do."[82] Father Callahan's humiliation brings us momentarily into this dysfunctional territory.

Nothing works in 'Salem's Lot because its vampires, like its mortals, have no palpable design and no identifiable leaders. Their invasion seems to follow the old xenophobic *Dracula* pattern: two evilly suave Europeans, Barlow and Straker, come to the Lot to open an antique store. Identified with un-American attributes like wit, homosexuality, and "old things, fine things" (p. 99), Barlow and Straker seem as contaminatingly foreign as Bela Lugosi was, but what is the role of the native Marsten House that seems to bring them? Is it, as Ben postulates, "a kind of psychic sounding board. A supernatural beacon, if you like" (p. 112)? And who is the Dark Father who, according to Matt (p. 319), is Barlow's Master?—is he Hubert Marsten or some sort of satanic essence (European or American?) hovering over the action?

This overdetermined chain of command is left undefined.[83] As in Rice's *Vampire Chronicles,* there are no rules and no clear vampire origin, demonic or divine. This vacuum of vampire leadership is the diffused authority of American democracy. Father Callahan muses on its Kafkaesque amorphousness: "It was all out of control, like a kid's soapbox racer going downhill with no brakes: *I was following my orders.* Yes, that was true, patently true. We were all soldiers, simply following what was written on our walking papers. But where were the orders coming from, ultimately? *Take me to your leader.* But where is his office? *I was just following orders. The people elected me.* But who elected the people?" (p. 305).

The vampires themselves have no doubt that they are under authority. Danny Glick explains to Mark, "*He* commands it"; Ed Miller awakens his wife into vampirism reassuringly: "Come on, darlin'. Get up. We have to do as he says" (pp. 240, 372). These vampires lack even the illusion of autonomy; they could never produce a wise and sophisticated Olivia, or even a Hammer woman welcoming her transformation with a knowing grin. Transformation in the Lot holds no promise of freedom. Yet, though these vampires are willingly led, Barlow could not be their Master, for after he is staked in a pseudo-climax, his creations survive him: in an egregious rejection of hierarchies of dominance, the death of the head has no effect on the creatures he made, who continue to drift around aimlessly, perhaps assuming they are still obeying orders.

These floundering, directionless killers pay occasional lip service to Dracula, but they have no access to his individuality, his efficiency, even his tyranny. Rather, they are cousins of the utterly American vampires in George Romero's possessed Pittsburgh, who in *Night of the Living Dead* (1968) and *Martin* (1978) devour, for no reason they know, the squabbling citizens of a city that has no authorities beyond woozy television and radio chatterers.

LIKE THE OTHER VAMPIRES born in the American 1970s—Weyland, Saint-Germain, Louis and Lestat—the citizens of Stephen King's Lot are wholly new creations, leaderless and lethal, uncertain what to do. The rules that control them are so indeterminate that they flow easily into the psychic vampires with whom this chapter began, the quintessence of twentieth-century predation who pervade everything in mortal life except mortality.

Whether they are lovable elitists like Frank Langella or ignorant shamblers like Stephen King's populace, vampires in the twentieth century inhabit a lush but senseless world. In the 1970s, humans and vampires seem to cry together for a leader, a master-vampire who will guide them beyond the corrupt morass of muttering voices that supposedly constitutes authority. When, in 1980, Ronald Reagan assumed that role, the vampires who had longed for him were systematically stripped of their powers.

4

Grave and Gay: Reagan's Years

Turning Back

THE NEW BEGINNINGS THAT MARKED vampire literature of the '70s settled into submission in the Reagan years. Like so much else in the leaderless 1970s, vampirism had been full of promise. After conservative leaders took hold of America and England, vampires, like many other species, enjoyed an apparent, inflated success story: there were more of them and they were more popular than ever.[1] Nevertheless, the vampires of the 1980s were depressed creatures. Constricted in their potential, their aspirations, and their effect on mortals, they were closer to death than to undeath.

Two movies about young male vampires—*Love at First Bite* (1979; dir. Stan Dragoti) and *The Lost Boys* (1987; dir. Joel Schumacher)—are, in their effect, worlds apart. *Love at First Bite* is that rarity, a genuinely funny spoof that doesn't mock its vampires out of existence. It can be both funny and vampiric because it embraces the comedy inherent in the 1970s vampire romance. *Love at First Bite* plays, in fact, like a high-spirited distillation of Badham's *Dracula,* which appeared the same year, but George Hamilton is less threatening than Frank Langella's sad-eyed sophisticate.

At the beginning of the movie, the communist government commandeers Castle Dracula, where the bored Hamilton, stuck in Bela Lugosi's accent and tuxedo, is mooning over photographs of an American model. Like most of his kind in the twentieth century, he emigrates from the old world to America. In grungy New York, this fastidious aristocrat can find no blood pure enough to drink; his florid anachronisms are a running joke; but he is neither predator nor buffoon. Like the finest vampires of his revisionist decade, he is a romantic redeemer. Aided by the usual sane '70s Renfield—who diagnoses society's madness rather than acting it out—

Hamilton manages to adapt to the city and save his beloved from it.

That druggie beloved is testament to the romantic fidelity of vampires in the '70s, for she is the same model whose picture he had mooned over in Transylvania. Dracula (who calls himself "Vladimir" in New York) rescues her from her sententious psychiatrist and fiancé (who, to certify his villainy, reveals himself as Van Helsing's grandson). Dracula's creed that "in a world without romance, it's better to be dead" carries the couple beyond the decaying city. We last see them transformed into bats, soaring through a gorgeous night sky. This Dracula is no loveless leech like his namesake, but a restorer of lost powers and a deliverer into new spaces.

Only the 1970s could produce an authentic comic romance about vampires. The motifs of the decade—the tarnished urban setting, the romantic emanation from the past who authenticates his tenderness by calling himself "Vlad," the crushing paternalistic psychiatrist, the shrewdly sane Renfield—come together in an oddly lovable movie, one whose parody surges with romantic hope. We need only compare *Love at First Bite* with a vampire spoof made ten years later—the grim *Vampire's Kiss* (1989; dir. Robert Bierman), in which Nicolas Cage, a smarmy yuppie convinced he's a vampire, is immobilized in psychosis—to see the joy drain out of vampirism in the 1980s. Even Cage's delusions inhibit him; romantic and social transfiguration are inconceivable to a character so beyond human or social contact that he cannot even prey efficiently. Not only in accounts of deranged adults, but even in visions of boys who fly, 1970s release becomes 1980s paralysis.

The Lost Boys was a popular teenage vampire movie of the 1980s, but its vampirism is ineffective predation that is joyless to the perpetrators: as in *Vampire's Kiss,* transformation is self-imprisonment rather than exaltation. The title comes from *Peter Pan,* but these West Coast high school students already live in Never Land, so they have no place to go. They drift around Santa Carla, their garish California town, where they prey on the fringes of the mortal population. Even when they fly, they do so with little elation, throwing themselves off a bridge down into a deadening fog rather than soaring upward as vampires did in the '70s. They spend most of their time fighting aimlessly, hanging out in trees, and playing sadistic mind-games with each other. The newcomer Michael is initiated into hallucinations like those of a bad drug trip, in which innocuous Chinese food turns to maggots and worms. After this repulsive meal, the blood Michael drinks is incidental and scarcely fortifying. For these young monsters, vampirism is as distasteful as living.

In 1958, in one of the usual Hammer teases, Peter Cushing's Van Helsing noted slyly that vampirism was "similar to addiction to drugs," a titillating possibility in the psychedelic age that was dawning. The lost boys of 1987, dull-eyed, stunted, and pale, have become casualties of the Republicans' war against drugs: they are so burned out that the antidrug message of official culture seems to have stifled *all* transformations or transforming perceptions. The metamorphoses of 1980s vampires are a cautionary warning, not an expansion of possibilities.

The ingrown vampire community lives in a plush underground resort buried in 1906 by the San Francisco earthquake. This opulent cocoon reflects Santa Carla itself, which consists of enclosed pleasure spots: malls, stores, amusement parks, showy houses. In 1975, Stephen King's 'Salem's Lot was equally ingrown, but it was nevertheless socially encompassing: incantations about Hiroshima, the Kennedys, Vietnam, and Watergate suggested horrible transformations in the nation that were refracted in an isolated town whose evil only comic-book-reading boys penetrated. In *The Lost Boys,* the same boys are, once again, vampire-hunters—only Sam, Michael's little brother, knows enough to declare, "You're a creature of the night, Michael, just like out of a comic book"—but there is no hint that something has gone wrong in the America these children inherit. Like the amusement park in which it begins, *The Lost Boys* offers insulated thrills.

From Christopher Lee to George Hamilton, vampires of the '60s and '70s were a soaring alternative to patriarchal families. But like so many '80s vampire visions, *The Lost Boys* admits no world beyond the family. Films of the 1970s were overburdened with the fathers Michael and Sam need; their only authority is their giddy divorced mother (Dianne Wiest) and her own father, a ghoulish eccentric with whom they have gone to Santa Carla to live. Wiest is so distracted by working and flirting that she abandons her boys to a vampire gang. In *'Salem's Lot,* vampirism accompanied national disasters no family could control or seal out. A single mother replaces Watergate as the catastrophic agent of *The Lost Boys,* for this silly woman not only loses her sons: the only male authority she provides turns out to be the head vampire.[2]

While Michael's transformation makes him sicker and sicker—not from loss of blood or depraved hunger, like Stoker's Lucy, but from paralyzing allergies to food, sun, and other sources of nourishment—his mother is gallivanting around with her pompous boyfriend, Max. Michael's little brother, Sam, and his vampire-hunting friends set out to kill the head vampire, who, Sam oedipally intuits, is not the tough teenage gang leader, but fatherly Max himself. In a climactic concluding fight, Sam proves to be right. He kills the bad father, saves his brother, and re-possesses his mother. This purified family is all we need to see: the ramifications of vampirism have shrunk from the political arena into the snug domestic unit.

Max's exposure as head vampire not only indicts the careless sexuality of the mother who exposes her sons to danger; it undermines the autonomy of vampires themselves. Vampirism is no longer the youth movement it was; the lost boys are pawns of an entrenched man. The renewed paternal authority in vampire films of the 1980s, an authority that had been eroding since the Hammer films' stylish mockery, nullifies the vampire gang itself, whose supposed freedom is orchestrated by an inescapable patriarch. Vampirism in *The Lost Boys* is no alternative to human society, but an illusion as fragile as a drug trip. Stripped of its hunger, its aerial perspective, its immortal longings, vampirism becomes more perishable than humanity.

The Lost Boys introduces a species that exemplifies the most important paradigm-shift of the 1980s: the half-vampire. Michael and his girlfriend, Star, are vampire initiates who have not yet turned because they have not made their first kill; thus, when Max, their head, is staked, they don't die with him as the old rules dictated; they return unscathed to their pristine teenage selves.[3] For the first time, vampirism itself is mortal.

POPULAR YOUTH MOVIES like *The Lost Boys* feature young men and their women[4] with neither energy nor dreams of change; even vampirism, their sole rebellion, is an impermanent condition governed by the respectable patriarch Max. When vampires do take power in the 1980s, they do not soar beyond society like George Hamilton in *Love at First Bite;* instead of confronting oppressors, they become oppressors themselves, taking on the inhibiting heaviness the 1970s had reserved for mortal tyrants. In the 1970s, writers like Fred Saberhagen and Chelsea Quinn Yarbro had exposed the tyranny within patriarchal history. After 1980, historical horror evolves in England into a grimmer genre, "alternative history," exemplified by such dense novels as Brian Stableford's *The Empire of Fear* (1988), Tim Powers's *The Stress of Her Regard* (1989), and Kim Newman's *Anno Dracula* (1992).

Yarbro's historical horror inserts a humane vampire into various epochs as a gauge of legitimized oppression. Though he is an aristocrat who dresses like an embodied work of art, Yarbro's Saint-Germain always sides with history's victims, especially when they are brutalized brilliant women. Alternative history is less social critique than origin myth: it inserts vampires into history, not to combat oppression, but to explain it. In their fundamental stupidity and inertness, the vampires in alternative history clog the fitfully aspiring spirit.

Brian Stableford defines alternative history with characteristic murkiness: it is the task of "trying to imagine how one alteration in the state of things might extend its consequences across centuries." He calls his own novel an "idol-infested story which we have created in order to give meaning to our own past."[5] In Stableford's alternative English history, a race of vampire aristocrats has always ruled common men. Even the halcyon Renaissance was a time of mortal subjection. Stableford's Englishmen are as eager as Yarbro's beleaguered women to turn into their rulers and acquire their powers, but a doomed freedom fighter insists upon vampires' fundamental torpor: "They have encouraged scholarship because they thought it a fit distraction; a deflection of our energy from resentful and rebellious ideas. They never looked for the kinds of reward which our learned men have begun to reap. Great changes are remaking the world;

changes wrought by artifice and discovery. But an empire of immortals loves constancy. Vampires mistrust the new, whenever it rises above mere novelty" (p. 8).

As the ensuing action proves, transformation is not redemption, but inertia. The long middle of *The Empire of Fear* involves a backward journey to vampire origins in Africa, but this mystic odyssey only confirms the tradition-bound mindlessness of the immortals. The end of the book leaps forward to the 1980s, when a miracle of genetic engineering endows mortals with vampire characteristics, but the evolving race is depleted of sexual and imaginative energy. The transformations that looked rapturous to many writers in the 1970s mean, in the 1980s, amalgamation with a power that is dullness. In the Reaganesque years, vampires represented an oppression so fundamental that no saving vitality could dislodge it.

Kim Newman's *Anno Dracula* also accepts vampire inertia as a given. Newman's alternative history is less encompassing than Stableford's; it deals only with fetid London in 1888, when Dracula has married Queen Victoria and made vampirism a prerequisite of power. Consequently, all the best people rush to turn. When Marie Corelli conforms, her novels deteriorate: "Vampires were rarely creative, all energies diverted into the simple prolonging of life."[6] As Prince Consort, Dracula is no reformer like Saberhagen's Vlad; he is as leaden a ruler as Marie Corelli is a writer. Class exploitation flowers and festers; the impoverished citizens of London's East End change in droves, but they gain neither sustenance nor power. Vampirism, for Newman, is an intensification of the devouring social norm.

Since the Prince Consort rewards his cronies, *Anno Dracula* treats us to a pageant of remembered monsters. Lord Ruthven is Prime Minister, one who spends his time alternately fawning and complaining about his subordination to a vampire of debased Carpathian blood; Varney is a sadistic colonial ruler in India. Carmilla, "a soppy girl, fearfully dependent on her warm lovers" (p. 185), has no political appointment; Newman never resurrects her as he does the males. Count Vardalek does return from Eric, Count Stenbock's "The True Story of a Vampire" (1894), playing the serpentine incarnation of the homosexual potential that vampires exuded in the 1890s. Dracula, who in

Stoker's novel was the outcast carrier of that potential, represents for Newman the homophobic establishment: avid to "crack the whip on . . . 'unnatural vice,'" he has Vardalek executed (pp. 50, 109–10). The vampires we knew as liminal outcasts are the Victorian ruling class in *Anno Dracula*. All have turned respectable with a vengeance.

The rampant conformity of Newman's British vampires corresponds to Max's patriarchal control of the vampire gang in California. In both *The Lost Boys* and *Anno Dracula*, entrenched power is insurmountable; no alternative communities are credible. The grim determinism of these Gothic fantasies reflects political and theoretical dogma in the 1980s. In America and England, powerful conservative leaders proclaimed that they had restored the patriarchal power that in the 1960s and '70s had seemed about to collapse. Like fantasy, scholarship in the 1980s responded to political fiat. Michel Foucault's anatomies of interlocking, inescapable structures of power pervaded academic thought. Like 1980s vampire works, Foucault discounts the possibility of rebellion: apparent ideological alternatives are mere offshoots of the tyrannical dominant discourse. Vampires who had been agents of change denied, in the Foucauldian 1980s, the very idea of revolution. They lost their immortality, but they embodied unalterable oppression.

Anno Dracula resurrects past vampires only to absorb them into its power structure. A self-reflexive return to origins, it discredits the autonomy of those origins: Newman's vampires were co-opted from their beginnings. Tim Powers's *The Stress of Her Regard* goes back still further, to vampire roots in Romantic poetry. His alternative history of Byron, Shelley, Keats, and Polidori involves their debilitating entanglements with an ancient, alternate species: the nephelim.

Neither the poets nor the nephelim who feed on them are the mercurial figures one associates with Romantic poetry. The poets are debilitated and depressed; the feeding nephelim are not the bloody vampires we know; they are stones. Scarcely sentient, they are always about to devolve into inorganic inertness: "Its torso seemed to be a huge bag at one moment and a boulder in the next, and the surface of it was all bumpy like chain mail; and when it had plodded its way on elephantine legs to the porthole, he could see that its head was just an angular lump with shadows that implied cheekbones and eye sockets and a slab of jaw."[7]

This mountainous hulk—which seems to the hero oddly female[8]—might be at home pursuing Wordsworth, but it seems out of place in the shimmering poetic world of the younger Romantics. The "angular lump" has little in common with volatile vampires like Byron's Darvell, Polidori's Ruthven, Coleridge's Geraldine, or Keats's Lamia. Stony, inanimate, subhuman, the nephelim belong to the 1980s, not to British Romanticism. *The Stress of Her Regard* is less overtly political than Stableford or Newman's alternative histories, but it too envisions vampires that are immutable obstructions. In these works blood is not the life: as the sediment of existence, vampirism demands not energy but cessation. Its need to kill desire and stop motion is the essence of 1980s conservatism.

None of these alternative histories can bear to look forward. Conceived in the 1970s, Yarbro's historical horror aspired to shine corrective light on the barbarities of the present, but the alternative histories of Stableford, Newman, and Powers are origin stories with no reformist potential. The hopeless determinism inherent in origin fiction suffuses even American works that are sheer exuberant myth-making with no historical pretensions: Anne Rice's *Vampire Chronicles*.

Despite his self-delighted solipsism in *Interview with the Vampire* and the egomaniacal stardom with which he begins his memoir, Lestat surprises us in the second half of *The Vampire Lestat*: turning from spectacle to audience, he sets out on a backward pilgrimage to uncover the origin of vampires. His predecessors would never have conceived such a quest; harboring imperial or sexual ambitions or scheming simply to stay alive, they looked toward the future. Only in the 1980s were vampires defined by their origins rather than their plots.

The Vampire Lestat is a series of temporal regressions in which Lestat, cynosure of twentieth-century America and pre-revolutionary France, embarks on a backward quest out of the knowable world. Like the enthralled boy who taped Louis's confessions in *Interview*, Lestat becomes an increasingly passive auditor of a series of tales that guide him beyond Western history

REFUND POLICY

HALF PRICE BOOKS

281 N Casaloma
Appleton, Wisconsin 54913-9675
920) 8301237

9 03:29 PM

#01 051KGK/00003

| 1 | 87.98 | UN | 7.98 |

3799-(used books at low prices)

SHIP/HAND	0.00
TAX (5% on $7.98)	0.40
TOTAL	8.38

PAYMENT TYPE

CASH   20.00

| PAYMENT TOTAL | $ | 20.00 |
| CHANGE DUE - CASH | $ | 11.62 |

THANK YOU!

Thanks for stopping by Half Price Books
on Casaloma. Enjoy the rest of your day.

END OF TRANSACTION

until he confronts his species' original parents, formed in pre-imperial Egypt.

Akasha and Enkil, known as Those Who Must Be Kept, are giant petrified figures, alive but immobilized: "Not in any sculpture anywhere had I ever seen such a lifelike attitude, but actually there was nothing lifelike about them at all."[9] A series of accidents turned these ancient rulers into blood-drinking demons composed of something like "flexible stone." These fossilized divinities have none of the animal vitality of Dracula, the originary vampire in his novel; they scarcely resemble their own preening, leaping, complaining progeny. Though they do move secretly and fitfully, their authority, like that of Tim Powers's inorganic nephelim, is their fixity.

The stony progenitors of *The Vampire Lestat* (a huge bestseller) might have inspired the immobilized vampire authorities of Britain's alternative historians. It is likelier, though, that the Reagan/Thatcher years fed all these marmoreal vampires. For most of *The Vampire Lestat,* Those Who Must Be Kept venerably oppress their caretaker Marius; to abandon them is to risk vampire holocaust, and so he lugs them wherever he goes, building them opulent shrines around the world. Though they no longer govern, their insentient authority remains absolute. Like the cumbersome past conservative leaders treasured, or perhaps like those leaders themselves, Akasha and Enkil are heavy husks of authority, arduous to preserve, dangerous to deny.

Uncomfortable parent-gods though they are, Akasha and Enkil are less frightening petrified than they are when they move. In *The Queen of the Damned,* the sequel to *The Vampire Lestat,* Akasha kills Enkil and returns to omnivorous life. Even before she reveals her Dracula-like plan to take over the world, her vitality terrifies Marius, who had cherished her as a statue: "Her cheek shone like pearl as she smiled, her dark eyes moist and enlivened as the flesh puckered ever so slightly around them. They positively glistered with vitality."[10] Those glistering eyes do not mesmerize as the old vampire eyes had done. In a decade when most vampires doze, their sheer energy horrifies.

We are supposed to believe that Lestat's exhibitionism arouses his sleeping progenitors, but when Akasha wakes, this primal mother utterly upstages Lestat and his crew. In her vengeful designs, particularly her plot to kill all men, the huge Akasha resembles those dreadful vampiric women who rose, reeking of feminism, in the British 1890s—Rider Haggard's Ayesha, for example, or Arthur Conan Doyle's Miss Penelosa in "The Parasite," or the "rag and a bone and a hank of hair" who will not understand the man she drains in Kipling's poem "The Vampire"—but Akasha is more one-dimensional than the female vampires of the British fin de siècle. Revived from her stony majesty, she has so little complexity that she is scarcely a vampire as Rice defines the species, but a depersonalized female force.

The Queen of the Damned is striking, and strikingly true to the 1980s, in the panoramic sweep with which it diminishes the vampires who were the stars of the first two *Vampire Chronicles*. Akasha is finally defeated by a ritual more ancient even than she is, one performed by female revenants from the prehistoric past. By the novel's ceremonial conclusion, Lestat and his friends have been reduced to the spectatorial role of humans in conventional vampire fantasies: they exist only to wonder and watch.

Like George Hamilton and Frank Langella in the 1970s, Lestat flies, but only under Akasha's grandiose instruction. "I am your true Mother, the Mother who will never abandon you, and I have died and been reborn, too," she proclaims, infantilizing him before dragging him up into the air. "But suddenly I felt her arm around me, and we were rising out of the tower up through the shattered roof. The wind was so fierce it cut my eyelids. I turned toward her. My right arm went round her waist and I buried my head against her shoulder" (p. 235). This terrified burial in shelter has none of the transcendent aspirations of earlier vampire flights. Even at the end, when Akasha has been extinguished and Lestat flies with Louis to London to initiate the plot of the sequel, flight is simply another one of the gadgets with which post-Akasha vampires amuse themselves. Its Shelleyan promise of renewal has become a toy.

Rice's vampires are diminished in the 1980s by the monumental power of their origins. The past for whose embrace they yearn extinguishes the energy that made them dazzling companions. In the 1980s, vampires, like the nations that imagined them, turn wearily back to a crushing past, not only because the future holds no promise, but because so many of them are ill.

Getting Sick

The AIDS epidemic, widely publicized by the early 1980s, infected the decade's already stricken vampires. The blood that had gushed out of Hammer movies was no longer a token of forbidden vitality, but a blight. Once the etiology of AIDS became clear, blood could no longer be the life; vampirism mutated from hideous appetite to nausea. AIDS bestowed nostalgic intensity on Anne Rice's eternally young, beautiful, self-healing men, whose boredom with immortality looked like a heavenly dream to young men turned suddenly mortal.[11] However diminished they became, Louis and Lestat were radiant exceptions to the vampires who shriveled in a plague-stricken, newly censorious culture.

Brian Aldiss's *Dracula Unbound* (1991) is an AIDS-saturated novel about ancient vampires who are newly loathsome. Hovering somewhere between alternative history and revisionist science fiction, *Dracula Unbound* depicts a cosmic evolution vulnerable to accident and steeped in disease. Set in the year 1999, Aldiss's account of time travel from the age of the dinosaurs to a distant sunless future resounds in catastrophes, both celestial and man-made: no regulating nature can repair a volatile cosmos no single tyrant controls.

At the center of this novel is Bram Stoker, a tormented visionary inflicted with "syphilis, the vampire of our amorous natures."[12] Through his illness and his terrifying contact with a Renfield helpless in the last syphilitic stage,[13] Stoker perceives vampire attackers and warns mankind. As Aldiss sees *Dracula,* "It had alerted people to the dangers of vampirism. At the same time, it contained Stoker's encoded message of personal sorrow, as he fell sick of the disease that had ravaged mankind for centuries. As well as the great vampire novel, Stoker had created the great nineteenth-century syphilis novel" (p. 227). In its day, *Dracula* was a compendium of emergent phobias. Twentieth-century America made it a bible of erotic, and then political, liberation. At the elegiac close of the American century it turned into a cry of mourning and warning.

Not only is Aldiss's Stoker defined by his disease; his vampires are sick by definition. Having evolved as predators on cool-blooded dinosaurs, they are allergic to the warm human blood they need to live. Thus they work stealthily and collectively to effect human extinction, a plot the heroic time travelers foil.

These scientifically defined vampires are scarcely individuals, but a mindless corporate body of which a huge horned Dracula is the head. As nonentities, they become the most unsympathetic vampires we have seen. Stoker's were ravenous; even the vampires of 'Salem's Lot bore an unnerving resemblance to their vicious human selves. With their rudimentary brains and collective consciousness, the vampires of *Dracula Unbound* are merely, dangerously, mindless. More absolutely than any of our authors, Aldiss segregates vampires from mortals. His ingenue, a fervent if naïve Christian, approaches the time-traveling Bram Stoker with a question that in the 1970s would have answered itself: "I suppose we should pity the poor vampires, doomed to such a miserable existence. They're really one more oppressed minority, aren't they?" Fred Saberhagen and Chelsea Quinn Yarbro wrote ambitious chronicles about this minority, but Aldiss's Stoker replies with oracular simplicity: "I simply thought of them as a bad lot—a disease, in short" (p. 255). By implication, Bram Stoker has devolved back to his old role as bard of a new homophobia. The urgent empathy of the 1970s has become at best unworldly, at worst politically correct.

The Reagan years oversaw a paradoxical mutation among vampires: they became nonhuman, obstructive, inert, but also susceptible to destruction. New rules sprang up, but now the rules protected vampires rather than protecting mortals against them. In Rice's *Chronicles,* Barbara Hambly's *Those Who Hunt the Night* (1988), and Jewelle Gomez's *The Gilda Stories* (1991), killing one's own kind, especially one's maker, is taboo. Like the wolves that had once sung so chillingly, vampires of the 1980s require the protective legislation of an endangered species. Like wolves—and unlike the lone individualists of the '70s—vampires hunt in packs in the '80s. The corporate body of *Dracula*

Unbound is an extreme instance of a new herd instinct among vampires: as in Anne Rice's gregarious male community whose members exist to fall in love with each other, to be solitary is to be exposed, to drift toward death.

But groups too are vulnerable. In Hambly's *Those Who Hunt the Night,* London's vampires are being murdered en masse: an amateur detective must save them from the manufactured vampire who feeds on them. In a culture turning from humanism to computers and cyborgs, in which authentic transcendence is associated not with nature or bodies, but with "a cybernetic organism, a hybrid of machine and organism, a creature of social reality as well as a creature of fiction," even uninfected vampires are debilitated because trapped in outmoded organicism.[14] Originally unnatural, vampires as a species are now abandoned in a nature withering before fabricated cybernetic brains.[15]

In the 1960s, the sun began to replace the increasingly problematic cross as authorized antivampire weapon. In Hammer movies, the sun was an elite killer: it both isolated Dracula and consecrated him while his female minions writhed and squirmed under the commonplace stake. By 1979, Frank Langella's solar death was an Icarus-like flight toward a center of energy that mirrored his own. The sun is less selective in the Reaganesque years: now associated with fire or explosives rather than glory, it becomes an efficient agent of mass destruction. The sun in *Interview with the Vampire* and Kathryn Bigelow's scorched western movie *Near Dark* (1987) is effective because it kills everyone equally. As vampires become perishable, the sun that kills them goes from a mythic agent of phoenixlike consecration to an indiscriminate explosive.

Increasingly susceptible to radiation burns, vampires sicken even when the sun doesn't shine. In Newman's *Anno Dracula,* most are born to rot: "Few vampires lived as long as they would have unturned" (p. 123), for "the bloodline of Vlad Tepes is polluted. . . . One would have to be addle-pated with disease to drink from such a well. But London is full of very sick vampires" (p. 166). In *Anno Dracula,* as in many recent works, vampire sickness is a sickness of the source. Like the origin quests that pervade Reaganesque vampire stories, *Anno Dracula's* obsession with bloodlines casts a pall of determinism even over metamorphosis. The sickness of Dracula's London is not a moral metaphor, but a state that is preordained.

But *Anno Dracula* also features a vampire with a pure bloodline: the aptly named Geneviève Dieudonné. As well-intentioned as Saint-Germain, though not as learned or percipient, Geneviève is a harmonizing alternative to Dracula's sick spawn. The contrapuntal Geneviève and Dracula exemplify the contradictory strains of vampirism in the AIDS years: they are diseases and carriers of disease, but at the same time, they are angelic incarnations of healing. In a culture haunted by the danger of pleasure and the deaths of the young, vampire immortality becomes both trespass and grace.

Patrick Whalen's *Night Thirst* splits its vampires into opposed species. The most common and dangerous are the New Ones, bestial mass devourers without consciousness whom no rituals can kill—only radiation. Their coming is that of a personified virus: "The disease was breaking out in Seattle like a virulent rampant plague."[16] But the two vampire Ancients, Gregory and Braille, are not only wise and loving: they have magical healing power.

An evil government agency abducts these angelic creatures, aiming to patent their blood. As one villain explains: "Think of it, John. Braille's living proof that there's a substance in this world with the properties to end every major disease we know about, make the body heal at an incredible rate, and might even end the aging process" (p. 18). The vision of vampires as inherently medicinal haunts works of this period. Like Whalen's Braille, Whitley Strieber's splendid immortal Miriam in *The Hunger* (1981) is ignominiously imprisoned in a hospital, her mystic body invaded by scientific probes that would turn her into a cure for mortality. The restorative and the infectious vampire—the angel and the germ—fight each other. The former is violated by humanity's overweening thirst for life; the latter, like AIDS or cancer, is a violator of that life. At least once, though, the two strains come together in an AIDS vampire romance. Dan Simmons's complex *Children of the Night* turns back to the vampire-saviors of the 1970s, but in keeping with his depressed

decade, Simmons makes his savior not a finely tuned consciousness like Yarbro's Saint-Germain, but a sick baby.

Children of the Night is not quite historical horror, nor is it
alternative history. Set in 1991 (the year of its composition), in
the chaotic demoralization of post-Ceauşescu Romania, it neither protests tyranny, as historical horror does, nor explains it
by inserting vampires, as alternative history does. In *Children of
the Night,* as in Simmons's earlier *Carrion Comfort* (1989), the
waste of history is assumed. Vlad Tepes, the immortal spirit of
Romanian oppression, does take over the narrative at times, but
if this gloating Vlad is not the savior he was in the 1970s, neither is he entirely unsympathetic: he is simply a tenacious political pro. The controllable theater of action is not politics, but
biology and genetics, as good doctors and evil fanatics struggle
for a blood whose holiness AIDS has reinvigorated. Kate Neu-
man, brilliant American doctor and paragon of womanliness,
explains this restored holiness: "Blood has—until recent decades—been the source of superstition and awe. . . . Now, with
AIDS, it's regaining that terror and mystery."[17]

The blood belongs to Joshua, a Romanian baby Kate has
adopted. The baby suffers from a rare AIDS-like disease, but he
possesses an ancient recessive gene—the biological origin of
vampirism—that transforms externally taken blood into a healing mechanism. Once, those with this gene drank blood; now
medical science can inject them with hemoglobin. Science re-
constitutes vampirism into a universal cure: like the violated Ancients in *Night Thirst,* Simmons's vampire baby is the personified
antidote to all diseases.

Though infection and political corruption appear intractable in *Children of the Night,* doctors are no longer oppressors,
but the only credible redeemers. They alone isolate the two
strains of vampirism, disease and healing, that converge in Joshua's mystic genes: "You have to be dying of a rare blood disease
in order to gain virtual immortality from the same disease," one
of the heroes explains. Moreover, unlike Dracula's vampirism,
"it's not catching" (p. 217). The medical science that had debased its prey in the 1970s is, in *Children of the Night,* the salvation of humans and vampires.

For Simmons as for so many writers in the '80s and early '90s, politics is despair. In *Carrion Comfort,* Simmons's psychic vampire epic, the vampires who both exemplify and inspire lust for power will never, as a species, disappear; in *Children of the Night,* post-Ceauşescu Romania is so corrupt that it scarcely matters whether Vlad Tepes survives. *The Vampire Lestat* looked for salvation in origins; *Children of the Night* finds it in genetics. Both novels seek hope only in predetermined structures, historical or biological, that neither mortal nor vampire can affect.

The infant angel/vampire with transfiguring power has antecedents in American myth-making: he is the giant Star Baby who floats down to the audience through space at the end of Stanley Kubrick's *2001: A Space Odyssey* (1968), and he is also the child Danny Glick in *'Salem's Lot* who, with a "high, sweet, evil laugh," sucks the life from a sick man. But the Star Baby and Danny Glick were, for better or worse, some kind of infantine extract of adult potential, while Simmons's utterly characterless baby exists only in his genetic makeup. He neither soars through space nor sucks blood; he is simply tossed back and forth like a football. In 1992, angel and vampire are not actors, but involuntary carriers of their own potential natures.[18]

Joshua, the most inadvertent of vampire/saviors, might cure AIDS with an extract of his blood, but he is not infected with it. This baby is and is not a vampire; he is and is not a savior; he is and is not an AIDS baby. Simmons's AIDS novel is purified of actual contact with AIDS, just as the novel's plot purifies AIDS from association with homosexual or any other transgressive sexuality. Like goodness and evil in *Children of the Night,* AIDS is refined into an involuntary condition detached from desire.

Like so many lost boys of the 1980s, Joshua needs a father. In the course of Kate's complicated medical, romantic, and maternal adventures, two of her prospective husbands are conveniently killed, leaving her with an activist renegade priest who is the novel's most seasoned authority and thus Joshua's best father. This implicit search for a sheltering family headed by the right patriarch is very much of its decade, but by the time Kate and the priest and Joshua soar—not on bat wings, but in a stolen helicopter—above Romania and all politics, with "no sense now of national boundaries, or of nations" (p. 375), the bad vampires have been blown up, while benevolent medicine has reconstructed the baby vampire. *Children of the Night* begins as a vampire story but ends, like so many Reaganesque plots, with vampirism and the urge that creates it domesticated out of existence. Authentic vampires of the '80s turned back to the shadows, proliferating on the margins of the restored patriarchal family.

Queer Shadows

On Valentine's Day, 1993, I attended a conference of Queer Theorists in the California desert at which a transsexual named Sandy Stone theorized her—and his—existence by summoning vampires. Sandy Stone is a performance artist who has not exchanged one gender for another: s/he embodies both. Shadows of a woman dart out of the man; glimpses of a man flicker in and out of the woman. Only by evoking the freedom of the vampire could s/he convey the transcendence of boundaries to which transsexuality aspires. Sandy Stone's vampires owe something to Anne Rice's, but for most of the conference members, they seemed to be a species of their own, one related only tangentially to the mainstream undead.

Sandy Stone did not so much describe vampires as attempt to embody them—"not the bloodsucking part, but the other part." As unnatural actors, vampires represent freedom from activity—even, it seems, from sexuality: "What do we get from listening to him [the vampire] talk about the fragrant blood thundering through [human] veins and watching the pulse in their temples and their throats and watching the silken skin going taut and the bones of their faces?" To emulate a vampire is to be a spectator disappearing into a spectator: we listen, talk, watch, without touching or becoming. Because they glide on the margins of activity, Sandy Stone's vampires dissipate rigid structures of gender and received identity, freeing their acolytes to "celebrate the change, the passing forms."[19]

Stone's incantatory presentation resembled a séance more than a conventional academic lecture, suggesting that for some believers, vampires have returned to the spectral form they adopted in the nineteenth-century theater. With the help of the vampire trap, Planché's Ruthven slithered through solid walls; Sandy Stone's slithers through solid constructions of gender and subjectivity. In the Reagan years and their aftermath, vampires' bodies wilted, but for one group of believers at least, they renewed themselves by retreating back into the shadows.[20]

The polarizing conservatism that intensified in America after 1980 generated its own antagonist: an autonomous, politically based homosexual culture that, like the women's movement of the 1970s, fought free of traditional medical and moral labels. Queer Theory (like the feminist theory that dominated academic feminism in the 1980s) is an abstraction of a political surge toward self-definition and determination. The provenance of Queer Theory is language, but as Teresa de Lauretis makes clear in her introduction to a special issue of the journal *differences,* its ambitions are sweepingly social: "[The word] elsewhere is not a utopia, an otherworldly or future place and time. It is already here, in the essays' work to deconstruct the silences of history and of our own discursive constructions, in the differently erotic mappings of the body, and in the imaging and enacting of new forms of community by the other-wise desiring subjects of this queer theory."[21] For de Lauretis, Queer Theory is a solvent, breaking down barriers and merging categories to produce transformations inconceivable in the Foucauldian academic mainstream. Its vampires are similarly unorthodox agents of reconstruction.

Queer Theorists like Sandy Stone adopt vampires just as many feminists did in the 1960s and 70s, but their vampires are far from the sexy, toothy transfigurers feminists embraced. Through the 1960s and '70s, George Stade's paradigm of Dracula as "an apparition of what we repress, traditional eros"[22] more or less held. Feminist writers like Yarbro and Charnas politicized Stade's paradigm, but they never rejected vampires who performed their social critique by becoming superior, tenderer, more versatile heterosexual lovers whose bloodsucking was a gesture toward seditious intimacy.

Like Sandy Stone, theorists of the AIDS years tend to excise "the bloodsucking part," turning instead to a slithery, polymorphous creature. Christopher Craft's seminal essay, "'Kiss Me with Those Red Lips': Gender and Inversion in Bram Stoker's

Dracula," exemplifies a vampire paradigm-shift by presenting a Dracula potent in his *non*-traditional eros. Craft's Dracula, like Lewis Carroll's Cheshire Cat, expresses his dynamic contradictions in a mouth so significant it scarcely bothers to bite: it simply *is.*

> With its soft flesh barred by hard bone, its red crossed by white, this mouth compels opposites and contrasts into a frightening unity, and it asks some disturbing questions. Are we male or are we female? Do we have penetrators or orifices? And if both, what does that mean? And what about our bodily fluids, the red and the white? What are the relations between blood and semen, milk and blood? Furthermore, this mouth, bespeaking the subversion of stable and lucid distinctions of gender, is the mouth of all vampires, male and female.[23]

This multigendered but scarcely toothed mouth defines the Reaganesque vampire at its most potent. Like Sandy Stone's transsexual engorger of subjectivities, Craft's Dracula, who exists to dissolve "opposites and contrasts," is more shadow than substance: his role is to expose the insubstantiality of the barriers that differentiate men from women, death from life. Dracula's own insubstantiality is implicit in Craft's title, which, like Sandy Stone's lecture, is more incantation than description, for "Kiss Me with Those Red Lips" is an imperative. Craft conjures his vampire as Stone does, praying that he will descend, kiss, and free his acolyte. Positioning himself as a polymorphous Renfield, Craft summons a Dracula so inclusive no melodrama can contain him.[24]

Men do their best to conjure a vampire they claim only to describe, but the most unabashedly mediumistic vampire-summoner I know is a woman, Sue-Ellen Case.[25] Like Craft's essay, Case's "Tracking the Vampire" is more incantation than argument. When I first heard it as a lecture at the University of Pennsylvania, Sue-Ellen Case read in a hushed, intent voice that led me to expect her vampire to materialize around her, irradiating Penn's dreary little lecture room.

This incantatory intensity survives on the page. The vampire Case tracks—the omnipresent but elusive "double 'she'"—

is always just about to enter the essay, but as the essence of the forbidden, she must lurk outside its boundaries. Like Craft's vampire, she is the shadow of acceptable substance: "the taboo-breaker, the monstrous, the uncanny. Like the Phantom of the Opera, the queer dwells underground, below the operatic over-tures of the dominant; frightening to look at, desiring, as it plays its own organ, producing its own music" (p. 3). Like the Opera Ghost who permeated Bela Lugosi's Dracula, Case's under-ground double "she" is most potent as sound. The echo, not the blood, is her life.[26]

Case's rather perfunctory survey of actual vampires in litera-ture and film finds them all inadequate to the charged presence in the wings or under the stage. Her bare concluding statement is, like Christopher Craft's title, more invocation than descrip-tion: "Finally, here, the vampire can enter" (p. 17). But she never does.

The spectral talisman of Queer Theory looks like the ghosts of the Victorian stage, but s/he performs the same function as the archetypal vampire whose solidity reassured Jungian critics in the 1960s. The volatile social changes of the '60s produced a Dracula who, to vampire-loving literary critics, was a reliably immutable presence in the unconscious. In the Reaganesque years, when reaction and AIDS seemed to petrify the future, crit-ics longed for *im*permanence: Queer Theorists apotheosized a phantasmal, unsettled spirit. Even the countercultural vampire is a product, if a resistant one, of its age.

Case's grand finale—"Finally, here, the vampire can en-ter"—is followed by a hopeful endnote: "This paper should have ended with a discussion of [Jewelle] Gomez's *Gilda Stories,* which appeared in print as my manuscript goes to press" (p. 19). *The Gilda Stories* is now in print. The stories offer a compelling ac-count of survival in a contaminated society, but because their vampires are infected with the anesthetizing virtue of the 1980s, they do not quite justify Case's occult flourish.

Jewelle Gomez's account of a black lesbian vampire and her chosen companions from slavery in 1850 to ecological catastro-phe in 2050 is, like other Reaganesque vampire fiction, a diluted vision of a benevolent endangered species. Gilda and her friends are givers, not killers. As a fledgling, Gilda learns her nurturing mission: "It is through our connection with life, not death, that we live. . . . We give what's needed—energy, dreams, ideas. . . . And when we feel it is right, when the need is great on both sides, we can re-create others like ourselves to share life with us."[27] Only bad vampires are violent and power-mad, and they are not so much authentic vampires as their creators' sick mistakes. A true vampire is a guardian angel.

Instead of killing mortals, Gilda and her friends bestow on them edifying dreams after taking fortifying sips of blood. Vampirism is not bloodsucking or feeding or the dark gift; it becomes "the exchange," an act of empathy, not power, whose first principle is, "feel what they are needing, not what you are hungering for" (p. 50). Like the construction of lesbianism *The Gilda Stories* celebrates, vampirism is purged of aggression. A model of collective restraint, Gilda's family seems far from the vampire Sue-Ellen Case is tracking, "the taboo-breaker, the monstrous, the uncanny" who lurks under the stage of visible society. Like the holy baby in Dan Simmons's *Children of the Night,* Gilda and her friends are medicinal.

Gilda is not the first good vampire we have met, but she is the most clannish good vampire: she exists entirely apart from antagonism. Yarbro's Saint-Germain mingled precariously in mortal culture, cherishing its beauty and deploring its destructiveness, but Gilda must shed her identification with mortals. As a result, the emphasis of *Gilda* falls on her virtuous extended family, whose primary antagonists are bad vampires, not the corrupted human world. As in Rice's *Chronicles,* vampirism in *Gilda* is a select club, but Gilda's club is purged of conflict and confrontation.[28]

Works like *Gilda* embody the vampires Queer Theorists invoke, but these vampires are more endangered than dangerous. At the end of *Gilda,* Gomez's saving remnant can only protect itself against a contaminated world: "The cities and the principles on which most societies are built have been poisoned. While this is of great concern to us, we have to remain apart to protect ourselves. We must all make safe places" (p. 214). The colony has gained defensive prudence, but it presents no threat to established power.

Gilda is clearly meant to be an enlightened response to the

sexism inherent in the lesbian vampire tradition, but Gilda's virtue defangs her into another paralyzing stereotype: that of the
good woman. Gomez's vampires are inhibited by their self-
righteous decade, whose protests dissipate in piety. In the nineteenth century, Coleridge's Geraldine and Le Fanu's Carmilla
had infiltrated father-ruled households, displacing hierarchical
authority by subversive intimacy with daughters. Gilda confronts no powerful patriarchs; she and her extended family
thrive by withdrawing into safe places. They gain each other's
approval, but they lose their diffusive menace. After 1980, even
countercultural vampires are segregated from anger and power.[29]

The segregation of vampires from mortal society, their complicity in a restorative ideology that re-erects barriers—not only
between vampire and mortal, but between male and female, rich
and nonrich, queer and straight, white Christians and alien
Others—affects even the vampires who spring from the homosexual culture that, in literature at least, came into its own in
the 1980s.

The recovery of vampire homoeroticism was itself a restoration in which a species that had been sanitized reclaimed its
literary origin from Stoker's influential bowdlerization. But Byron and Polidori's gentleman-predators and Le Fanu's ardent
Carmilla were above all interpenetrative: their power was the
response they aroused in mortals. Their late-twentieth-century
counterparts Lestat and Gilda have learned identity politics.
They live and love in enclaves of their own, scarcely bothering
to infiltrate mortal drawing-rooms or bedrooms or boardrooms.
In the Reaganesque years, they are so clannish and self-enclosed
that they present no threat.

Near Dark: Vampires Die

> "I ain't a person anymore; don't know what I am. . . . I'm sick."
> "Those people back there, they wasn't normal."
> Caleb and his father in *Near Dark*

Vampires' co-optation by a conservative social enterprise
that aims to restore discredited authorities is scarcely new, nor
is it necessarily life-threatening; it is the impetus of Stoker's *Dracula*. *Dracula* lives on in so many incarnations precisely, I think,

because of Stoker's doomed attempt to place more faith in manliness than he does in vampires. I want to end with a similar
work from the late 1980s, Kathryn Bigelow's *Near Dark*. In my
opinion, *Near Dark* is the best vampire work to come out of the
Reaganesque years, not because it will ever be as influential as
Dracula—few besides vampire aficionados have heard of this re-
markably original movie—but because, like *Dracula*, it tries so
strenuously to submerge its vampires in paternalistic morality
that it makes us cry out for something new.

In fact if not in stereotype, *Near Dark* is a woman's film;
Kathryn Bigelow not only directed it, but coauthored the screenplay with Eric Red, making her our first female creator of cinematic vampires.[30] In fiction, by 1987, novelists like Chelsea
Quinn Yarbro and Suzy McKee Charnas had absorbed vampires
into a female tradition; Anne Rice had become a famous vampire mage; but in film, the few woman directors who managed
to make movies steered clear of horrors, voluntarily or not.

Bigelow's vision is scarcely feminine: she is not, like Jewelle
Gomez, horrified by violence, nor does she refine murder into
aestheticism as Anne Rice does. *Near Dark* is full of a gratuitous
macho slaughter Bigelow's camera relishes as much as her vampires do. A long fight sequence in which her hillbilly vampires
kill the inhabitants of a bar with sickening ingenuity reminds
us that vampires are cannibals before they are anything more
high-minded. Still, as she does in her later *Blue Steel* (1990),
Bigelow handles conventionally masculine genres with a sly infusion of parody. Like George Romero's living dead, her vampires enjoy their food; one of them slurps blood off his fingers
with the down-home appreciation, "It's finger-lickin' good!"
Moreover, like a populist cousin of Anne Rice, Bigelow makes
her account of vampire predation a recovery of origins.

Unlike *The Vampire Lestat*, nothing in *Near Dark* is un-
American or antidemocratic; no one visits glittering Europe or
worships jeweled Egyptian statues. Bigelow's vampire gang ca-
reens around the Southwest plains in a series of banged-up vans;
Caleb, the stricken young hero, tries to take a bus from Texas to
his Oklahoma home, but he is too sick to travel; these vagrants
cling to their American roots, moving only in aimless circles.
Their origin is the Southwest itself: Bigelow fixes them in the

western genre, with its rigid polarization of good vs. bad, settlers vs. aliens, the family home vs. the open spaces. Cast in this primary American melodrama, deprived of exotic countries and times, Bigelow's vampires play melodrama's traditional villainous role. They are robust and funny, as villains often are, but they cast no shadow on the good.

The good in *Near Dark* is exemplified by Caleb's strong father, his pretty little sister, and the family dinner table, at which milk is the prominently displayed drink. Unlike his counterparts in earlier, more iconoclastic films, this paradigm of paternal authority has nothing in common with vampires. In *'Salem's Lot,* a more comprehensive account of vampire democracy in another American heartland, the young hero ruefully admits his father's proximity to vampirism: "'My father . . . he would have made a very successful vampire. Maybe as good as Barlow, in time. He . . . he was good at everything he tried. Maybe too good.'"[31] Fathers in the Reagan years are spared such penetrating sons. The untouchable patriarch in *Near Dark* is, like so many good characters of his era, a celebration of segregation.

In his protective perfection, Caleb's father needs no wife. In *The Lost Boys,* which also appeared in 1987, a single mother carelessly exposes her sons to evil, but a single father is an altogether different figure, one who not only guards his son, but knows how to cure him. In *Near Dark,* vampirism is unquestionably a disease, not an empowering endowment. Unlike Lucy and Mina in Badham's 1979 *Dracula,* whose medical fathers specialized in sadistic malpractice, Caleb is lucky enough to have a father who is not only an authentic authority, but a good doctor.

Mae, the vampire who infects him, is no buxom temptress like the Hammer women, thrusting out her cleavage and popping her fangs; she is a boyish teenager licking a Dairy Queen.[32] Mae's boyishness makes her less threatening to an innocent like Caleb—though his innocence doesn't stop him from some coercive maneuvers suggestive of date rape. When, despite her pleading, he refuses to drive her home without a kiss, Mae gives him the kiss he demands, then leaves him to stagger around the plains retching in agony as the morning sun blazes into the sky. "He looks sick," his little sister Sarah remarks in ladylike understatement as the vampire commune abducts him into their van.

He stays sick through most of the movie. For Caleb at least, vampirism is an even more uncomfortably debilitating transformation than it was for Michael in *The Lost Boys*. Like Michael, Caleb makes a terrible vampire, for he is too squeamish to kill. Anne Rice's vampires surged instantaneously into their new identities, but though Mae prods him to discover his instinct— "Just feel, feel what's in you"—he has no instinct. He lurches around getting weaker and whiter while Mae kills for him, letting him drink from her wrist. He wins the gang's approval at last by getting them out of a police raid. Just as he is beginning to enjoy his new life, his father rescues him from a motel portentously named "Godspeed," entering just as "America the Beautiful" blares on television over a grand American flag.

When Caleb asks plaintively, "Daddy; Daddy; did you ever transfuse a person?" his father proceeds to do just that, infusing Caleb with his own healthful blood and expelling the vampire poison. Caleb's father is no specialist like Van Helsing; he is a mere veterinarian, schooled in neither science nor the occult. Nevertheless—and for the first time in vampire literature—his bizarre medical treatment succeeds. De-transformed and rehumanized, Caleb is miraculously cured of what should have been terminal vampirism. In the literary history of the vampire myth, no father or doctor, since Stoker or before him, was able to undo vampirism. This patriarch's triumphant transfusion reverses a tradition of consistent failure; his healing powers rest on no traditional base, signaling not the restoration of the patriarch, but his metamorphosis. He can make things un-happen, turn back the clock.

Like the homesteads in all westerns, the father's house is pure but not secure. Caleb walks in the sun with Sarah, but Mae returns for him. All vampire allegiance transfused away, he says simply, "I belong here, Mae. This is my family," but while he and Mae embrace on the lawn, the gang is kidnapping Sarah upstairs. In the classic western confrontation, Caleb destroys the vampire posse and rescues his sister: one gang member explodes in his truck while the sun incinerates the others. Mae saves Sarah and survives the conflagration. Tenderly, Caleb takes her back to his father's house where his good blood transfuses her back to mortality. The movie ends with a still of the de-transformed Mae perched unsteadily on the paternal operating table with the sun falling on her. Caleb, who has taken on his father's protective role, engulfs her unsteady figure in a sheltering embrace.

Though we see her only through Caleb's eyes, Mae is the central character in *Near Dark*. Whereas Caleb has no vampire instinct, she is adept at undeath. As Jenny Wright plays her, Mae is more than a tomboy: most of her fellow vampires are clods, but she is close to the lithe, mercurial, androgynous vampires of 1980s Queer Theorists. Her mouth might be the one featured in Christopher Craft's gender-blending "'Kiss Me with Those Red Lips'"; Mae rather than the solid, single-minded Gilda should walk into Sue-Ellen Case's essay at its incantatory conclusion. Jenny Wright's Mae lacks fangs, snarls, and the usual accoutrements, but she suggests another order of being.

Her attraction to vampirism has less to do with bloodthirst than with thirst for immortality. She seduces Caleb by emptying Dracula's paean to night: "Listen to the night; listen hard; it's so bright it'll blind you," she whispers. "Hear the night; it's death." There are no distracting children of Mae's night; she has no control over animals or interest in them; unlike Dracula but like Max Schreck's Nosferatu, she repels horses. Le Fanu's Carmilla cuddled into her incarnation as a strangely elongated cat, but Mae reaches away from animalism toward inhuman vastness: "I'll still be here when the light from that star gets down here to Earth in a billion years." Her disaffection for animals, her awe at night and immortality, are nullified when, at the end, a paternalistic veterinarian restores her to the sun and an organic life span.

When they first meet, Caleb lassos Mae with bullying affection, but she resists him with her superior vampire strength. As his vampire mentor, she patiently props him up, defending him from the others and covering for his ineptitude. Undead and in control, she need not defer to male supremacy. Like Yarbro's Olivia and those other freestanding vampire women of the 1970s, Mae is immunized against patriarchy. In the restorative ending, though, Caleb and his father lasso her in earnest.

In the final still, where the father-controlled Caleb looms paternally around her, Mae's powers are gone and she has been surgically restored to a proper daughterly place. So, by implication, are all those flying, biting, self-directing women who came before her, and so are women in the world outside the theater. Kathryn Bigelow's account of a vampirism that is medically reversible is a story of spaces lost. The astronomical immensity of the night sky, the empty amplitude of the western plains, contract into a freeze-frame of enfolding arms.

Homer and Sarah, the children in *Near Dark*, repeat Mae's reversion to confinement. Homer is a chunky child-vampire who out-machos the tough adults around him; he smokes, plays cards, kills, and bursts into antic dances when the vampires torch a bar. Like the little girl who eats her parents in *Night of the Living Dead,* Homer with his blood-smeared mouth is a deceptively cute camera subject. Like Anne Rice's Claudia, he grumbles about being an adult trapped in a child's body. Homer exemplifies a lesson familiar to vampire aficionados at least: with their mask of innocence, children are the most successful vampires of all.

Anyone who has followed vampires to this point would expect Homer to be at least as committed a vampire as Stephen King's Danny Glick. The child-vampires of the 1960s and '70s implicitly refuted sentimental constructions of innocence; the prototypical psychic vampires, these children exemplified in its original form the monstrous energy of dependency. The child-monsters popular in the 1970s, of which child-vampires were breed champions, abetted that decade's ideological erosion of paternalism. Like women, children who were monsters broke free of controlling patriarchal definition. They did not need to be taken care of and told who they were. In however antisocial a manner, child-vampires fed themselves.

Homer is one of those defiantly self-sustaining creatures until he meets pretty little Sarah, with whom he falls devoutly in love. All innocence and sweetness, Sarah has none of Claudia's savagery: like a classic movie daughter, she exists to cuddle, to play and pose, to be abducted and rescued by men. Homer kidnaps her into the vampire gang, not to molest her but to adore her. When she is rescued, he flings himself after her into the blazing sun, crying her name as he shrivels and burns. Finally, he explodes. We are meant to see Homer's macho protestations as a cute, Tom Sawyer–ish pose: underneath, he is a child after all as patronizing adults want to see them—innocent, needy, unable to take care of himself. Like Mae after her transfusion, Homer shakes off vampirism and reverts to the human being that controlling adults love. For both woman and child, the consequence of shedding vampirism is suicide.

The happy ending of *Near Dark* is as checkered as its title. Stereotypes that never existed are restored: crouching daughterly women, innocent children, omnipotent doctors, and benignly caretaking men. If vampirism is a wasting disease like AIDS, its cure is a blessing, but if it contains immortality, secret strength, and forbidden identities, its domestication is a death more painful than Homer's. Bigelow's title carries the same mixed message, for in the sun-struck ending, the cured lovers are nowhere near a dark that in this movie is less assaultive than day. At the end, like vampirism, dark is lost.

If, however, a restored patriarch has gained control, exerting powers no patriarch has had before, healing out of existence a myth that for two centuries has allowed us to envision lives beyond the constraints of death and social expectations, then we are indeed near dark, for Bigelow's paternalistic happy ending is the end of enlightenment.

NEAR DARK IS NOT AN ELEGY for the death of vampires, but it is, I think, a proclamation of the end of the vampire cycle that began with revisionist éclat in the 1970s. In 1987, vampires were already suffering the loss of will that accompanied the dominance of Reaganism and AIDS. The wisest of them were fatigued: unable to bear continual changing times, the elders in Anne Rice's and Jewelle Gomez's novels crawled out of their stories to die. The vampires who live on are afflicted by this same lapse of initiative. The reversibility of vampirism in 1980s movies—in *The Lost Boys* and *Fright Night* as well as *Near Dark*—suggests that at the end of the twentieth century, vampirism is wearing down and vampires need a long restorative sleep. They will awaken; they always have; as Stoker's Dracula boasted,[33] time is on their side.

Notes

Introduction

1. Quoted in the *Philadelphia Inquirer* (May 7, 1991), p. A24.
2. Matson cartoon in the *New York Observer* (September 7, 1992), p. 1.
3. James Twitchell, for instance, acknowledges that adolescents of both genders go to horror movies, but he goes on to explain their appeal by a Freudian "Ur-myth of adolescence" that is clearly based on the fantasies of boys. See *Dreadful Pleasures: An Anatomy of Modern Horror* (New York and Oxford: Oxford University Press, 1985), pp. 99–100. David J. Skal is more assured in quarantining girls like myself from vicarious bloodlust: "In a suburbanized, plasticized America [of the 1950s], monster culture answered a need among *male* baby boomers for haunted houses instead of tract houses, an ancient, Europeanized structure of meaning." *Hollywood Gothic: The Tangled Web of* Dracula *from Novel to Stage to Screen* (New York and London: W. W. Norton, 1990), p. 190; my italics. Walter Kendrick barely qualifies the maleness of his "horror maven": "This character exists in various subspecies, though *he is most likely to be male,* to be between fifteen and forty-five years old, and American." Walter Kendrick, *The Thrill of Fear: 250 Years of Scary Entertainment* (New York: Grove Weidenfeld, 1991), p. 257; my italics.
4. See Noël Carroll, *The Philosophy of Horror, or Paradoxes of the Heart* (New York and London: Routledge, 1990), p. 2: "But what seems to have happened in the first half of the seventies is that horror, so to speak, entered the mainstream. Its audience was no longer specialized, but widened, and horror novels became increasingly easy to come by."
5. *The Penguin Book of Vampire Stories,* ed. Alan Ryan (New York: Penguin, 1988), and *Vampyres: Lord Byron to Count Dracula,* ed. Christopher Frayling (London: Faber and Faber, 1992).

Chapter 1

1. George Gordon, Lord Byron, "Fragment of a Novel" (1816; reprinted in *The Penguin Book of Vampire Stories,* ed. Alan Ryan [New York: Penguin, 1988], p. 2). This volume hereafter cited as *Penguin.*
2. Eve Kosofsky Sedgwick, *Between Men: English Literature and Male Homosocial Desire* (New York: Columbia University Press, 1985), p. 91. Sedgwick's canon—"*Caleb Williams, Frankenstein, Confessions of a Justified Sinner,* probably *Melmoth [the Wanderer],* possibly *The Italian*"—perplexingly omits the homoerotic vampire tales that were being written at the same time. Technically, these are part of Sedgwick's story; from the Byron-Polidori accounts of young men traveling with vampires to Jonathan Harker's encounter with one at the end of his journey—an encounter chaster in Stoker's novel than in the films it generated—nineteenth-century male vampires surely persecute and compel other males. The sensuous lure of their friendship, however, is more complex than the anality that engages Sedgwick's haunted heroes.
3. David Pirie indulges in the usual hasty confusion of vampires in *A*

Heritage of Horror: The English Gothic Cinema, 1946–1972 (New York: Avon, 1973), p. 83: "[Polidori's] *The Vampyre* reveals the link between Byron and Dracula to be so close that it is impossible not to regard them as literary cousins; for Stoker's novel brought to a temporary fruition the strain of the Fatal Nobleman with piercing eyes and deadly ambitions which Byron had earlier lifted from the pages of Mrs. Radcliffe and turned into a major character cult." Vampires, like other minorities, may look alike to outsiders, but the differences among them are more telling than the surface similarities.

4. Quoted in D. L. Macdonald, *Poor Polidori: A Critical Biography of the Author of "The Vampyre"* (Toronto: University of Toronto Press, 1991), p. 102. Hereafter cited in the text as "Macdonald."

5. See Paul Barber, *Vampires, Burial, and Death: Folklore and Reality* (New Haven and London: Yale University Press, 1988), p. 67.

6. *The Poetical Works of Lord Byron* (London: Oxford University Press, 1960), p. 259, ll. 755–60.

7. "With few exceptions, folkloric vampires do not travel. They are not itinerants, like Dracula, and nothing is said of their being able to circumvent their obligation to remain in their graves by taking with them a supply of earth. . . . Like ghosts, vampires are usually bound to a particular location[.]" "The dead are most dangerous, as a rule, to those closest to them in life" (Barber, *Vampires, Burial, and Death*, pp. 67, 194). See also James B. Twitchell, *The Living Dead: A Study of the Vampire in Romantic Literature* (Durham, N.C.: Duke University Press, 1981), p. 10: "The vampire never wantonly destroys—in fact, his initial victims are preordained; they are those whom he loved most when alive." Byron's Darvell and Polidori's Ruthven are, as far as I know, the first vampires who re-create their desires by ignoring their genealogical and emotional origins: their mobility is psychic as well as geographical. Bram Stoker will have his cake and eat it by making his Dracula an itinerant who must nevertheless drag along on his travels cumbersome cartons of earth from his homeland, creating annoying logistical problems for vampires in the twentieth century.

8. Macdonald makes the similar point that Ruthven is the first of many traveling vampires. He is also the first aristocrat and the first vividly individualized vampire, as opposed to the automatonlike animated corpses of folklore (pp. 192–96).

9. It is a Freudian cliché, and a lazy one, to assert that all horror literature is a disguised reenactment of a universal fear of incest. See, for instance, James B. Twitchell's disappointingly reductive *Dreadful Pleasures: An Anatomy of Modern Horror* (New York and Oxford: Oxford University Press, 1985), p. 93: "The fear of incest underlies all horror myths in our culture that are repeatedly told for more than one generation." One might just as well say that the fear of *anti*-incest—of being carried beyond one's family, genetic or special—"underlies all horror myths." There are, however, too many forces shaping our fears to universalize them by any single unchanging formula.

10. Demons like Keats's Lamia do bring intensity to some Romantic marriages, which seem to come alive when they are marriages to the dead. For a more detailed account of the perversities of Romantic marriage iconography, see my "Jane Austen and Romantic Imprisonment," in *Jane Austen in a Social Context*, ed. David Monahagan (London: Macmillan; New York: Barnes and Noble, 1981), pp. 9–27.

11. Twitchell, *The Living Dead*, pp. 145–60, reads *The Rime of the Ancient*

Mariner wittily and plausibly as a vampire tale in which the Mariner recounts his journey into vampirism. Perhaps because predator and prey are women, the vampirism of Coleridge's *Christabel* moves to the surface of the narrative, rather than remaining subterranean.

12. "Sensuality, promise, terror, sublimity, idyllic pleasure, intense energy: the Orient as a figure in the pre-Romantic, pretechnical Orientalist imagination of late-eighteenth-century Europe was really a chameleonlike quality. . . . But this free-floating Orient would be severely curtailed with the advent of academic Orientalism[,]" which began to crystallize in the 1830s. Edward W. Said, *Orientalism* (1978; reprint, New York: Vintage, 1979), pp. 118–19.

13. See, for instance, the sixteenth-century Prussian tale "The Shoemaker of Silesia," in which a returned, predatory, and very fleshly husband is referred to merely as a "ghost." Quoted in Barber, *Vampires, Burial, and Death,* pp. 10–13.

14. Mary Shelley, introduction to the third edition of *Frankenstein; or, The Modern Prometheus,* ed. James Rieger (1818; reprint, Chicago and London: University of Chicago Press, 1982), p. 225. Christopher Frayling reminds credulous readers that Mary Shelley's account of the genesis of modern horror contains more legend than fact, not least because there were *five*, not four, in the ghostly party: in her later zeal for respectability, Shelley omitted either the unprepossessing commoner Polidori or the still more disreputable Claire Clairmont. See Frayling, ed., *Vampyres: Lord Byron to Count Dracula* (London: Faber and Faber, 1992), pp. 12–17.

15. Our own ghosts are a specialized species. For example, Peter Straub's *Ghost Story* (1979) is as rationalized a story of recurrence and revenge as *Hamlet:* a young girl, Eva Galli, returns in various forms to destroy the men who raped and murdered her. To Straub, a ghost *means* the return of a particular person from the dead, generally to rectify an abuse. Byron's "ghosts," like Mary Shelley's creature, are not returned emanations of once-living beings. They are originals, as alive in their peculiar ways as the humans they obsess, though unlike Hamlet's father or Straub's Eva, they have no particular reason for being.

16. For an account of the iconography of Byron's Turkish transvestism, see Marjorie Garber, *Vested Interests: Cross-Dressing and Cultural Anxiety* (New York and London: Routledge, Chapman and Hall, 1992), pp. 316–17.

17. Macdonald, p. 86, discusses Polidori's attraction to the contemporary idea of a "life fluid," which, while remaining matter, tends to merge with spirit, "present[ing] life as a very subtle material substance." In nineteenth-century terms, this life fluid is more ghostly than vampiric, resembling the refined ectoplasm Victorian mediums and occultists claimed was the substance of ghosts.

18. Planché's melodrama claimed to be an English translation of a French adaptation of Polidori by Pierre François Adrien Carmouche, Charles Nodier, and Achille de Jouffroy titled *Le Vampire: mélodrame en trois actes avec un prologue* (1820). For an account of some of the many melodramas and operas Polidori inspired, see Pamela C. White, "Two Vampires of 1828," *Opera Quarterly* 5 (Spring 1987): 22–57.

19. Roxana Stuart claims that the overt eroticism of stage vampires, "the simultaneous longing for—and terror of—being devoured," is the heart of their subversive popularity, but their suggestive friendship with young men

was too subversive to be popular, or even, until the twentieth century, to be dramatized at all. See "The Eroticism of Evil: The Vampire in Nineteenth-Century Melodrama," *Themes in Drama 14: Melodrama* (Cambridge: Cambridge University Press, 1992), pp. 223–44.

20. J. R. Planché, *The Vampire; or, the Bride of the Isles,* reprinted in *The Hour of One: Six Gothic Melodramas,* ed. Stephen Wischhusen (London: Gordon Fraser, 1975).

21. Walter Kendrick, *The Thrill of Fear: 250 Years of Scary Entertainment* (New York: Grove Weidenfeld, 1991), p. 126.

22. See Michael R. Booth, *Theatre in the Victorian Age* (Cambridge: Cambridge University Press, 1991), p. 78.

23. Dion Boucicault, *The Phantom* (1856; New York: Reader Microprint, 1969), i, V, p. 14.

24. *The Poems of Samuel Taylor Coleridge* (London: Oxford University Press, 1960), pp. 197–98. Future references to this edition of Coleridge's complete poems will appear as *Coleridge.*

25. Charlotte Brontë, *Jane Eyre* (1847; reprint, Middlesex: Penguin, 1966), p. 311.

26. *The Wolf Man* (1941), dir. George Waggner, starring Lon Chaney, Jr., as Larry Talbot.

27. *Popular Writing* (June 1842). Quoted in Frayling, *Vampyres,* p. 145. Until recently, *Varney* was attributed to Thomas Preskett Prest, but Frayling and Alan Ryan agree that "recent scholarship has established Rymer as almost certainly the author" (Ryan, ed., *Penguin,* p. 25).

28. James Malcolm Rymer, *Varney the Vampire; or, The Feast of Blood* (1845–47; reprint, New York: Arno Press, 1970), p. 61.

29. According to Robert Tracy, "Loving You All Ways: Vamps, Vampires, Necrophiles and Necrofilles in Nineteenth-Century Fiction," in *Sex and Death in Victorian Literature,* ed. Regina Barreca (Bloomington and Indianapolis: Indiana University Press, 1990), p. 40.

30. Elsewhere *Varney* claims that vampirism originated in Norway, Sweden, and the Levant. The indeterminate origin of vampires, and their affinity for Nordic countries, distinguishes Rymer's geography from that of Byron's Turkey or Stoker's Transylvania. Vampires do not emanate from a single exotic spot in the alien Orient, but from various possible nations with strongly Anglo-Saxon affinities.

31. Karl Marx, *Capital: A Critique of Political Economy,* vol. 1, trans. Ben Fowkes (1867; reprint, Harmondsworth: Penguin, 1990), p. 342.

32. George Dibdin Pitt, *The String of Pearls; or, The Fiend of Fleet Street* (1847), in *The Golden Age of Melodrama: Twelve Nineteenth-Century Melodramas,* ed. Michael Kilgarriff (London: Wolfe, 1974), p. 248.

33. Earlier he claims to have murdered not his son but his wife. The numerous inconsistencies of *Varney the Vampire* make vampirism less grotesque and more representative: any number of causes bring it to birth in any number of countries. Moreover, though the moon can give birth to vampires, as can vampires themselves—as Varney does at the end, in the story of the resuscitated Clara, a blatant anticipation of Stoker's Lucy—vampirism, like hell, is also a punishment for earthly sins, making us wonder how many ordinary characters in this sardonic narrative will become after death the vampires they already are.

34. Quoted in David J. Skal, *Hollywood Gothic: The Tangled Web of Dracula*

from Novel to Stage to Screen (New York and London: W. W. Norton, 1990), p. 15.

35. J. Sheridan Le Fanu, *Carmilla* (1872); reprint, *Penguin*, p. 87.

36. Early Hollywood vampire movies repeat this gender division. Gloria Holden as *Dracula's Daughter* was allowed far more erotic, even homoerotic, license than her self-absorbed father had been. John L. Balderston, the author of the screenplay, makes clear audiences' greater comfort with female sex and violence: "The use of a female Vampire instead of male gives us the chance to play up SEX and CRUELTY legitimately. . . . In *Dracula* these had to be almost eliminated. . . . We profit by making Dracula's Daughter amorous of her victims." (Quoted in David J. Skal, *The Monster Show: A Cultural History of Horror* [New York: W. W. Norton, 1993], p. 197.)

37. In *The Vampire Lovers* (directed by Roy Ward Baker), the 1970 Hammer remake of *Carmilla*, this fleetingly glimpsed black woman is replaced by a male devil-figure, usually on horseback, on whom the camera dwells as he repeatedly tells Carmilla how to proceed in her vampiric activities. Thus, in the supposedly enlightened 1960s, Hammer substitutes for Le Fanu's undefined female collusion a single male devil regulating the women whose impassive faces and absurdly inflated breasts make them indistinguishable, whether they are predators or prey.

38. See Richard Dellamora's superb chapter, "Poetic Perversities of A. C. Swinburne," in *Masculine Desire: The Sexual Politics of Victorian Aestheticism* (Chapel Hill: University of North Carolina Press, 1990), pp. 69–85. Though Dellamora does not talk specifically about "strangeness," he does treat lesbianism as a trope of gender transformation for Victorian men in a manner that illuminates Le Fanu's vampire romance.

39. Mario Praz, *The Romantic Agony*, trans. Angus Davidson (1933; reprint, Ohio: Meridian, 1968), p. 77: "In the second half of the nineteenth century the vampire becomes a woman . . . ; [but] the stronger sex remained such, not only in name, till the time of the Decadence, when . . . the roles appeared to be reversed."

40. Eve Kosofsky Sedgwick makes this shrewd point about Proust's Albertine in *Epistemology of the Closet* (Berkeley and Los Angeles: University of California Press, 1990), p. 234.

41. *A Choice of Kipling's Verse*, ed. T. S. Eliot (London: Faber and Faber, 1941), p. 109. Bram Dijkstra, *Idols of Perversity: Fantasies of Feminine Evil in Fin-de-siècle Culture* (New York and Oxford: Oxford University Press, 1986), pp. 333–51, provides a compendium of evilly heterosexual devourers and drainers of men.

42. *The Vampire's Ghost* (1945; dir. Lesley Selander), an obscure, low-budget film, tried to revive vampires' lunar bond and their phantasmal affiliation, but after the tactile Carmilla, these conventions fall away in the best-known works. See Alain Silver and James Ursini, *The Vampire Film from Nosferatu to Bram Stoker's Dracula*, rev. ed. (New York: Limelight Editions, 1993), pp. 91–92.

43. See Jack Sullivan's *Elegant Nightmares: The English Ghost Story from Le Fanu to Blackwood* (Athens: Ohio University Press, 1978), p. 49: "The modern ghost story [as Le Fanu inaugurates it] conjures up an inexplicably horrible world whose inhabitants follow their own mysterious rules. The only principle of consistency seems to be a self-referential system of cruelty, capable of constantly regenerating itself as it seeps into the natural order of things."

44. An ingenious TV movie of *Carmilla* (1989; dir. Gabrielle Beaumont) is the only adaptation I have seen that is true to Victorian intensities of friendship. In the spirit of Le Fanu's furious turbaned black woman, Jonathan Furst's script transposes the action to the antebellum American South, rife with furtive voodoo rites even before Carmilla enters. Carmilla seduces Laura (here called Marie) Byronically, with promises of travel, adventure, rebellion against her father's pathological possessiveness. "I can take you to worlds beyond your dreams," she whispers as she playfully dematerializes. Marie's father is not Le Fanu's cloudy, laughing obstruction, but a neurotic tyrant who madly sequesters his daughter "like one of his paintings" and lusts after Carmilla. Marie's mother has not died, but run away from him—to become a vampire in league with Carmilla, we learn at the end. The script equates vampirism not with lurid sex but with women's friendship as a rebellion against paternal control. Marie does ostensibly submit to her father, inadvertently staking Carmilla herself, but the story ends when she repeats Carmilla's earlier enigmatic self-assertion: "That was another lifetime; I'm much happier now." As Le Fanu hints, Marie overcomes Carmilla by becoming her.

This modernization of Le Fanu is shrewdly true to his essence. On the one hand the script courts media feminism by caricaturing all the men so that no one can take them seriously—Roddy McDowell does an especially overplayed turn as a boorish vampire killer—but the easy bond among the women is a superb realization of Le Fanu's lyrical hints. Le Fanu, though, cannot be called feminist in our contemporary sense, which is radically aware of power inequities; his preternatural web of women is an image of impossible equity, a variant of his century's unacknowledged dream of friendship.

45. James B. Twitchell, *The Living Dead,* affirms categorically, and, I think, correctly, that *Carmilla* is a "conscious attempt to render Coleridge's *Christabel* into prose," though he goes on to strangle both in censorious pseudo-diagnoses. Initially, he finds the eroticism of *Christabel* so disturbing that he recasts Christabel as a man, perhaps "the poet himself," acting out incestuous fantasies about his mother (pp. 44–45). But the more literal *Carmilla* forces him to read both works, if uneasily, on their own terms: "For *Carmilla,* like *Christabel,* is the story of a lesbian entanglement, a story of the sterile love of homosexuality expressed through the analogy of vampirism" (p. 129). Not only do these ambiguous love stories offer abundance rather than sterility; the passionate identification between vampire and prey lies at the heart of nineteenth-century vampire iconography, although Twitchell fastidiously quarantines female homoeroticism from the unrealized entanglements of male vampires.

46. Lillian Faderman's *Surpassing the Love of Men: Romantic Friendship and Love between Women from the Renaissance to the Present* (New York: William Morrow, 1981) traces ideologies surrounding romantic friendship between women from sentimental idealization to medicalization and taboo. The obsession with female romantic friendship in vampire literature by men is a symptom of both attitudes.

47. Andrea Weiss, *Vampires and Violets: Lesbians in Film* (1992; reprint, Middlesex: Penguin, 1993), p. 87.

48. Lesbian vampires are, at this writing, a thriving species in feminist

theory, fiction, and film, but they represent utopias beyond Le Fanu's imagination, not adaptations of his quintessentially Victorian tale of terror—a man's dream of a friendship so compelling and terrible that only women can embody it. Among adaptations, however, the *Carmilla* Gabrielle Beaumont directed in 1989 for Showtime's Nightmare Classics is an intelligent exception to the usual erotic exhibit. Beaumont revises Le Fanu through the prism of twentieth-century feminism, a modernization truer to Le Fanu's tone than more superficially authentic versions. There is nothing inscrutable or mystified about Marie's cry to her father: "Let me have a friend; that's all I'm asking." Beaumont's abandonment of mediating male observers captures the intensity and exhilaration, as well as the danger to family ties, of Victorian erotic friendship. Unfortunately Beaumont's shrewd dramatization has never reached theaters. Compressed into an hour time slot, it played only in the relative obscurity of cable television.

49. Pauline Kael, *5001 Nights at the Movies* (New York: Henry Holt, 1991), p. 812.

50. See S. S. Prawer, *Caligari's Children: The Film as Tale of Terror* (1980; reprint, New York: Da Capo, 1980), p. 162. Prawer's reading of *Vampyr* (pp. 138–63) is a particularly sophisticated tribute to Dreyer's consummate control over his dream tale.

51. *Lust for a Vampire* is the most interesting film in Hammer Studios' "Karnstein Trilogy," of which the other two are *Vampire Lovers* (1970; dir. Roy Ward Baker) and *Twins of Evil* (1971; dir. John Hough). Made as Hammer's cheeky *Dracula* series, which I shall discuss in chapter 3, was trailing off, the Karnstein trilogy seems to me relatively languid and conventional.

52. My awareness of these spectatorial vampire movies echoes Laura Mulvey's influential theory that the male gaze confines and determines women's performances in *all* "classic" films, but my point is less sweeping than Mulvey's: in contrast to the wonderful variety of movies, lesbian vampire films in the aesthetic or commercial mainstream justify their existence by making gazing men, not desiring women, their subject. See Laura Mulvey, "Visual Pleasure and Narrative Cinema," *Screen* 16 (1975): 6–18. For a mordant affirmation of the shaping power of a female gaze, see Linda Williams, "When the Woman Looks," *Re-visions: Essays in Feminist Film Criticism,* ed. Mary Ann Doane, Patricia Mellencamp, and Linda Williams, American Film Institute Monograph Series, vol. 3 (Frederick, Md.: University Publications of America, 1984). Jackie Stacey, *Star Gazing: Hollywood Cinema and Female Spectatorship* (London and New York: Routledge, 1994), counters Mulvey's abstract psychoanalytic assertions with a historical account of the ardor with which women have always looked.

53. Whitley Strieber, *The Hunger* (1981; reprint, New York: Avon, 1988), p. 189.

54. Miriam's chic murder-by-jewelry recalls Gloria Holden's fastidious attacks with a hypnotic ring in *Dracula's Daughter* (1936; dir. Lambert Hillyer). Holden is surrounded by all the iconography of aestheticism that stood for homosexuality in 1930s Hollywood: she is large, dark, and "aristocratic"; she lives in Chelsea, in a studio as sinister (because as remote from ordinary experience) as her father's Transylvanian castle; she seizes our visual attention by playing turbulent music on the piano by candlelight; she prowls after a soft blond woman, her model and visual antithesis. But

though Dracula's daughter stalks women, her ring does her work for her: she never touches her prey or expresses commonality with them, turning them, as Scott's Miriam does, into remote objects to stare at.

55. Weiss, *Vampires and Violets*, p. 98, was disappointed to learn that a body double was intercut with shots of Catherine Deneuve in the love scene. I find so little relation between body parts and persons that it scarcely matters.

56. Bram Stoker, *The Essential Dracula*, ed. Leonard Wolf (1897; reprint, New York: Penguin, 1993), p. 53. Dracula denies this taunt, as will many of his later acolytes, but the sister-bride is right; he loves no one in his novel.

Chapter 2

1. Bram Stoker, *The Essential Dracula*, ed. Leonard Wolf (1897; reprint, New York: Penguin, 1993), pp. 49–50.

2. Recent critics assiduously confine Dracula in his century; New Historicism or blindness to Dracula's role in shaping our present inhumanity inspires ingenious readings that see in him the spirit of 1897, Victoria's Diamond Jubilee year. Dracula has never been recognized as Stoker's bequest to a future that includes ourselves. Franco Moretti, for instance, sees in *Dracula* an allegory of 1897 capitalism; Christopher Craft brilliantly exposes its homoerotic undercurrents, "a pivotal anxiety of late Victorian culture," without acknowledging the more compelling and explicit homoeroticism of a tradition Stoker does his best to purge from *Dracula;* Stephen D. Arata reads *Dracula* as a late-Victorian nightmare of "reverse colonization," whereby "primitive" races supplant enervated Anglo-Saxons; Judith Halberstam analyzes Dracula's convergence with late-nineteenth-century anti-Semitic constructions of the smelly, parasitical Jew. See Franco Moretti, *Signs Taken for Wonders*, trans. Susan Fischer, David Forgacs, and David Miller, 2d ed. (New York: Verso, 1988), pp. 83–108; Christopher Craft, "'Kiss Me with Those Red Lips': Gender and Inversion in Bram Stoker's *Dracula*," *Representations* 8 (Fall 1984): 107–33; Stephen D. Arata, "The Occidental Tourist: *Dracula* and the Anxiety of Reverse Colonization," *Victorian Studies* 33 (Summer 1990): 621–45; and Judith Halberstam, "Technologies of Monstrosity: Bram Stoker's *Dracula*," *Victorian Studies* 36 (Spring 1993): 333–52.

3. See, for instance, Christopher Frayling's tidy genealogy in *Vampyres: Lord Byron to Count Dracula* (London: Faber and Faber, 1992), pp. 3–84.

4. *The Poems of John Keats* (London: Oxford University Press, 1961), p. 162, ll. 49–50.

5. Bram Stoker, "Dracula's Guest" (1897; first published 1914), reprinted in *Penguin*, pp. 163–74.

6. See, for instance, Robert Tracy, "Loving You All Ways: Vamps, Vampires, Necrophiles and Necrofilles in Nineteenth-Century Fiction," in *Sex and Death in Victorian Literature,* ed. Regina Barreca (Bloomington and Indianapolis: Indiana University Press, 1990), p. 42. William Veeder assumes that Van Helsing derives from Le Fanu's Dr. Hesselius and Baron Vordenburg, but long before Le Fanu's time, the vampire expert was a stock character in the theater: Planché's helpful chorus of spirits tells us what the vampire is, as does Boucicault's more accessible Dr. Rees. Keats's nasty expert Apollonius in *Lamia* is the most canonical example of the vampire hunter who kills by

expertise. See William Veeder, Foreword, *Dracula: The Vampire and the Critics,* ed. Margaret L. Carter (Ann Arbor: UMI Research Press, 1988), p. xvi.

7. An assumption I, like Frayling (p. 351), find implausible.

8. In Stoker's *Essential Dracula,* p. 51, editor Leonard Wolf suggests that the blond vampire "may have something in common with Lucy"; Gerold Savory's thoughtful 1977 adaptation, starring Louis Jourdan and directed by Philip Saville, superimposes on the slavering vampire a memory of Mina's face as she demurely brushes her hair.

9. Ellen Terry's "About H. I.," her diary during the 1890s, which her daughter appended to the final edition of her autobiography. See *Ellen Terry's Memoirs,* with a preface, notes, and additional biographical material by Edith Craig and Christopher St. John (1932; reprint, New York: Benjamin Blom, 1969), pp. 270–71.

10. David J. Skal, *Hollywood Gothic: The Tangled Web of Dracula from Novel to Stage to Screen* (New York and London: W. W. Norton, 1990), pp. 26–27. Also see my *Ellen Terry, Player in Her Time* (New York: W. W. Norton, 1987), esp. pp. 190–200.

11. Quoted in Phyllis A. Roth, *Bram Stoker* (Boston: Twayne, 1982), p. 5. Roth goes on to claim "that Stoker's friendship with Irving was the most important love relationship of his adult life" (p. 136), though she suggests shrewdly (p. 14) that *Dracula* somehow sapped Irving's imperial potency.

12. His great-nephew claims that Stoker died of syphilis caught from the prostitutes to whom he turned when his chilly wife refused further sexual relations after the birth of their son. See Daniel Farson, *The Man Who Wrote Dracula: A Biography of Bram Stoker* (New York: St. Martin's Press, 1975).

This rehearsal for Ibsen's *Ghosts* is a suggestive genesis of the most theatrical vampire ever created, but the rigidly polarized roles—frigid wife and contaminating whore—allotted to the women of this biographical script are probably the consequence, not the cause, of Stoker's consuming hero worship of Irving. We should not condescend to Stoker's supposedly "Victorian" definitions of women without remembering their entanglement in Irving's theater and Irving's own emotional and imperial magnetism. Many Victorian men reduced their women to labels; few had their imaginations aroused by a compensating Irving.

13. In Fred Saberhagen's wonderfully witty and astute novel *The Dracula Tape,* in which Dracula gets to tell the story Stoker refuses to include, the vampire complains sardonically about his doltish guest: "He misinterpreted these oddities, but never asked openly for any explanation, whilst I, wisely or unwisely, never volunteered one. . . . My little Englishman was tolerant of it all, but he was dull, dull, dull. A brooder, but no dreamer. There was no imagination in him to be fired." *The Dracula Tape* (1975; reprint, New York: Ace, 1980), pp. 16, 31. Saberhagen's Dracula wants to restore the communion with mortals that was the birthright of earlier vampires.

14. Christopher Craft, "'Kiss Me with Those Red Lips,'" pp. 110–16, is particularly ingenious in describing, and thereby authorizing, the homoerotic contact that does *not* take place in *Dracula.*

15. Stoker's "original Foundation Notes and Data for his *Dracula*" in the Rosenbach Library in Philadelphia, quoted in Frayling, p. 301; reprinted by permission (see n. 40 below).

16. Two of the most stylized *Dracula* films, directed by Tod Browning

(1931) and Francis Ford Coppola (1992), advertised themselves as love stories: Browning's was billed as "the strangest love story ever told," while Coppola's ads reassured us that "love never dies." In both, though, the vampire
performs on a plane so remote from the other characters that one can
scarcely imagine vampire and mortal touching or even conversing, much
less biting or loving.

17. These Jonathans are presumably uninfected at the redemptive end-
ings of their movies, but later film Jonathans amplify Murnau's suggestive
variation by actually becoming vampires. See especially Terence Fisher's *Horror of Dracula* (1957), the first of the brightly colored Hammer films that
illuminated the 1960s, in which Jonathan, here a susceptible vampire-
hunter, is easily seduced by a chesty vampire woman who wears a tunic;
Dan Curtis's TV movie (*Bram Stoker's Dracula,* 1973), starring Jack Palance,
which follows the Hammer tradition by abandoning Jonathan to the three
ravenous vampire women so that he can become a snarling monster Van
Helsing must stake at the end; and, most dramatically, Werner Herzog's
Nosferatu the Vampyre (1979), a searing remake of Murnau's film. In Herzog's
revision, a grinning, fanged Jonathan ends the movie by galloping off
to become king of the vampires after his wife has sacrificed herself in
vain. Only Herzog follows Murnau by discarding the three intermediary
female vampires, allowing Dracula himself to transform his vulnerable
guest.

These later Jonathans are all oafish revisions of Stoker's supposedly heroic civil servant, who obeys a paternalistic employer by bringing to a wild
country the light of British law. In the 1960s and 1970s, movie Jonathans,
like the imperial mission they represent, are corrupt and vulnerable. Although, unlike Stoker's pure survivor, they become vampires with scarcely
a whimper of protest, they resemble Stoker's character, who exists to belong
to someone in power, more than they do the passionate friends of the generous Byronic gentry.

18. I use Stoker's names here for the reader's convenience. *Nosferatu* was
a pirated adaptation of *Dracula* whose original titles muffle its debt to Stoker
by renaming the characters; Dracula, for example, becomes Graf Orlok.
Some later prints revert to the Stoker names, though "Mina" mutates into
the more powerful and euphonious "Nina." Skal, *Hollywood Gothic,* esp. pp.
43–63, provides a thorough and witty account of Florence Stoker's Van Helsing–like pursuit of Murnau's elusive film.

19. Stoker's Van Helsing affirms that the vampire's "power ceases, as
does that of all evil things, at the coming of day" (p. 290), but the sun is no
threat to Dracula's life: it merely limits his shape-shifting capacity.

20. Gregory A. Waller writes eloquently about the wives in Murnau's
original *Nosferatu* and Werner Herzog's remake, whom he sees as solitary
warriors, independent of traditional weapons and of the wise directing father figures who contained Stoker's women. According to Waller, *Nosferatu's*
women are as isolated in bourgeois society as the vampire, sacrificing themselves ironically—and, ultimately, tragically—to institutions that ignore
and silence them; see Gregory A. Waller, *The Living and the Undead: From
Stoker's Dracula to Romero's Dawn of the Dead* (Urbana and Chicago: University of Illinois Press, 1986), p. 225.

Waller's excellent account of mutating vampire representations is sometimes sentimental about victimized women, who, in both versions of *Nosfer-*

atu, seem to release through self-sacrifice their own rebellious vampiric allegiance, though they refrain from snarling and growing fangs.

21. Siegfried Kracauer's *From Caligari to Hitler: A Psychological History of German Film* (Princeton: Princeton University Press, 1947) reads *Nosferatu* prophetically, as an allegorical warning against the plague of Hitlerism. Kracauer's influential reading is truer, perhaps, to the coldly imperial Dracula than it is to Murnau's ravished ghost.

22. Waller, *The Living and the Undead,* p. 92, notes astutely that in the American film, Renfield is maddened by Dracula, while in Stoker's novel the vampire manipulates a madness, embodied in Renfield, that lurked in England before his coming. This contrast holds if one reads the screenplay alone, but Dwight Frye's performance is so bacchanalian from the beginning that it is difficult to call the pre-Dracula Renfield "sane."

23. In the so-called "Spanish *Dracula*" (1931, dir. George Melford)—a Spanish-language adaptation for Mexican distribution that was filmed at night, on the same set and from the same shooting script as the Hollywood version—Dracula feeds Renfield generously, but Pablo Alvarez Rubio's affable chicken-chewing dispels any erotic tension between himself and Carlos Villarias's vampire. Accordingly, Villarias's Dracula leaves Renfield's prone body to his sister-brides.

The Spanish *Dracula* is technically superior to the Hollywood original: its photography is more sophisticated, its women are sexier, and its narrative is slightly more logical. It ignores, however, the subterranean attraction between the vampire and his guest that invigorates Browning's version.

24. The jarring shift of rhythm and focus after the movie leaves Transylvania is due in part to the producer's squeamishness; on the final shooting script, Carl Laemmle, Jr., wrote the Van Helsing–like rule, "Dracula should only go for women and not men!" David J. Skal, *The Monster Show: A Cultural History of Horror* (New York: W. W. Norton, 1993), p. 126. Early Hollywood movies allow emotional complexity to spill out in improbable countries like Transylvania or King Kong's Africa or Oz, but it is barred from home.

25. This shift of authority from an egalitarian vampire-hunting community to Van Helsing's autocratic leadership is the thesis of Waller's analysis of *Dracula*'s immediate descendants in film (*The Living and the Undead,* pp. 77–109).

26. Jonathan Dollimore writes compellingly about the rise of perversity as a creed in the 1890s, a decade in which the rigid categories erected by new experts in sexology came to restrain the play of affection. Because of Oscar Wilde's imprisonment and its aftermath, the willful evasion of categories that the creed of perversity proclaims is at best fragile, at worst doomed: "So in creating a politics of the perverse we should never forget the cost: death, mutilation, and incarceration have been, and remain, the fate of those who are deemed to have perverted nature." *Sexual Dissidence: Augustine to Wilde, Freud to Foucault* (Oxford: Clarendon Press, 1991), p. 230.

27. Bram Dijkstra, *Idols of Perversity: Fantasies of Feminine Evil in Fin-de-siècle Culture* (New York and Oxford: Oxford University Press, 1986), p. 351.

28. Judith Weissman notes that in *Dracula,* "the one group of people that [female vampires] never attack is other women." Weissman, "Women and Vampires: *Dracula* as a Victorian Novel" (1977), reprinted in Carter, ed., *Dracula: The Vampire and the Critics,* p. 75.

29. Hume Nesbit, "The Vampire Maid" (1900), reprinted in *Dracula's*

Brood: Rare Vampire Stories by Friends and Contemporaries of Bram Stoker, ed. Richard Dalby (London: Crucible, 1987), p. 221.

30. F. G. Loring, "The Tomb of Sarah" (1900), reprinted in *The Undead: Vampire Masterpieces*, ed. James Dickie (London: Pan, 1971), p. 100.

31. Phyllis A. Roth suggests plausibly that since Dracula is not staked, but only stabbed with a bowie knife, he does not die at all: he simply turns himself into mist after sending his captors a last look of triumph. See her "Suddenly Sexual Women in *Dracula*" (1977), in Carter, ed., *Dracula: The Vampire and the Critics*, p. 67, n. 27.

By so flagrantly ignoring his own elaborate rules, Stoker was probably leaving room for a sequel he lacked the heart or energy to write. Dracula's anticlimactic death, if it is a death, reminds the reader that once he has been silenced, even a vampire is easy to kill.

32. Many critics and novelists, even more loyal to the vampire, perhaps, than Renfield, have reconstructed Dracula's suppressed narrative. The most persuasive critic to do so is Carol A. Senf, "*Dracula*: The Unseen Face in the Mirror" (1979), reprinted in Carter, ed., *Dracula: The Vampire and the Critics*. Senf claims that *Dracula* is dominated by a series of unreliable, even criminal narrators who suppress their vampire/victim: "Dracula is *never* seen objectively and never permitted to speak for himself while his actions are recorded by people who have determined to destroy him and who, moreover, repeatedly question the sanity of their quest" (p. 95).

Senf's persuasive essay could be a gloss on Saberhagen's *Dracula Tape* (1975), whose urbane Dracula reinserts himself into Stoker's narrative, exposing with relish the incompetent dolts who persecuted him in the 1890s. This Dracula plays Van Helsing by telling Van Helsing's story: "When I have made you understand the depths of the idiocy of that man, Van Helsing, and confess at the same time that he managed to hound me nearly to my death, you will be forced to agree that among all famous perils to the world I must be ranked as one of the least consequential." Fred Saberhagen, *The Dracula Tape* (1975; reprint, New York: Ace, 1980), p. 101. Like Senf, Saberhagen accuses Van Helsing of murdering Lucy with incompetent blood transfusions, then exploiting vampire superstition to cover up his own malpractice. Like most Draculas in the 1970s, Saberhagen's is, emotionally and intellectually, a superior being who genuinely loves Mina. He transforms her to save her from the mortal idiots who bully and adore her.

Saberhagen's iconoclastic Dracula paved the way for garrulous and glamorous vampires like Anne Rice's Armand and Lestat, who not only tell their own stories, but initiate them, thus becoming culture heroes in a manner impossible to Stoker's compliant Count.

33. The word *homosexual* had been part of medical jargon since the 1870s, but it began to infiltrate popular discourse in the 1890s. The first reference to it in the *Oxford English Dictionary* is dated 1897—*Dracula's* year—in which Havelock Ellis apologizes for using this "barbarously hybrid word." There is an abundance of studies exploring the emergence of homosexuality as a new clinical category in the late nineteenth century. All acknowledge their debt to Michel Foucault's pioneering *History of Sexuality*, 2 vols., trans. Robert Hurley (New York: Vintage, 1980, 1986). In writing about nineteenth-century constructions of homosexuality as a clinical monster, I am especially indebted to Lillian Faderman, *Surpassing the Love of Men: Romantic Friendship and Love between Women from the Renaissance to the Present*

(New York: Morrow, 1981), and Richard Dellamora, *Masculine Desire: The Sexual Politics of Victorian Aestheticism* (Chapel Hill: University of North Carolina Press, 1990).

34. Eve Sedgwick claims that in literature, 1891 was a watershed year in the construction of "a modern homosexual identity and a modern problematic of sexual orientation." Eve Kosofsky Sedgwick, *Epistemology of the Closet* (Berkeley and Los Angeles: University of California Press, 1990), p. 91. For most nonliterary observers, however, 1895—in which homosexuality was publicly, even theatrically, defined, isolated, and punished in the famous person of Oscar Wilde—was surely the year in which the public learned what writers had sensed four years earlier. Talia Schaffer's essay "'A Wilde Desire Took Me': The Homoerotic History of *Dracula*" (*ELH: A Journal of English Literary History* 61 [1994]: 381–415) demonstrates in persuasive detail the association between *Dracula* and the Wilde trials.

35. Eric, Count Stenbock, "The True Story of a Vampire" (1894), reprinted in *The Undead*, p. 169.

36. H. Montgomery Hyde, *Oscar Wilde* (London: Methuen, 1975), p. 374.

37. In the theater at least, Wilde's disgrace seems to have had, if anything, a freeing impact on the next generation of women, in part because the Labouchère Amendment ignored lesbianism: the new constraints on men freed women to experiment with new theatrical idioms. As they did when they were vampires, women acted uninhibited roles that were taboo for men. See, for instance, my account of Edith Craig's unabashed—if admittedly professionally marginal—community of homosocial and homosexual women in *Ellen Terry, Player in Her Time*, esp. pp. 364–436.

38. Skal, *Hollywood Gothic*, pp. 34–38, discusses the affinities between Stoker and Wilde, two Irishmen who adored Whitman and loved the same woman: Wilde proposed to Florence Balcombe, whom Stoker later married. Skal does suggest that Wilde's trials motivated the strident antisex rhetoric of Stoker's later career, but he ignores the power of the trials over Stoker's imagination of Dracula, a conjunction Schaffer analyzes with depth and thoroughness.

39. This aesthetic animalism evokes Henry Irving's famous performance in *The Bells*, in which, during his reenactment of murder, he is said to have thrown back his head and howled when he reached the line: "'How the dogs howl at Daniel's farm—like me they are hungry, searching for prey.' And then [continues the enthralled observer] he howled. It makes my hair stand on end when I think of it." Like Irving, Dracula turns animalism into a compelling art form. Quoted in Marius Goring, Foreword to *Henry Irving and* The Bells, ed. David Mayer (Manchester: Manchester University Press, 1980), p. xv.

40. Stoker's working notes include typed excerpts from a "Goldon Chersonese" by "Miss Bond," many of which deal with transfiguration and animal worship: "The Malays have many queer notions about tigers, and usually only speak of them in whispers, because they think that certain souls of human beings who have departed this life have taken up their abode in these beasts, and in some places for this reason, they will not kill a tiger unless he commits some specially bad aggression. They also believe that some men are tigers by night and men by day!" Stoker's own commentary makes clear that this animal possession generates not degradation, but awe:

"It almost seems as if the severe monotheism to which they have been converted compels them to create a gigantic demonology." Quoted by permission of the Rosenbach Museum and Library, Philadelphia, Pa. (Stoker, Bram, *Dracula: ms. notes and outlines* [ca. 1890–ca. 1896], EL4/f.s874d/MS).

41. Leonard Wolf makes this connection in *The Essential Dracula*, p. 47.

42. Sir Frederick Treves, "The Elephant Man" (1923); reprinted in Michael Howell and Peter Ford, *The True History of the Elephant Man* (Middlesex: Penguin, 1980), p. 190.

43. Leslie Fiedler, *Freaks: Myths and Images of the Secret Self* (1978; reprint, New York: Anchor, 1993), p. 174.

44. Howell and Ford, pp. 210, 110, 206. On p. 35, Howell and Ford make explicit what Treves's memoir discreetly implies: that Merrick's "penis and scrotum were perfectly normal."

45. Harriet Ritvo, *The Animal Estate: The English and Other Creatures in the Victorian Age* (Cambridge, Mass.: Harvard University Press, 1987), p. 6.

46. Quoted in James Turner, *Reckoning with the Beast: Animals, Pain, and Humanity in the Victorian Mind* (Baltimore: Johns Hopkins University Press, 1980), p. 133.

47. Rudyard Kipling, *Jungle Books* (1894–95; reprint [*The Jungle Book*], Middlesex: Penguin, 1987), pp. 81, 93.

48. Adaptations that use the release of the wolf feel the need to rationalize it more clearly than Stoker does. In Dan Curtis's 1973 TV movie (*Bram Stoker's Dracula*), for example, Jack Palance's Dracula uses the wolf to attack and distract the vigilant *Arthur*, his primary antagonist, while the vampire finishes off Lucy. Stoker's Bersicker only frightens to death Lucy's innocent mother, which Dracula surely could have done himself.

49. In the exuberantly revisionary 1970s, vampires regained hints of their animal powers. Louis Jourdan, in Philip Saville's BBC *Dracula* of 1977, was the first cinematic Dracula to crawl down his castle walls in the lizardlike manner Stoker described. Saville, however, insulates his human characters from vampiric transformations more chivalrously than Stoker did: his Jonathan never attempts to emulate Dracula's crawl, but instead jumps awkwardly, feet first, out of the castle window, retaining his humanity at the cost, one imagines, of a painful fall.

50. J. Sheridan Le Fanu, *Carmilla* (1872; reprinted in *The Penguin Book of Vampire Stories*, ed. Alan Ryan [New York: Penguin, 1988]), pp. 102, 130.

51. Elisabeth Bronfen claims that dead women are powerful artistic subjects because of their otherness: "Because the feminine body is culturally constructed as the superlative site of alterity," it both expresses death and deflects it from the artist and viewer, who are inevitably male. *Over Her Dead Body: Death, Femininity and the Aesthetic* (New York: Routledge, 1992), p. xi. I doubt whether, even in the most patriarchal societies, men have a premium on seeing. I suggest instead that women are culturally constructed vehicles of intimacy rather than otherness, and thus—in art, at least—are freer than men to act out embarrassments like desire or death.

Chapter 3

1. Matthew Bunson, *The Vampire Encyclopedia* (New York: Crown, 1993), which is not always reliable, claims (p. 215) that the earliest psychic vampire was Etherial Softdown in Webber's *Spiritual Vampirism* (1853).

2. See Karl Edward Wagner's story "The Slug" in *A Whisper of Blood*, ed. Ellen Datlow (New York: Berkley, 1991), pp. 23–33. In this witty tale, an affable creep barges in on his writer friend so persistently that he ends up devouring not only the writer's energy and time, but his career. Killing the creep does not restore the writer, who goes on to enervate a woman sculptor, the next victim in the chain.

3. Alice and Claude Askew, "Aylmer Vance and the Vampire" (1914), reprinted in *Dracula's Brood: Rare Vampire Stories by Friends and Contemporaries of Bram Stoker*, ed. Richard Dalby (London: Crucible, 1987), p. 287. Dalby is a discerning collector of early psychic vampire stories that, on the face of it, have little to do with Stoker's antihuman account of conquest. But the abundance of psychic vampires between 1867 and 1940 suggests that the Victorian fin de siècle, like our own, canonized the rigid, rulebound Dracula while imagining more comprehensive vampires in daily life. Despite Dracula's official absence from these tales (many of which are love stories), Dalby's title slyly identifies him as the monstrous parent of ordinary parasites.

4. George Sylvester Viereck, *The House of the Vampire* (1907; reprint, New York: Arno Press, 1976), p. 185.

5. Fritz Leiber, "The Girl with the Hungry Eyes" (1949; reprint, *Penguin*, pp. 347–48).

6. Sir Arthur Conan Doyle, "The Parasite," in *Dracula's Brood*, p. 124.

7. Mary E. Wilkins-Freeman, "Luella Miller," in *Penguin*, p. 176.

8. Bram Stoker, *The Essential Dracula*, ed. Leonard Wolf (1897; reprint, New York: Plume, 1993), p. 69.

9. It takes a more pervasively fearful age even than 1914 to acknowledge the psychic vampirism of the young. Stephen King's *'Salem's Lot* (1975) was shocking in the gleeful alacrity with which its children (like Stoker's women) adapted to vampirism. More recently, in such stories as Edward Bryant's "Good Kids," children upstage their vampire attackers. Mr. Vladisov, a suave foreigner with "the kind of accent I've heard actors working in restaurants goofing around with" (p. 162), tries to feed on a group of girls who turn out to be more adept energy-drainers than the monster. As the narrator—a devoted reader of Stephen King—explains: "It's funny sometimes about old folktales. . . . Like the one forbidding adults to sleep in the same room with a child. They had it right. They just had it backwards. It's *us* who suck up the energy like batteries charging." "And then we fed," she concludes complacently. (In *Blood Is Not Enough: 17 Stories of Vampirism*, ed. Ellen Datlow [1989; reprint, New York: Berkley, 1990], pp. 170–71).

That late-twentieth-century phenomenon, the child-vampire, not only insinuates vampirism into the life cycle: it forbids us to believe in a redemptive future. "Good Kids" suggests that Mina's baby boy, whom the end of *Dracula* offers up as an antidote to the vampire, might smilingly devour the heroic hunters who collectively engendered him for their own salvation.

10. Algernon Blackwood's wealthy, robust Mr. Frene in "The Transfer" (1912) is one of the more Philistine Edwardian psychic vampires. His greed is indistinguishable from simple gregariousness: "For this Mr. Frene was a man who drooped alone, but grew vital in a crowd—because he used their vitality. He was a supreme, unconscious artist in the science of taking the fruits of others' work and living—for his own advantage. He vampired, unknowingly no doubt, every one with whom he came in contact; left them exhausted, tired, listless. Others fed him, so that while in a full room he

shone, alone by himself and with no life to draw upon he languished and declined" (*Penguin*, p. 207).

No human can resist Mr. Frene, but unlike most psychic vampires, he is brought down by a superior antagonist: an energy-draining plant.

11. By 1990, when (as we shall see) "classic" vampires are perhaps the last credible feminist heroes, vampire writers try to revoke the ancestral bond between the bloodsucking Dracula and his psychic brood. For example, *Children of the Night* (New York: Tor, 1990), Mercedes Lackey's vampire romance, juxtaposes a lovable "real, classical, blood-sucking vampire" (p. 52) with a dangerous community of psychic vampires, or, in New Age parlance, "psivamps." The bloodsucker is sufficiently gentle, sexy, and vulnerable to become the lover of the heroine, a spunky sensitive; the psivamps are evil antihumans who, like Stoker's Dracula, exist only to be destroyed by the community of the good.

Like Algernon Blackwood's Mr. Frene, psivamps are in their element at parties: "Like the kind of person who walks into a party and leeches off the liveliest person there, and when he leaves, he's feeling wonderful and his 'victim' feels like the bottom of the biorhythm court. I've known psychic vampires that could drain you so low that you'd catch every germ that walked by, just because the immune system is so tied to the emotional system. And ones that left you ready to commit suicide but too tired to pick up the knife to do it" (Lackey, *Children of the Night*, p. 61). By contrast, "classic" bloodsuckers shine in intimate relationships. At the end of the twentieth century, only vampires whose most vampiric traits are siphoned away achieve untainted intimacy with mortals.

12. Dan Simmons, *Carrion Comfort* (New York: Warner, 1989), p. 610.

13. *Blood Is Not Enough*, ed. Datlow, pp. 2–3. More pithily, Datlow asserts in her introduction to *A Whisper of Blood*, p. xi, that "the concept of vampirism can be seen as a metaphor for negative relationships," a category that, like other attempts to encompass psychic vampires, never seems to end.

14. In *Blood Is Not Enough*, see especially Garry Kilworth, "The Silver Collar"; Harlan Ellison, "Try a Dull Knife"; Sharon N. Farber, "Return of the Dust Vampires"; Susan Casper, "A Child of Darkness"; Leonid Andreyev, "Lazarus"; Joe Haldeman, "Time Lapse"; Chet Williamson, ". . .To Feel Another's Woe"; in *A Whisper of Blood*, J. W. Jeter, "True Love." These are not necessarily the best stories in two superb collections, but they may be the most representative.

15. See too the more encompassing incantation in Tanith Lee's wonderful "The Janfia Tree" (in *Blood Is Not Enough*, p. 196): "A demon which vampirized and killed by irresistible pleasures of the flesh. What an entirely enchanting thought. After all, life itself vampirized, and ultimately killed, did it not, by a constant, equally irresistible, administration of the exact reverse of pleasure."

16. I don't feel that *Nosferatu* belongs in this pageant of Draculas. Neither F. W. Murnau's 1922 silent film nor Werner Herzog's brilliant 1979 remake exemplifies Anglo-American taste. Prints of both are relatively inaccessible, and so, I fear, is the phantasmal, almost passive vampire they feature, who owes more to the ghostly conventions of the Victorian stage than to our own bloody-minded century. Two large classes of University of Pennsylvania undergraduates, vampire lovers all, who giggled politely through Max Schreck's sad-eyed glidings, forced me to accept *Nosferatu*'s marginality.

I am also omitting Gary Oldman's similarly shadowy Dracula in Francis Ford Coppola's 1992 *Bram Stoker's Dracula*. James V. Hart's screenplay is so reliant on that of the 1973 TV movie of the same name, starring Jack Palance, that discussion would be redundant. Moreover, the fundamental illogic of Coppola's kaleidoscopic cinematography, and of Oldman's Dracula himself, suggests that a postmodern Dracula may be a contradiction in terms. Audiences who believe absolutely in Anne Rice's Louis and Lestat seem to relish a Dracula in a perpetual state of visual and ontological decomposition. It may be that Coppola has killed Dracula at last and that he will fade out with the twentieth century.

17. As David J. Skal claims in *Hollywood Gothic: The Tangled Web of Dracula from Novel to Stage to Screen* (New York: W. W. Norton, 1990), p. 81. See also Alain Silver and James Ursini, *The Vampire Film: From* Nosferatu *to* Bram Stoker's Dracula, rev. ed. (New York: Limelight Editions, 1993), p. 60.

18. Gaston Leroux, *The Phantom of the Opera*, trans. Alexander Teixeira de Mattos (1911; reprint, New York: Harper Perennial, 1987), p. 14.

19. James Malcolm Rymer, *Varney the Vampire; or, the Feast of Blood* (1845–47; reprint, New York: Arno Press, 1970), p. 134.

20. Lugosi's Dracula was, of course, born on the American stage: American audiences first met him in 1927, in Hamilton Deane and John F. Balderston's popular play; Raymond Huntley, the first Dracula to wear a tuxedo and cape, had played a more demonic vampire in the London production. Skal's *Hollywood Gothic*, pp. 65–109, provides an exhaustive account of the intricate stage history of this leaden play.

When Lugosi's Dracula mutated to film, he underwent a lucrative class descent. All Americans, not merely wealthy New Yorkers who giggled while they shivered, were haunted by this alien figure. When he displayed himself before mass audiences of moviegoers, who were often provincial and poor, Lugosi forfeited the knowing complicity with sophisticated spectators that he, like the vamp Theda Bara, had enjoyed in the '20s. A theatrical character in a movie is, of course, more alienated—thus funnier and more horrible at once—than theatrical characters in the theater.

21. Dracula's Erik-like association with music is even more pronounced in *Dracula's Daughter* (1936; dir. Lambert Hillyer). Though Lugosi never appears in this sequel, his presence hovers over his tormented daughter (Gloria Holden). She succumbs to that spirit while playing the piano with a candlelit, histrionic flair reminiscent of Lon Chaney in the 1925 *Phantom of the Opera*. She begins by playing what she calls "normal music"—her mother's song—but despite herself her song turns romantic and sinister. Once Dracula descends on her music, she abandons herself to tragic postures, homoeroticism, and death.

In the Italian/Spanish/German *Count Dracula* (1970; dir. Jess Franco), instead of flying into Mina's bedroom, Christopher Lee takes pains to lure her to the opera and bite her there—in tribute no doubt to his musical master Lugosi.

22. Skal, *Hollywood Gothic*, p. 85. In 1926, the *Chicago Sunday Tribune* ran a vitriolic article denouncing the corrupting effect on American men of Valentino's effeminacy; see Marjorie Garber, *Vested Interests: Cross-Dressing and Cultural Anxiety* (New York and London: Routledge, 1992), pp. 361–62. By 1931, vampires could kill women and win love for it, but their manhood had to look inviolate.

23. George Stade, Introduction, in Bram Stoker, *Dracula* (New York: Bantam Classics, 1981), p. vi.

24. David J. Skal, *The Monster Show: A Cultural History of Horror* (New York: W. W. Norton, 1993), p. 169. Skal's characterization of the strange amorphousness and pervasive repulsiveness of Stoker's Dracula—an utterly antisocial creature worlds away from the many movie stars who seduce us in his name—is stunningly accurate: "Dracula spends little time on social niceties and is physically repellent, a cadaverous old man who grows younger as he drinks blood but who never becomes attractive" (p. 83).

25. Kim Newman, "Bloodlines," *Sight and Sound* (January 1993), p. 12. Newman's own mordant vampire novel, *Anno Dracula* (1992), is suffused with this belief that social crises breed vampirism: in Newman's "alternate" Victorian England, which is oppressed at every level, vampirism has become not only tyrannical but chic, for Dracula has married the queen and appointed Lord Ruthven prime minister.

26. Like most commentators on popular horror, Noël Carroll relegates to mere forerunners the few vivid monsters of the late 1960s. He valorizes as a true horror cycle the swarm of innovative works that, in the '70s, entered the mainstream, dominating popular, not just specialized, culture. See Noël Carroll, *The Philosophy of Horror, or Paradoxes of the Heart* (New York and London: Routledge, 1990), pp. 2, 103–7.

27. Visual shadows of the Depression may be too easy to find. Skal, *The Monster Show*, p. 159, calls Dracula "a sanguinary capitalist" and the Frankenstein monster "a poignant symbol for an army of abject and abandoned laborers, down to his work clothes and asphalt-spreader's boots." But such topical assertions merely repeat Franco Moretti's incorporation of both Frankenstein's creature and Dracula into the iconography of *nineteenth-century* capitalism (*Signs Taken for Wonders: Essays in the Sociology of Literary Forms*, rev. ed., trans. Susan Fischer, David Forgacs, and David Miller [1983; reprint, New York: Verso, 1988], pp. 83–108).

Only *King Kong* is actually set in Depression-era America rather than Ruritanian Europe, and though economic desperation leads the imperial Americans to capture Kong and imprison him in New York, Kong himself is, I think, intended to represent fears more primal than economic.

28. King Kong continually threatens to violate these taboos: the central non-event of the movie is his intercourse with the diminutive Fay Wray. When, in a sequence cut from the original print, he tweaks her nipple affectionately, this anatomical impossibility is almost realized onscreen. Just as Kong embodies the animalism Lugosi purged from Dracula, he almost performs the act *Frankenstein* and *Dracula* purged from our visual imagination.

29. Tod Browning's next film, *Freaks* (1932), forces on viewers this forbidden interaction between creature and human. The freaks' refrain as they engulf and absorb the perfect statuesque woman is the telling chant, "One of us." *Freaks* was considered so obscenely terrifying that it ended Browning's Hollywood career.

30. This happy phrase is Gregory A. Waller's in *The Living and the Undead: From Stoker's Dracula to Romero's Dawn of the Dead* (Urbana and Chicago: University of Illinois Press, 1986), p. 87.

31. Lane Roth writes with some disdain of the materialism of *Horror of Dracula*, opposing it to the cinematic self-consciousness of *Nosferatu:* "Where in *Nosferatu* reality is subjective and mind-dependent, in *Horror of*

Dracula, reality is matter." See "Film, Society and Ideas: *Nosferatu* and *Horror of Dracula,*" in *Planks of Reason: Essays on the Horror Film,* ed. Barry Keith Grant (Metuchen, N.J., and London: Scarecrow Press, 1984), p. 249.

There was surely a certain klunkiness in Hammer films that intensified as they became more formulaic, but for teenagers in 1958, Hammer Studios' primary American audience, the realization that vampires had bodies was thrilling.

32. Lane Roth notes acutely, p. 246, that with *Nosferatu* the ritual hour for vampire-killing changes from dusk to dawn. Stoker's Dracula, who dies (if he does) just as he is coming to life, shows a vitality absent in Max Schreck and his sun-scorched progeny, who die at the same time they would normally fall into a deathlike trance. Here and often, Stoker's rituals commemorate the life in his Undead, while those of his successors dwell on somnolence.

33. In the next Hammer film, *Brides of Dracula* (1960), Peter Cushing's Van Helsing has his finest moment when he cauterizes his vampire bite with a red-hot poker and holy water—a treatment he might have learned from his contemporary, Emily Brontë, who cauterized in the same way the bite of a rabid dog, though she omitted the holy water.

34. He also notes, with an equally secular emphasis, that vampirism is "similar to addiction to drugs," an analogy more important, and far more sinister, in vampire literature of the 1980s.

35. In 1979, Frank Langella's Dracula gives a highly sophisticated explanation of his ability to function around the clock: "It is always daylight somewhere on earth, Professor. After my rest my need is only to stay in darkness." Stoker's xenophobic characters were aware only of the sun's rising and setting *in their homelands*. Langella's Dracula has acquired a global perspective.

36. Drake Douglas, *Horror!* (New York: Macmillan, 1966), p. 35.

37. *The Rime of the Ancient Mariner,* Coleridge's vampire-tinged epic, may be the source of both the Planché moon and the Hammer sun. In *The Ancient Mariner,* "the moving Moon" is generally a fulfilling presence, while the sun is huge, static, and assaultive.

38. My own unsystematic research has uncovered three quite disparate children of the night in the early 1990s alone: Mercedes Lackey's adventure-romance (1990); a lurid video about vampires pursuing nubile teenage girls in a midwestern town called "Allburg, USA"; and Dan Simmons's ambitious epic account of Vlad the Impaler, Romanian history, and AIDS (1992). See Mercedes Lackey, *Children of the Night* (New York: Tor, 1990); *Children of the Night,* written and directed by Tony Randel (1991); and Dan Simmons, *Children of the Night* (New York: G. P. Putnam's Sons, 1992). All assume that children of the night are vampires, not wolves.

39. Roth, "Film, Society and Ideas," p. 252, defines the probable working-class audience of Hammer films in England. I suspect that British students would have found them trite; I know only their curiously powerful impact in America. When they were imported to the United States, they became a wicked addiction for middle-class '60s students like myself. Conventional and sexist as they ostensibly were, their fatuous patriarchs, ravenous women, and modish Dracula flooded viewers like me with ineffable feelings of rebellion. *The Rocky Horror Picture Show* (1975) institutionalized this rebellion for the next generation, but in the inchoate early '60s, Hammer

provided no costumes, songs, or mass rituals that told us even before the movie began that we were there to transgress.

40. Fisher's claustrophobic Holmwood family harboring vampires it doesn't recognize anticipates a dreadful family in a quite different vampire movie: George Romero's *Night of the Living Dead* (1968). Superficially these films could not be further apart. The hordes of reanimated corpses that rise to eat the living in Romero's America have none of the dashing individuality of Hammer vampires: they are disposable and indistinguishable. Hammer's opulent colors look garishly old-fashioned next to Romero's grainy, *cinéma vérité* black-and-white; Hammer's beautiful predators pale before Romero's slovenly ghouls; and the opulent Hammer Victorian England looks like Disneyland next to Romero's grainy Pittsburgh.

Nevertheless, Romero's awful Cooper family springs from the Hammer Holmwoods. Mr. Cooper, a bullying idiot, takes refuge in an abandoned house. Unlike the more enterprising refugees, Cooper boards his family in a sealed cellar. Mrs. Cooper's complaint—"There's a radio upstairs and you boarded us in down here?"—translates into the language of modern America the unexpressed complaint of Fisher's boarded-in Lucy and Mina. This later wife is at least free to grumble, "We may not enjoy living together, but dying together isn't going to solve anything."

The vampire they harbor as they bicker is not Christopher Lee in a clean white coffin, but their own wounded daughter, who, transformed into a ghoul, rises and eats her parents. The other ghouls are automata; this child alone shows relish for the kill, grinning with her bloody mouth as adorably as a child in a TV commercial, then grabbing a trowel to stab her mother enthusiastically. In 1968 America, a year whose political idiom was violent denunciation, George Romero was free to make explicit the monsters bred in the ordinary cloistered family, but these monsters rose first, if more demurely, in the stylized and remote Hammer ambience.

41. Waller, *The Living and the Undead,* p. 142, emphasizes Hammer films' stabilizing endorsement of the couple, "an exceedingly safe image that underlies and perpetuates bourgeois society's all-important reliance on the discrimination between sexual roles and on monogamous, heterosexual relationships." In my opinion, he makes too little of the resonant images of potent transformation that erode all bourgeois couples.

42. Walter Kendrick, *The Thrill of Fear: 250 Years of Scary Entertainment* (New York: Grove Weidenfeld, 1991), p. 229. Of course, as Kendrick goes on to remark, Victorian England was grayer and grimmer than its Oz-like Hammer image. The most famous Victorian literature features the dreary contours of England blurred in rain and fog. For Victorians themselves, Italy was the land of color and arousal.

43. Including S. S. Prawer, who devotes a thoughtful chapter to this sequence in *Caligari's Children: The Film as Tale of Terror* (Oxford: Da Capo Press, 1980), pp. 240–69.

44. Ira Levin's obstetrical thriller, *Rosemary's Baby,* became a best-seller in America in 1967, only a year after *Dracula, Prince of Darkness.* Images of women violated by husbands, doctors, churches, and other institutionally sanctioned bodies of men entered the American consciousness through horror literature before they became part of the feminist political platform in the 1970s. David J. Skal's *The Monster Show,* pp. 287–305, has a fascinating chapter on gynecological violations and 1960s horror conventions.

45. Chelsea Quinn Yarbro remembered his urbanity vividly enough in 1978 to dedicate her first Count Saint-Germain novel, *Hôtel Transylvania: A Novel of Forbidden Love,* to Christopher Lee. Perhaps she remembered Lee's interior decoration more vividly than his Dracula: her supercivilized Count Saint-Germain passes from one historical epoch to another, always in consummate taste. The hungry reader envies not only his vampiric powers and his erotic tenderness, but his perfect clothes and elegant villas. Christopher Lee was the first Dracula for whom vampirism and taste were synonymous.

46. Drake Douglas, *Horror!* p. 10. Leonard Wolf's *A Dream of Dracula: In Search of the Living Dead* (Boston and Toronto: Little, Brown, 1972) is a still more rigidly Stoker-bound horror anatomy. Wolf's book swings around wildly in time and space, from 1960s Berkeley to the biblical beginnings of Western culture. Its sole anchor is Dracula, timeless and archetypal: "There he stood, enfolded in darkness. Dracula. Our eidolon, the willing representative of the temptations, and the crimes, of the Age of Energy" (p. 302). The disorder of Wolf's dream depends on the stability of Dracula, who is given the role of God. A wider range of vampires would throw Wolf's quest into hopeless confusion.

47. Robin Wood, "Return of the Repressed," *Film Comment* (July–August 1978), 28.

48. Raymond T. McNally and Radu Florescu, *In Search of Dracula: A True History of Dracula and Vampire Legends* (Greenwich, Conn.: New York Graphic Society, 1972), p. 12.

McNally and Florescu's influential book, identifying Stoker's Dracula with the Wallachian ruler Vlad the Impaler, appeared the same year as Leonard Wolf's *A Dream of Dracula.* Thus, seventy-five years after Stoker's novel, American writers reincarnated Dracula as monarch in both the unconscious and medieval history.

49. All references to Stoker's working notes are reprinted by permission of the Rosenbach Museum and Library, Philadelphia, Pa. (Stoker, Bram, *Dracula: ms. notes and outlines,* EL4/f.s874d/MS).

50. Francis Ford Coppola's appropriation, in 1992, of the 1973 TV movie's title and central idea turned the quest for authenticity into a sad joke. Nineteen years later, Coppola simultaneously borrowed and mocked the heroic hopes of the early '70s.

The most authentic *Dracula* of the 1970s, a three-part British television serial (1977; dir. Philip Saville), had no relation to Vlad Tepes, but an unusual respect for Bram Stoker. Louis Jourdan is a genteel, only faintly foreign Dracula whom reverse negative shooting transforms, at intervals, into a red snarling mouth and an all-seeing eye: the camera performs the same horrible metamorphoses that evocations of animals did in the novel. Gerald Savory's screenplay is intelligently faithful to Bram Stoker's own crosscutting structure, adding only a strain of piety alien to both Stoker's fin-de-siècle pragmatism and the secular hero worship of the American 1970s.

51. For Chelsea Quinn Yarbro's achingly loving Count Saint-Germain, an inability to weep is one of the pains of the vampire condition: vampirism dries up his tears along with his semen. But Saint-Germain is always weeping inwardly over the brutality of mortals.

52. Stephen King, *Danse Macabre* (1979; reprint, New York: Berkley, 1982), p. 317.

53. *I Am Legend* was also an inspiration for Stephen King's *'Salem's Lot*

(1975), a quite different brand of '70s vampire revisionism. *'Salem's Lot* is less concerned with Matheson's solitary survivor, whom King fragments into four or five not very effective vampire-hunters, than with the hordes of engulfing vampire-citizens who in their mindless uniformity form the new community. The two disturbing innovations of *I Am Legend*—the lone monster/hero who embodies humanity's last days, and the collective, now-normal vampirism of the new species—become the norm of 1970s horror.

54. Like its ostensible source, Balderston and Deane's 1927 play, this *Dracula* is set not in Victorian England, but in the 1920s. In Badham's 1920s, the romantic, tactile nineteenth century that Langella represents is being overrun by gramophones, cars, and common little men.

55. As Waller puts it, Langella's Dracula liberates Lucy "from a male-dominated society that imprisons and suppresses all that it deems mad" (*The Living and the Undead,* p. 100).

56. This too is a restoration, one that goes back to Stoker's novel: Badham's adaptation is the first to highlight the residence of Stoker's Dr. Seward in his own madhouse, though Stoker's doctor is no patriarch, but a wistful family man manqué.

57. Renfield does appear in Philip Saville's 1977 *Dracula,* whose fidelity to Stoker makes impossible the omission of a major character. Saville's Renfield is less lunatic than vampire acolyte. Once he has given Louis Jourdan's Dracula access to Mina, he becomes the bitten Mina's virtual confessor: the two are bound by shared spiritual guilt and fear. Saville's religiosity makes Renfield less a barometer of England's sanity than an index of its stricken soul.

58. Klaus Kinski's mute Renfield in Jess Franco's otherwise unimaginative *Count Dracula* (1970) is a forerunner of these knowing madmen. The screenplay drains Renfield of his mysterious vitality; he is no longer a vehicle of uncontrollable life-hunger, but simply a victim of Dracula, who drove him mad by murdering his daughter. Nevertheless, Kinski's delicate mime, all in white in a white room like Pierrot, seems to embody an awareness denied to the wise men who diagnose him. In 1979, Kinski went on to play a poignant Dracula in Werner Herzog's remake of *Nosferatu.*

59. See Paul Barber, *Vampires, Burial, and Death: Folklore and Reality* (New Haven and London: Yale University Press, 1988). In many movies, folklore vampires were replacing glamorized Hammer corpses; Romero's *Night of the Living Dead* (1968) is overrun with these awkward, festering, feasting revenants. Graphic footage of the war in Vietnam, the assassinations and rumblings of civil war at home, had made corpses revert to the rot and dread they had embodied before the so-called enlightenment of the eighteenth century, when they gained the potential to become uplifting icons.

60. In all the prints I have seen, Mina seems, confusingly, to die twice: some time after the scene I have just described, Lucy watches in horror as the men cut the heart out of a ruddy, unstaked and undecomposed Mina. Moreover, this Mina does not reflect in a mirror, while the decomposing Mina revealed herself to her father by her reflection in water. Is this a glitch in editing, a bit of Wonderland logic to dislodge our expectations, or a Cubist attempt to juxtapose a folkloric with a literary vampire?

61. In the 1990s, my University of Pennsylvania students, tougher than I am, found no romance in what one of them called "granola vampires." But in its time, during the first wave of the women's movement, this *Dracula*

gave me at least assurance that all stories and relationships were in the process of transformation.

62. Chelsea Quinn Yarbro, *The Palace* (New York: St. Martin's Press, 1978), p. 152. Yarbro's ellipses.

63. Since the gorgeous Sabella is an extraterrestrial from a future planet known as "Novo Mars," she doesn't quite belong in this discussion of a superior species intersecting with contemporary human society. See Tanith Lee, *Sometimes after Sunset* (New York: Doubleday, 1980).

64. Quoted in Joan Gordon, "Rehabilitating Revenants, or Sympathetic Vampires in Recent Fiction," *Extrapolation* 29 (1988): 227–34. In Gordon's view, Saint-Germain is so nonviolent that these novels are scarcely horror fiction at all. Gordon's exclusive focus on vampires prevents her from investigating the plausible horror of Yarbro's violent mortals.

65. Gordon finds sympathetic vampires largely a phenomenon of the 1980s, as does Margaret Carter in her "What Makes a Vampire 'Good'? Sympathetic Vampires in Contemporary Fiction" (delivered at the International Conference of the Fantastic in the Arts, 1993). But like so many pious fictions of the Reagan-Bush years, sympathetic vampires are dilutions of a once-potent reformist impulse: they originated as social scourges in the bolder 1970s.

66. Chelsea Quinn Yarbro, *Better in the Dark* (New York: Tor, 1993), p. 286.

67. Suzy McKee Charnas, *The Vampire Tapestry* (1980; reprint, New York: Pocket, 1981), p. 74.

68. In February 1991, Suzy McKee Charnas described to my class at the University of Pennsylvania her own dramatization-in-progress of *The Vampire Tapestry* in which Floria's unprofessional embrace of the vampire is unequivocally destructive, not the hinted-at release through romance it almost becomes in the novel.

69. Whitley Strieber, *The Wild* (New York: Tor, 1991), p. 250.

70. Michael Talbot's *The Delicate Dependency: A Novel of the Vampire Life* (New York: Avon, 1982) is a more extravagant epic of salvation by vampires who are virtual angels. For Talbot, who sweeps over human history with the assurance (though not the detailed accuracy) of Yarbro's historical horror, vampires are the *illuminati* who by elaborate mind-control have always saved humans—whom they need in order to reproduce—from their own self-destructive tendencies. Like Saint-Germain and Strieber's intense aliens, Talbot's vampires are healers, not diseases.

71. Anne Rice, *Interview with the Vampire* (1976; reprint, New York: Ballantine, 1977), p. 16.

72. *The Tale of the Body Thief* ((New York: Alfred A. Knopf, 1992), the fourth book of *The Vampire Chronicles,* is a definitive statement of the incompatibility between vampires and humans. After an awkward attempt at union through a body exchange between Lestat and the mortal David, Lestat forces a happy ending by turning David into a vampire. Only then is communion between them possible.

73. The later novels in *The Vampire Chronicles* (1985–) strenuously expand the airless world of the self-contained *Interview,* but these later works express a different historical moment than the elitist yearnings of the late 1970s.

74. In the decade of its publication, Robin Wood called *'Salem's Lot* "un-

ambiguously reactionary" because "the novel's monster is unequivocally evil and repulsive, and onto him are projected all the things of which the book is clearly terrified (including gayness, which provides the novel with a whole sub-text of evasions and subterfuges)" ("Return of the Repressed," p. 25). Had Wood called "the monster" "the *monsters*," an entire community of stalwart if corrupt citizens, he would have gotten closer to the heart of King's fear.

Homosexuality is spread more widely in *'Salem's Lot* than Wood suggests: the decadent Barlow and Straker surely suggest a gay couple invading small-town America from wicked Europe, but despite his peripheral love affair with a town girl who eagerly becomes a vampire, the hero, Ben Mears, is similarly implicated in homoerotic couplings—first with the high school teacher, Matt, then with Mark, the monster-ridden child who alone recognizes vampires and evades them. Focusing on families, King's novels generally have little interest in homosexuality, but like *Interview, 'Salem's Lot* steeps vampirism in male homoeroticism. If that homoeroticism makes villains villains, it also makes heroes heroes.

75. Stephen King, *'Salem's Lot* (1975; reprint, New York: Signet, 1976), p. 149.

76. In *Danse Macabre,* for example, pp. 38–39.

77. On p. 322, a well-meaning doctor claims coyly to Ben that Matt Burke, the local schoolteacher, reminds him of Van Helsing, but since Matt is at that point hospitalized with a terror-induced heart attack, he is scarcely Stoker's monumental knower; he is even further from those invulnerable paragons, Edward Van Sloan and Peter Cushing. Moreover, Matt has to cram, futilely, to learn the rules that were the stuff of Van Helsing's wisdom. "And now, if you don't mind, I'm very tired. I was reading most of the night," he tells his perturbed friends. This "authority" would do better to abandon his rule books for Mark Petrie's horror comics.

78. *Bare Bones: Conversations on Terror with Stephen King,* ed. Tim Underwood and Chuck Miller (New York: Warner, 1988), p. 5.

79. Of whom David J. Skal writes superbly in *The Monster Show,* pp. 287–305, though he excludes vampire children like Danny Glick and Rice's Claudia from his infantine company.

80. King's vampires adjust to changing idioms. *Stephen King's Sleepwalkers* (1992), a TV movie, is set in the timeless small town typical of the Reaganesque years. Like most '80s and early '90s horror, it limits its focus to the family: incest replaces politics as the vampire breeding ground. The handsome teenage vampire and his sexy mother are reassuringly un-American: they look like extraterrestrials and, like many '80s vampires, they come from ancient Egypt.

81. One of my students at the University of Pennsylvania was so dismayed by this breakdown of the rules that she wondered whether Father Callahan simply ranked too low in the hierarchy. "It would have worked if he'd been a bishop or something," she claimed, searching for controlling hierarchies in a book that valorized, for a time at least, tongue depressors and toys.

82. Robert Lucid's seminar on popular literature, University of Pennsylvania, April 1, 1991.

83. In one of the best *'Salem's Lot* spin-offs, Robert R. McCammon's *They Thirst* (1981; reprint, New York: Pocket, 1988), whose vampires take over

Los Angeles, Stoker's imperial rules and hierarchies are restored: there is a definite head vampire, Vulkan, who aims to conquer the world by creating a new dominant race. Does McCammon graft Stephen King's nightmare American epic to the new decade of the '80s that aimed to restore the rules flouted in the '60s and '70s?

Chapter 4

1. David J. Skal reminds us of Ronald Reagan's fondness for economic blood-draining metaphors and his "call for a mass purification [that] struck a deep response in a public that suddenly believed much of the nation's blood was indeed rotten, and as black as its sins." *The Monster Show* (New York: W. W. Norton, 1993), pp. 344–45. As usual, political faith both inspired and reflected the vampires who proliferated in popular culture.

2. *Fright Night* (1985; dir. Tom Holland) also features a ditsy divorced mother who dates a vampire while her adolescent son watches in horror. William Peter Blatty's best-selling novel, *The Exorcist* (1971), had featured a divorced working mother who left her child vulnerable to diabolical possession, but until the vampire films of the 1980s, popular culture was not responsive to Blatty's Catholic moralism. The abandoned and abandoning mothers of sons in the '80s are far from those earlier vampire-embracing wives and daughters whose surge for freedom was the heart of the story.

3. *Fright Night* and *Near Dark* (1987; dir. Kathryn Bigelow) also feature these vampire fellow-travelers, characters who seem to have turned but whose humanity is magically restored at the end of the movie. *The Hunger* (1983; dir. Tony Scott) features a vampirism that suddenly runs down, resulting in agonizing accelerated aging. Even its head vampire, Miriam, who is indestructible in Whitley Strieber's novel, inexplicably runs out of vampirism at the end. So, by implication, does Anne Parillaud in *Innocent Blood* (1992; dir. John Landis), whose gamine vampire suppresses her blood-drinking instinct when she finds true love with an understanding policeman.

4. Whether they are vampires or vampire-hunters, most protagonists in the patriarchy-restoring Reagan/Bush years are men and their women. Often, as in the British 1890s, those women are particularly horrible vampires whose destruction we should not mourn. Lesbian vampires are a dynamic if often separatist exception.

5. Brian Stableford, *The Empire of Fear: An Epic Vampire Novel* (1988; reprint, New York: Carroll and Graf, 1991), p. 289.

6. Kim Newman, *Anno Dracula* (1992; reprint, Carroll and Graf, 1993), p. 319.

7. Tim Powers, *The Stress of Her Regard* (1989; reprint, New York: Ace, 1991), p. 76.

8. Theoretically the nephelim are hermaphrodites, but their associations with such prehistoric female monsters as the Graie and Medusa, along with their proclivity for turning into female statues, marrying men, and draining them, connote femininity in a manner typical of Reaganesque vampire stories, which demonize women—even, at times, at the expense of their own plots.

9. Anne Rice, *The Vampire Lestat* (New York: Alfred A. Knopf, 1985), p. 338.

10. Anne Rice, *The Queen of the Damned* (New York: Alfred A. Knopf, 1988), p. 27.

11. Skal, *The Monster Show*, p. 346, reads Rice's *Chronicles* as myths of consolation: their "sympathetic portrayal of an alternate, supernaturalized sexuality that survives a world of death conveys a complicated healing message to a community which has suffered, and continues to suffer, a concentrated level of human loss unprecedented outside of wartime—or medieval plague."

12. Brian W. Aldiss, *Dracula Unbound* (1991; reprint, New York: Harper, 1992), p. 118.

13. In the Reaganesque years, Renfield devolves from social seer to invalid. Ellis Hanson's "Undead," which contextualizes *Dracula* in relation to late-Victorian homophobia and early Freudianism, constructs a Renfield who performs "the ideal sickrole of the homosexual hysteric. He is a sort of gay male Anna O., passing perversely from semiotic howling to a polysemous formality." Ellis Hanson, "Undead," in *Inside/Out*, ed. Diana Fuss (New York: Routledge, 1991), p. 326.

14. Donna J. Haraway, *Simians, Cyborgs, and Women: The Reinvention of Nature* (New York: Routledge, 1991), p. 149.

15. In the Guadalajaran film *Chronos* (1994; dir. Guillermo Del Toro), the vampire is a golden artifact, somewhere between an insect, a bomb, and a wind-up toy. Its visual motif is not blood, but wheels and gears. The "device," as the characters call it, is more vividly potent than its grisly but predictable organic effects. Lesbian theorists like Sue-Ellen Case similarly restore power to vampires of the late twentieth century by taking them out of nature and bestowing on them the dynamism of artifacts.

16. Patrick Whalen, *Night Thirst* (New York: Pocket, 1991), p. 226.

17. Dan Simmons, *Children of the Night* (New York: G. P. Putnam's Sons, 1992), p. 137.

18. Caryl Churchill's brilliant play *Mad Forest: A Play from Romania* (1990; reprint, London: Nick Hern, 1991), also set in Romania after the fall of Ceaușescu, presents a more mordant union of angel and vampire. The angel, who knows only "flying about in the blue," is seductively apolitical, though it sometimes flirts with fascism; the vampire, "undead and getting tired of it," feeds, in his bored way, on the blood of revolution. At the end they dance together while the newly liberated mortals construct fresh narratives of hurt and hate. Unlike *Children of the Night,* Churchill's play is profoundly political, but it too disbelieves in change. Churchill's alternative to political hope is, like Simmons's, a collaboration between angel and vampire, but her collaborators are ancient predators rather than infant saviors.

19. "Unnatural Acts," conference at the University of California at Riverside, February 14, 1993.

20. Ellis Hanson is less celebratory, but though his Dracula is a product of the homophobic revulsion of the British fin de siècle and the American AIDS years, he too is associated less with blood than with shadowiness: Hanson's "homosexual as revenant" "is afraid of mirrors because his absence in them reminds him of his own unrepresentability." He is cursed and empowered by being specter rather than substance. Ellis Hanson, "Undead," in *Inside/Out,* ed. Fuss, p. 328.

21. Teresa de Lauretis, Introduction to "Queer Theory: Lesbian and Gay

Sexualities," *differences: A Journal of Feminist Cultural Studies* 3, no. 2 (1991): xvi.

22. George Stade, Introduction to Bram Stoker, *Dracula* (New York: Bantam Classics, 1981), p. vi.

23. Christopher Craft, "'Kiss Me with Those Red Lips': Gender and Inversion in Bram Stoker's *Dracula*," *Representations* 8 (Fall 1984): 109.

24. The line from *Dracula* that gives Craft his title expresses a similarly unrealized desire, though like all Stoker's explicit wishes it is scrupulously heterosexual. Entranced by the three vampire women, Jonathan Harker dissolves in an erotic reverie: "I felt in my heart a wicked, burning desire that they would kiss me with those red lips" (*The Essential Dracula*, p. 51). Of course, they don't; Dracula separates them at the critical moment, leaving this kiss as unconsummated in Stoker's novel as it is in Craft's essay.

25. Sue-Ellen Case, "Tracking the Vampire," "Queer Theory: Lesbian and Gay Sexualities," *differences: A Journal of Feminist Cultural Studies* 3, no. 2 (1991): 1–19.

26. Both male Queer Theorists like Craft and lesbian theorists like Case insist that their vampires are multigendered, but the vampires they conjure adopt the genders of their authors. Even Sandy Stone's vampire is generally a "he," while Case's resolves herself into "she."

27. Jewelle Gomez, *The Gilda Stories: A Novel* (Ithaca, N.Y.: Firebrand, 1991), p. 45.

28. Jody Scott's *I, Vampire* (1984; London: Women's Press, 1986) is a similarly nonconfrontational lesbian vampire story. The insubordinate vampire Sterling O'Blivion swoops up into space fiction when she is taken over by the dynamic Benaroya. Benaroya may or may not be Virginia Woolf; she is undoubtedly not a vampire, but a tutelary extraterrestrial. Like other '80s vampires—including Lestat in the grip of Akasha—Scott's tough-talking protagonist lacks the power to initiate her own story. Her allegiance to a higher being saves her from a society impossible to confront, even for a vampire.

29. The discrepancy between the invocations of theorists like Sue-Ellen Case and the retrograde vampires they summon is replicated in the discrepancy between the two parts of the play *Angels in America,* Tony Kushner's "Gay Fantasia on National Themes." Part 1, *Millennium Approaches,* ends gorgeously, with an angel crashing into the sickroom of an AIDS patient, intoning the thrilling prophecy: "A marvelous work and a wonder we undertake, an edifice awry we sink plumb and straighten, a great Lie we abolish, a great error correct, with the rule, sword and broom of Truth!" (p. 62).

But in part 2, *Perestroika,* the angel reveals itself as the spirit of reaction. Plagued by obstructing coughs, it can cry only: "YOU MUST STOP MOVING! . . . HOBBLE YOURSELVES!" (p. 52). See Tony Kushner, *Angels in America, Part One: Millennium Approaches* (1991; New York: Theatre Communications Group, Inc., 1993) and *Part Two: Perestroika* (1991; New York: Theatre Communications Group, Inc., 1994).

For the most vivid fantasists of the 1980s and '90s, AIDS and backlash generate only retrograde revelations. Whether the messianic apparitions are angels or vampires or—as they often become—a compound of both, they cry in some form, "HOBBLE YOURSELVES!"

30. Gabrielle Beaumont's provocative 1989 *Carmilla* is blocked from the-

atrical distribution by the hour-long format of Showtime Nightmare Classics.

31. Stephen King, *'Salem's Lot* (1975; reprint, New York: Signet, 1976), p. 382. Ellipses are King's.

32. The vampires in *Near Dark* ignore most of the traditional rules; they eat, drink, and smoke, seem indifferent to holy objects, and, since they live in their homeland, have no need to travel with coffins of native earth: they sleep in their truck and in motels. They are, however, violently susceptible to the sun that flames over most of the movie.

33. "My revenge is just begun! I spread it over centuries, and time is on my side" (p. 365).

Index